BANTU BUREAUCRACY

Plate I. Zibondo, Ruler of Bulamogi.

BANTU BUREAUCRACY

A Century of Political Evolution among the Basoga of Uganda

LLOYD A. FALLERS

THE UNIVERSITY OF CHICAGO PRESS
CHICAGO AND LONDON

Library of Congress Catalog Card Number: 65–25124

THE UNIVERSITY OF CHICAGO PRESS, CHICAGO & LONDON
The University of Toronto Press, Toronto 5, Canada

Preface to 1965 Edition ©*1965 by The University of Chi-*
cago. All rights reserved. Published 1965. Original edition
published 1956 in England for East African Institute of
Social Research by W. Heffer & Sons Ltd. Printed in the
United States of America

PREFACE TO THE 1965 EDITION

If we were starting to carry out a study of the political institutions of the Basoga today, the result would be a book quite different from this one, for both Soga politics and our intellectual equipment for understanding them have undergone important changes since the period 1950–52, when the data presented here were gathered. Since that time, the Basoga, like so many other African peoples, have passed from colonial tutelage to citizenship in an independent state, caught up in all the cross-currents of intra-African and international politics. During the same period, the comparative study of political systems has changed from a rather narrow field of study, pursued in mutual isolation by political scientists concerned with modern European and American governments and by anthropologists concerned with traditional non-Western ones, to a broad interdisciplinary concern, engaging the attention of subject and area specialists of many kinds. The two developments are, of course, related: the decolonization of Africa and Asia, by creating a host of new sovereign states in socio-political environments unfamiliar to students of Western government and politics, has served both to expand the empirical basis for comparative political studies and to raise novel problems for analysis.

The political developments of the past decade and a half have not, of course, affected all aspects of Soga society and culture to the same degree. Much of the description in this book of the texture of village life—its principal institutions and the agricultural economy upon which it rests—doubtless remains as valid today as it was then, but the political institutions that relate the village community to Uganda and to the world have changed radically. In the period 1950–52, participation in politics meant, to the average Musoga, the attempt to influence the colonial bureaucracy and its local extention, the Busoga African Local Government, through informal pressure and on behalf of personal, familial, or local community ends. Formal participation in the formation of public policy was limited to the indirect election of representatives to councils, whose functions were still largely advisory. Popular political groups were only beginning to form. Accounts in Uganda's newspapers of events in Ghana (then still the Gold Coast), where Kwame Nkrumah had been released from prison to lead the first post-colonial African government, were received by the politically articulate Basoga with great interest but with little sense that similar developments were imminent in their own country.

Similar developments were, of course, much more imminent than anyone then realized. Once begun, the process of decolonization spread across the continent with surprising rapidity. By 1952, the first popular, Uganda-wide political party, the Uganda National Congress, had been formed. By 1956, partly as a result of the crisis precipitated by the deportation of the Kabaka of Buganda in 1953, serious negotiations concerning the constitutional shape of a self-governing Uganda were in progress. Finally, in 1962, just a century after the first European explorer entered the area and seventy years after the establishment of British colonial rule, Milton Obote, leader of the Uganda Peoples' Congress, took office as Prime Minister of the new state.

As a result of these developments, the Musoga villager's political universe has expanded greatly and his participation in it has quickened. Today, political parties compete for his vote, urging him to take positions on issues, both national and international, involving factors quite outside his experience. A study of present-day Busoga would not only still concern itself, as this one does, with the politics of administration, for bureaucracy has not, of course, disappeared with independence, but it would also necessarily be much more concerned with the interplay between bureaucracy and popular political organizations.

In analyzing this interplay, a present-day investigator would find much stimulation in the recent expansion of comparative political studies. Our thinking about bureaucracy, for example, has advanced considerably beyond the classical Weberian analysis, upon which the present study is principally based. The growth of political sociology, stimulated in part by the revival of interest in the work of de Tocqueville, has greatly increased our understanding of the politics of social stratification, while anthropologists working in Africa and Asia have begun to interest themselves in the ways in which such primordial social units as tribes, castes, and ethnic and religious groups behave under conditions of populistic political competition. Political scientists and economists have developed new ways of thinking about the politics of economic growth. All this gives grounds for hope that the intellectual challenge presented by the emergence of the new states will be met by an appropriate increase in the depth and range of social science understanding.

PREFACE TO THE 1956 EDITION

A social anthropologist's indebtedness to others is particularly great. Firstly, like other scholars, he is indebted to his teachers, his fellow-students and his colleagues for the training and stimulus without which scholarly research would be an impossibility for him. In this regard, my greatest debt is to Audrey Richards, Director of the East African Institute of Social Research, under whose guidance the study reported in this book was carried out. For ideas, for practical advice and consolation in the inevitable trials of field research, and for creating at the Institute an atmosphere of stimulating intellectual exchange, I am most grateful to her and to other members of the Institute staff. The present study was financed in part by the Institute and in part by the United States Educational Commission in the United Kingdom (the "Fulbright Program"). I acknowledge with deep gratitude the assistance of both organisations.

To my teachers and colleagues in the universities in which I have been privileged to work, I owe such competence in social science research as I may have achieved. At the University of Chicago, Professors Robert Redfield, Fred Eggan, Sol Tax and William Lloyd Warner introduced me to social anthropology and, at a later stage, guided me in the preparation of an earlier version of this study as a doctoral dissertation, while Professors Edward Shils and Gerhard Meyer led me through the writings of such sociologists as Weber, Durkheim, Simmel and Parsons. At the London School of Economics, where I was enabled by the United States Educational Commission in the United Kingdom to spend a year of graduate study, I acquired my interest in Africa and was privileged to work under Professor Raymond Firth and Drs. Audrey Richards and Edmund Leach. As a lecturer at Princeton University I benefited greatly from discussions with Professors Fred Stephan, Wilbert Moore, Marion Levy and Gresham Sykes. To Marion Levy I owe a special debt for inviting me to participate in a seminar on "The Structure of Society," sponsored by the Social Science Research Council, during the summer of 1953. Parts of this study were presented at the seminar and benefited greatly from criticism received there.

An anthropologist also acquires a second, and very deep indebtedness to the people among whom he works. At the very least, he imposes upon people's hospitality and time. More seriously, he may, in addition, be disruptive of normal social relations, particularly during the early stages of his work when he unavoidably blunders about in a social system whose rules he does not yet understand. For their open-hearted hospitality and constant help to an inconvenient guest, I am everlastingly grateful to Owekitiibwa Ezekeri T. Wako, Zibondo, and Omwami Stanley Wandira, then Sub-County Chief Ssabawaali of Kigulu. Valuable advice and assistance were also given by Isebantu W. W. K. Nadiope, Kyabazinga of Busoga; Owekitiibwa W. P. Mwangu, Secretary-General of the Busoga African Local Government; Owekitiibwa Y. K. Lubogo, Treasurer of the Busoga African Local Government; and by my paid assistants, J. Mugadu, H. J. Kagoda, M. Magola, D. Wabulembo, S. Kamusala, S. Mukupya, E. Nyende, G. W. Mugadya, E. Ngatia, Z. Kalireko, J. Isoba, S. Walugyo, H. Sajabbi, Y. Kagona, K. Mutaka, and J. Ntende. Others, far too numerous to mention, gave freely of their time and friendship.

To the administrative officers in charge of Busoga District during my visit, I am also indebted for their great patience and for their willingness to discuss problems encountered in the course of research. It is difficult for anyone without first-hand experience of colonial life to appreciate the extent and complexity of the responsibility borne by the colonial civil servant, a responsibility which I have tried to document in Chapter IX of this study. In this situation, the presence of a strange European at large in his area is inevitably a source of worry and distraction. Mr. T. R. F. Cox, Provincial Commissioner, Eastern Province, and Mr. D. Marshall and Mr. R. F. Roper, who served as District Commissioner, Busoga, at different times during my visit, bore the added burden of my presence with great tolerance and courtesy and freely shared with me their knowledge of Busoga.

Finally, I must thank Dr. Audrey Richards, Mr. John Beattie, Dr. Edward Winter, Mr. T. R. F. Cox, Mr. R. F. Roper, Mrs. E. M. Chilver, Mrs. Jean Robin and my wife, Margaret, for reading the manuscript and offering valuable criticisms, and Miss Beryl Berrange for her care and diligence in helping me prepare it for publication.

The data upon which this study is based were collected between November, 1950, and July, 1952. The methods of research used were mostly the conventional anthropological ones: interviews with individuals, observation of social interaction, the collection of genealogical and biographical materials and the study of published and unpublished documents. Since much of the work was centred upon current politics, a sensitive topic in any colonial situation, it was essential that I be wholly identified with neither the British administration nor the Soga. To the extent that a "neutral" rôle was achieved, this was due in large part to the generosity and forbearance of the officers of the Busoga District Administration, who provided every possible assistance "with no strings attached," and to the very kind assistance of several prominent Soga, including those mentioned above, who acted as my sponsors and helped me to explain to others the purposes of the research. The time spent in the field was divided more or less equally between Busambira, in the south-central part of the District, and the area around Kaliro, in the north-central County of Bulamogi. Shorter visits to other parts of the District provided material for comparison with these areas.

Two other sources of data, in addition to those listed above, should be mentioned. Although I was primarily interested in political structure, it was also necessary, since Busoga had not been well-described in the literature, to assemble a basic body of information concerning the life of ordinary Soga in the villages. Much of this, of course, had to be acquired by the usual methods of interviewing and observation and by the "soaking up" process of residence among villagers and learning their language. But since Busoga is a relatively large and heterogeneous country, it was also desirable to gather, wherever possible, statistical data concerning the variations in patterns which were observed impressionistically. This was accomplished through the use of a questionnaire which was filled out for all the homesteads in five villages. The questionnaires (reproduced in Appendix I) were printed in the Ganda language and were completed with the help of several literate Soga assistants who, by good fortune, had had experience as interviewers in the population census carried out in 1948. In addition to the statistical material, this homestead survey provided a valuable "laboratory" for the observation of the social structure in action. It provided a situation in which I could legitimately be involved as a participant. Once the support of a few prominent persons had been secured, these persons were able to act as guides to the local authorty system, indicating to me whose support was necessary for the success of the operation and in many cases using their influence to mobilise this support. The actual interviewing was not begun until the sponsors were satisfied that the support of all opinion leaders in the community had been acquired. From the point of view of the survey itself, this preliminary organisation was most valuable. Only two persons in the five villages refused to be interviewed.

A second valuable source of data was the records of litigation kept by the African Local Government courts. The Soga are a litigious people. Wherever social relations are strained, people are apt to go to court for a settlement. The records, written in Ganda, are quite voluminous and accurate, providing reasonably close approximations to the questions asked by the court and the testimony of the litigants and witnesses. The record of one case is reproduced in Appendix IV. Such records proved to be of great value, both in the study of the substance of Soga customary law and as records of types of social situations in which authority is exercised.

TABLE OF CONTENTS

LIST OF TABLES

LIST OF FIGURES

LIST OF PLATES

LIST OF MAPS

CHAPTER I

THE PROBLEM: INSTITUTIONAL CONFLICT AND CHANGE

AIMS OF THE STUDY.

This is a study of integration and conflict among some of the institutions of an East African people, both prior to their experience with the West and to-day, after nearly a century of ever-deepening Western influence.

The Soga are a Bantu-speaking people of the Inter-Lacustrine group, numbering somewhat more than half a million and inhabiting the area to the east of the Victoria Nile between Lakes Victoria and Kyoga in the Eastern Province of Uganda (see Map 1). Before the entry of Europeans into the area, Busoga was divided among a series of small kingdom-states and its people were subsistence agriculturalists and keepers of cattle, sheep and goats.[1] With the establishment of British administration at the end of the nineteenth century, the country was unified politically and integrated into the newly-formed Uganda Protectorate. During the half-century which has since elapsed, new institutions have been introduced and old ones altered; the majority of Soga have become peasants in the commonly accepted sense of the term, cultivating small holdings both for subsistence and for the market, and their political system has become an amalgam of traditional indigenous structures and modern Western ones.

The aim of this study is twofold. First, I hope that it will provide a case study of interest to the growing number of social scientists

---

[1] Like other Bantu languages, those of the Lake Victoria region have class prefixes. Thus the people about whom I write are called *basoga* (singular: *musoga*), their language *lusoga* and their country *busoga*. Still other prefixes occur when the root is used adjectivally, e.g. *ente ensoga* (a Soga cow), *ekibbo ekisoga* (a Soga basket). In the interests of simplicity, I shall, with one exception, use only the root form and speak of "the Soga" and "things Soga." The exception will be the name of the country, which I shall call "Busoga" in order to avoid such etymological hybrids as "Soga-land." It should be noted that the practice of using the root form in referring to Bantu peoples has been far from universally followed, so that in bibliographies one must look for "Basoga" and even "Wasoga" (the Swahili form) as well as "Soga."
Since no standard orthography for the Soga language has been developed, I have, in reproducing Soga words, followed the practice of *Ndi Mugezi*, a newspaper published at Kamuli in Bugabula County. Ganda words are written according to the orthography used in Mulira, E. M. K., and Ndawula, E. G. M., *A Luganda-English and English-Luganda Dictionary*, 1952, and in Ashton, E. O., Mulira, E. M. K., Ndawula, E. G. M., and Tucker, A. N., *A Luganda Grammar*, 1954.

1

who concern themselves with the nature and limits of conflict and
integration in societies, in particular in those undergoing rapid
change. The quickening pace of change in most non-Western
societies under Western influence, or in reaction to it, and their
growing prominence on the international scene, have brought these
problems to the fore with greater practical urgency, while àt the
same time social scientists have been attempting to develop adequate
conceptual tools for dealing with such societies. A single case study
cannot, of course, provide answers to the more general questions
which arise in this connection; such questions can only be answered
through the accumulation and analysis of data drawn from many
societies undergoing change. A case study can, however, stimulate
new hypotheses. I present this one in the belief that it contains
elements which, if not unique, are at any rate not well described in
existing literature. If this is so, the present study may contribute
to wider comparative analysis by suggesting new ranges of variation
with which such analysis must deal.

This study has a second aim. In coming years the Soga and the
British administrators under whose tutelage the colonial situation
has placed them will be faced with many decisions, and the choices
which are made will be full of consequences for the future of Busoga.
It is certainly not the business of a foreign academic to say which will
be the right choices, and I most emphatically deny any intention
in this direction. As a brief visitor and outsider, I have tried to
view the situation with appropriate humility and detachment.
But in the nature of the case I shall concern myself with the situation
in which the Soga and their British tutors find themselves, and thus,
inevitably, with the nature of some of the decisions which face
them. Such "loading of the dice" cannot be avoided; it is a necessary concomitant of any attempt to describe and analyse. It is not,
however, the same thing as an explicit concern with policy. I may,
of course, be wrong in my view of the situation. Indeed, in view
of the complexity of the processes which are under way in Busoga
and in other colonial areas, and taking into account the rudimentary
state of our understanding of such processes, I am more than likely
to be wrong. It is my hope, however, that those who must make
decisions concerning areas under administration will find profit
in this study, if only as a stimulus to disagreement.

INTEGRATION AND CONFLICT AMONG INSTITUTIONS.

I do not wish at this point to enter into an extended discussion of
concept and theory. In the final chapter of this book I shall take
up again what I consider to be some of the major theoretical problems upon which the study bears, but for the moment it will suffice

merely to introduce a few technical terms and ideas which I wish to use in descriptive exposition. This much seems necessary because to-day sociology and social anthropology (I should use these terms interchangeably) are passing through a phase of rapid and extensive theoretical development, while central trends and terminological conventions have not yet clearly emerged.[1] This circumstance, while it promises much for the future, makes it incumbent upon anyone writing in the field to identify himself, so to speak—to make clear how he uses terms and what he means by them. I shall, therefore, briefly introduce the categories of thought which I bring to the situation which I shall describe.

This book is concerned, first of all, with certain social institutions. "Institution" means to me a pattern of behaviour which a group of persons consider "right" or "correct"—a norm or pattern of conduct. For a pattern of behaviour to be institutionalised means that persons approve of its being followed and disapprove of its not being followed. Institutional norms may, of course, be either positive or negative; they may prescribe acts to be carried out or proscribe acts to be avoided. And such norms are always defined by persons in relation to situations. They never say: "You must at all times and places do this." Rather they say: "At these times and places and with regard to these persons, you must do this." Finally, an institution defines the social rôle of an individual. By rôle, I mean that behaviour which is imposed on an individual both by the expectations of others and his own desire to conform, and which he is expected to display under certain circumstances. If an individual fails to carry out the expectations associated with his rôle, he is punished, both by sanctions applied by others and by his own feelings of remorse or uneasiness at having broken a rule which is "built into him"—which has become part of his personality by virtue of his having grown up in a community in which the rule is institutionalised.[2]

---

[1] I should use the two terms interchangeably because, though sociologists and social anthropologists often work in different kinds of societies and use different research techniques, the problems with which they are concerned seem to me to be ultimately the same. The point is of some importance because the increasing inter-penetration of Western and non-Western societies would seem to give rise to social situations which can best be studied through the use of concepts and techniques derived from both fields. In a limited way, I believe, the present study illustrates the desirability of such an approach.

[2] Institutional rules, of course, vary greatly in the degrees and kinds of sanctions which support them. At one extreme are explicitly formulated "moral" or "ethical" rules, the breach of which outrages a society's members and brings into play severe sanctions. At the other extreme are patterns of dress and the like which people may not "feel strongly" about but which

Continued on page 4

As I am chiefly concerned, in this book, to describe and analyse political institutions, I had better explain what I mean by the word "political." The dominant tendency, particularly among students of Western political systems, has been to think of "things political" as pertaining, not just to particular institutions, but to special concrete social units, usually those entrusted with the legitimate use of the ultimate sanction of force for the maintenance of social order. Such special social units we normally speak of as "government" or "the state." In modern Western societies, this association of political institution with government as a special sub-unit of society has some justification. In those societies, authority, the legitimate use of power backed by sanctions, is to a high degree allocated to special social units consisting of special persons. Government is a specialist occupation.

Similarly, in such societies "the economic" tends to be associated with other special social units which we call "firms," and "the religious" with still others which we call "churches." But such is not the case in many societies. In Africa, for example, it is common for the same social unit, say a clan or lineage, to be in nearly equal measure "economic," "political" and "religious." Such would appear to be the case among the Nuer, the Gusii and the Tallensi, among whom lineage groups of various degrees of extension have simultaneously the functions of "churches," "states" and "firms." Elsewhere, local village communities may form such "multipurpose" social units. Ultimately, of course, this is also true of modern Western societies if one focuses upon "the nation" as a whole as the social unit. The modern nation as a whole has economic, political and religious aspects. But within it, one may distinguish particular sub-units which are specialised in one or another of these directions, while in the African societies cited above such specialised sub-units may not be found. Finally, the specialised social sub-units of the modern West do not wholly exhaust the

Continued from page 3

nevertheless are followed by most members of the society. A person who does not follow them is not "bad" but merely "a bit odd." Following Levy and Parsons, I use the term "institutional norm" for this whole range of phenomena. (See Levy, Marion J., Jr., *The Structure of Society*, 1952, pp. 102–105; Parsons, Talcott, "The Motivation of Economic Activities," *Canadian Journal of Economics and Political Science*, Vol. VI, No. 2, 1940, pp. 187–203).

As I explain below, "institutional norms or rules" in my sense specify the individuals and groups to which they apply, but are not the same as such persons or groups. Likewise, such norms or rules may relate to non-human physical objects such as land, money or livestock, so that in order to talk about an institution one may have to describe the typical geography of a local community or typical methods of cultivation. Again, however, such objects are not themselves institutions but rather things about which there are institutions.

economic, political and religious aspects of their societies.   Churches have economic and political aspects, governments have religious and economic aspects and firms have religious and political aspects. Even in the modern West the specialisation is relative.[1]

With such considerations in mind, I find it useful to define "political institutions" simply as the rules governing the legitimate use of power and not as the social units to which such rules apply. As I have already said, institutions specify the persons, and hence the social units, to which they apply.   But such social units may be, and probably always are in some degree, also the units to which particular economic institutions (which I define as the rules governing the distribution of goods and services) and religious institutions (which I define as setting forth the ultimate or highest-order values of a society) apply.   Thus, in my terms, the British Parliament is not a political institution but rather a specialised social unit to which British political institutions allocate overriding legitimate power.   British political institutions, in my terms, also allocate legitimate power, though in lesser degree, to social units which are not so obviously "political."   An employer, for example, may legitimately apply the sanction of dismissal to an incompetent or dishonest employee, and a father may, within limits, legitimately apply sanctions to ensure his son's good behaviour.   In Soga society, with which this study is concerned, political institutions allocate legitimate power to specialised social units more than is the case in many African societies, though to a lesser degree than in the modern West.   But in attempting to describe the political institutions of Soga society as a whole, I shall have to deal with the family, the lineage and the village as well as with the state, for all these social units clearly have political as well as other aspects. Furthermore, their political aspects may be related to their economic and religious aspects and so it may be necessary to discuss these as well.

Finally, this study is concerned with integration and conflict among some of the institutions of Soga society.   It has been one of the most fruitful notions of modern social science that the component institutions of any society constitute, not a random collection of discrete elements, but an ordered system such that (a) the constituent institutions fit together more or less harmoniously and (b) they combine to satisfy the minimum conditions for the society's

[1] My distinction between concrete social units (persons and groups) and the institutions which apply to them is similar to, but not identical with, Levy's distinction between concrete and analytic aspects of social systems. (See Levy, op cit., pp. 88–100.)   My thinking about this and many other matters touched upon in this chapter owes a great deal to Levy's stimulus, both through his writings and through personal discussion.

continued existence. By providing a framework for analysis independent of Western institutional peculiarities this idea has contributed greatly to the scientific understanding of non-Western institutions, and among students of Western societies has produced analyses of institutions which, perhaps because of their very familiarity, had gone unrecognised or been misunderstood. It has also, however, been productive of a great deal of rather acrimonious debate among social scientists and misunderstanding among their readers, by virtue of the different interpretations which have been given to such terms as "system," "integration," "function," and the like. Again, this is not the place for discussion of various points of view. I want merely to make clear how I intend to use these ideas in the present case study.

One aspect of the part played by an institution in the society in which it is found is its relationship to other institutions—its consequences for other institutions and vice versa. It is my view that such consequences must be discovered, not assumed to exist. One rather extreme view among social scientists has held that all the institutions of a society are intimately bound up (by implication, equally bound up) with all other institutions of that society.[1] I do not believe that this is so. For example, the rules governing entrance into and participation in the Bird Watchers' Society of Bournemouth (if such exists, and I am sure it must) can hardly be said to be intimately connected with the conventions governing election to the House of Commons. Of course, it is undoubtedly true that the entire body of institutions which go to make up the British Constitution have important consequences for the formation and continued existence of private "interest" associations in Britain, but this is not the point. The Bird Watchers' Society and the House of Commons are each governed by some institutions peculiar to themselves and one may legitimately claim that in their particulars each of these two bodies of institutions might vary considerably without consequence for the other. Both their relative independence of one another in detail and their ultimate connection through the wider institutions with which each is related are important social facts. One looks, then, for connections between institutions but one does not assume that they exist.

A second rather extreme view among social scientists has implied that the consequences which a society's component institutions have for one another "must" in some sense be harmonious consequences,

---

[1] See, for example, Kluckhohn, Clyde, "Navaho Witchcraft," *Papers of The Peabody Museum of American Archaeology and Ethnology*, Vol. XXII, No. 2, 1944, pp. 46–47. See also Merton's summary and critique of this and other simplistic versions of "functionalist" social science; Merton, R. K., *Social Theory and Social Structure*, 1949, pp. 21–81.

that they must mutually support one another.[1] Let it be admitted at once that there is undoubtedly a tendency in this direction. Everything we know about human behaviour would lead us to believe that human beings behave with some consistency, though how much we cannot yet say. Through processes which students of the central nervous system are beginning to discover, neural connections come to be established in such a way that what an individual does at one time or in one situation is related to what he does at another time or in another situation. Perhaps there is thus a biologically-rooted "need" for consistency among the social situations through which individuals pass. Other roots of the human tendency towards some degree of consistency or patterning have been found by some at the level of the society at large. For whatever reason, human beings come to have "ends" or "wants" or "goals" and it seems to be the case that the ends, wants or goals of a society's component individuals cannot vary quite at random and still be in any substantial degree realised. Hobbes' famous paradox states that the attainment of ends by individuals is only feasible if individuals subordinate themselves to a common body of rules: rules, of course, limit individual freedom to attain ends of certain kinds. We recognise this whenever we speak of "institutions" in the sense outlined above, for "institution" means patterning, rules and sanctions.

These tendencies towards consistency or harmony in a society's institutions must certainly be admitted. What is not clear is the degree of harmony needed. Granted that there is a tendency toward consistency, what are the dimensions and limits of this tendency? We do not know, and until we do, it seems to me pretentious to speak, as some social scientists do, as if we knew. Certainly an utter lack of social rules or an utter lack of consistency among social rules (which comes to the same thing) would produce Hobbes' "war of each against all." But who has seen a society which came to such an impasse? Writers have described the "lawless" urban slums of industrial Europe and America, the "disorganisation" among American Indians swamped by immigrant Europeans, the "detribalised" populations of shanty-towns around modern African cities. But somehow social life goes on in such situations. Somehow, the complete "war of each against all" seems never to occur. On the other hand, no reliable observer has claimed to have discovered a society which worked with perfect smoothness and regularity, where all institutional rules were perfectly consistent with one another, where there was no deviation from the rules. Parsons has argued with great cogency that such

[1] See note 1, p. 6.

a perfect state of integration is impossible of realisation in human society due to the partial independence of "personalities" and "societies" as systems.[1] He might have noted also the difficulty of any society's making sufficient rules (and individuals' learning sufficient rules) to cover all possible situations. Somewhere, apparently, between perfect integration and the "war of each against all" there are limits within which human societies vary, but at present we are able to place those limits only with great vagueness and uncertainty. When, therefore, we study a concrete society, we can look for integration and conflict, but we must think of our society as falling somewhere along a continuum bounded on the one hand by perfect integration and on the other hand by utter conflict, just as we must think of the connection between any two institutions as falling somewhere along a continuum bounded on the one hand by mutual irrelevance and on the other by intimate involvement.

There is another dimension to the place of an institution in the wider society of which it forms a part. Taken together with other institutions, it may in varying degrees contribute or fail to contribute to the realisation of particular ends or conditions, including the maintenance of the society in a steady state. Here again, some social scientists have tended to take extreme positions. Some have written as though it could be assumed that a society's component institutions, individually and severally, and each in equal measure, contribute to the maintenance of that society in a steady state.[2] In a certain tautological sense, of course, this is true. A society is maintained in every detail only in so far as all its institutions and all the relationships between its institutions are maintained. But this is only to say, "if it were not so, it would not be so," a rather unprofitable assertion which leads us no further. And of course it remains true only if the society is looked at in flat time-perspective—if the time dimension is neglected. Some societies, at any rate, have "built-in" tendencies towards change. In the modern West, technological innovation, and perhaps even social innovation, are quite clearly institutionalised. Innovation is an institution and the innovator the occupant of a clearly institutionalised social rôle.[3] While many of the world's societies have undoubtedly remained for substantial periods in relative stability, there is little evidence of absolute stasis anywhere or at any time. In any case, a static view of society would have little relevance to the modern African (or indeed, the general modern non-Western) scene. As far back as history allows us to look, East Africa has

[1] Parsons, Talcott, *The Social System*, 1951, pp. 44–45.
[2] See note 1, p. 6.
[3] Parsons, Talcott, *The Social System*, Chapter 11.

been the scene of constant flux and, of course, such tendencies are being intensified to-day. Nor does the future hold out any hope of "steady states" for African societies. If the present period is one of "readjustment" for such societies, this can hardly be a readjustment to a new equilibrium; it can only be an adjustment to steady change. I therefore find it useful to ask, not "how do a society's institutions act to maintain it," but rather "how far do a society's institutions act to maintain it in a steady state and how far do they act to change it in what ways?"

Both equilibrium and change in various directions may of course be either implicit and unintended or explicit and intended for a society's members.[1] And various members may have different views. These differences in intention may be of much importance. As a recent Governor of Kenya Colony has pointed out, early treaties between non-Western peoples and representatives of Western nations can often be explained only by assuming that neither party foresaw with any clarity the consequences of his acts.[2] One might, of course, cite many other, less spectacular, examples from many societies. For present purposes, the point is simply that whether or not persons perceive or intend the consequences of and inter-relationships among acts and institutions may be of great moment for the direction which a society takes.

Let me briefly recapitulate the questions which I shall ask of Soga society and note some of the guideposts which 1 hope to use in finding answers to them. I have said that I shall try to analyse Soga political institutions in terms of the degree to which they are in harmony or in conflict among themselves and with other institutions. I have defined political institutions as the rules governing the distribution of legitimate authority and have noted that institutions always define the circumstances and persons to which they apply. Where then does one look for harmony or conflict among institutions? Primarily, it seems to me, one looks for situations in which two or more institutions claim the adherence of the same persons or groups, or where they bring different persons or groups into relations with one another by defining overlapping fields of interest. For example, religious and economic institutions may so define the persons to whom they apply that the same persons or groups are simultaneously bound by the rules of both. In such circumstances, economic and religious institutions are mutually related and they may be in harmony or in conflict.[3] Different

---

[1] Merton, R. K., *Social Theory and Social Structure*, 1949, pp. 61 ff.

[2] Mitchell, Sir Phillip, *African Afterthoughts*, 1954, p. 56.

[3] The famous Tawney-Weber discussion concerning the relationship between the "protestant ethic" and capitalism concerns just such a connection between economic and religious institutions. (See Weber, Max, *The Protestant Ethic and the Spirit of Capitalism*, 1930; Tawney, R. H., *Religion and the Rise of Capitalism*, 1938.)

political institutions within a society may be in harmony or conflict with one another, likewise.   Where such overlapping institutions are in harmony, the rôles which individuals are expected to play will mutually reinforce one another; where they are in conflict, persons will be expected to play more or less incompatible rôles.

Even where institutions do not overlap in the sense of applying simultaneously to the same persons, they may define overlapping fields of interest.   For example, different persons or groups bound by different institutions may both claim the use of a single scarce resource.   Where such uses are compatible or complementary, there is no conflict; indeed, the two sets of persons, though in other respects bound by different, and even conflicting, institutional rules, may have a common, harmonious interest in maintaining the resource.   The example of roads and other "public utilities" comes to mind.   Thieves and priests may have a common interest in maintaining them, though in other ways thieves and priests are bound by quite incompatible institutional rules.   On the other hand, overlapping interests may bring institutions into conflict. In the history of Christendom, the definitions of God's and Caesar's claims upon scarce resources have often enough been such as to produce conflict.   Again, persons and groups bound by conflicting institutional norms may each claim universal applicabliity for their norms over the whole of a society's membership, thus making collision inevitable.   In all such cases, a crucial rôle is played by what may be called "referee institutions."   In the modern Western liberal democratic state, a degree of conflict of interest is accepted and even institutionalised, but it is and can be so because there are referee institutions, such as the ballot box with all its attendant rules, which contain and canalise conflict.   "Conflict" and "harmony" are thus not simple variables.   Their nature and significance in a society can only be assessed through painstaking unravelling of institutions and their interconnections.

I am also enquiring into the contribution of political institutions in Busoga toward maintaining the total society in a steady state, or toward changing it in particular ways.   Either persistence or change, of course, involves survival of a society's members.   There are thus certain basic prerequisites for any human society such that, whatever else happens, there must be institutions to satisfy them.   These include the biological necessities of human life, such as food and, depending upon the environment, clothing and shelter, and also, if inter-generational persistence is considered, provision for reproduction and the rearing of children in terms of some definition of the proper adult.   In addition, for some combination of the reasons discussed above, a minimum degree of order among the institutions satisfying these biological prerequisites would seem to be necessary. Beyond these minimum necessities, however, the possibilities become very diverse. Various states of society, including persistence in a steady state, are possible, and one must consequently analyse the part played by institutions in contributing toward these various states. This is my understanding of the meaning of the "comparative method" in anthropology and sociology. One cannot, however, analyse institutions in terms of their contributions to all possible states of society. A choice must be made lest analysis become almost infinitely complex.

For example, it would seem relatively unprofitable to analyse Soga society in terms of the contributions, negative or positive, of its component institutions toward changing Soga society in the direction of seventeenth-century Chinese society. In terms of "pure" sociological science—the comparative method in its fullest sense—such an analysis might be quite useful. Indeed, it might well be argued that such "unrealistic" comparative analysis across wide stretches of time and space is necessary for the progress of sociology and social anthropology toward true scientific status.[1] It is, however, outside the scope of a monograph mainly concerned with the analysis of a single society to compare that society with all others or even with all others of a broadly similar type. In addition, I hope that this study may have some practical relevance to the problems of Soga society's immediate future. I shall therefore select, arbitrarily from the pure science point of view, only certain particular possible future states of Soga society against which to analyse contemporary Soga political institutions. Among these will be, on the one hand, persistence in a steady state and, on the other, the various future states of the society seen by Soga and the British administration to be desirable. Soga aims for the future often disagree, among themselves and with the aims of the administration, and it is of course no part of my task to choose among these various views. I hope only to discover something of what the achievement of various of these possible future conditions might involve for Soga political institutions as they operate to-day.

There remains one final problem, arising out of the above

[1] This, however, would seem to me to be a very long-range aim. Ideally, one would choose for comparative analysis societies having features relevant to the hypothesis one wished to test, without regard to their time-space location. Something like this kind of "pure" comparative analysis may be possible with regard to restricted aspects of social structure about which a great deal is known. Many anthropologists, however, would argue that, initially at least, comparative analysis can best be carried out with regard to societies known to be historically related so that more of the unknown number of factors influencing social structural variation may be held constant. I subscribe to this view.

paragraphs. I have spoken of "Soga society" as if it were a clearly defined unit about whose boundaries there were no doubt. This was of course an incautious way of speaking. Even before it came under British protection, Busoga was not a unit which could be clearly defined. As will be seen in later chapters, traditional Busoga, from some points of view, consisted of several "societies" since there were within its boundaries several small, more or less autonomous states. At the same time, there was among these units enough cultural similarity to set them off from neighbouring social units, and a frequent interchange of persons. In connection with modern Busoga, other problems of unit definition arise. Is modern Busoga a separate society or is it part of some larger society such as the Uganda Protectorate or the British Commonwealth? Are British administrators members of Soga society or are they not? These are weighty problems, and not entirely "academic" ones. I shall attempt to deal with them in the final chapter of this study, but for the moment let me be content to say arbitrarily that my analysis pertains to the political institutions relevant to the social system which operated, and operates to-day, within the geographical limits of the area called "Busoga."

So much for the general ideas which I bring to this study. Let me now, before plunging into the description of Soga society, briefly outline some of the major institutional complexes in traditional and modern Busoga, and some of the inter-relations among these institutional complexes which will be discussed in the chapters which follow. I shall focus upon two principal cases of institutional inter-relatedness which seem to me to have been prominent in Soga politics at different times over the past century. In later nineteenth century Busoga (the earliest period for which it appears possible to gather reliable information), legitimate authority seems to have been distributed in terms of two main institutional complexes: on the one hand, authority for certain purposes resided in patrilineal kinship groups or lineages; on the other hand, for certain other purposes it was organised about the centralised, hierarchical kingdom or state. In modern Busoga, under the administration of the British Protectorate, a third type of organisa-tion of authority has been added to these: the Western type of local government organisation involving electoral representation and bureaucratic civil service. Let us briefly examine each of these types of organisation of authority.

TRADITIONAL BUSOGA: LINEAGE AND STATE.

Every known human society has a kinship system; that is to say, every known human society allocates *some* social rôles on the basis of real or assumed biological relatedness.   The reasons for this universality of kinship-structured institutions are not yet thoroughly understood, though some of them undoubtedly relate to the absence in man (as well as in some higher primates) of a delimited mating period—making for stability of mating pairs—and to the helplessness at birth and slow maturation of the human infant—making for a relatively long period of parental care.[1]   In addition, given human society, some kinship group may be a prerequisite for adequate socialisation.   But for whatever reasons, either the nuclear family (parents and children) or some group of consanguineal kin and their children is everywhere an institutionalised unit.[2]   Everywhere also, such units are differentiated internally; distinct social rôles are assigned to their members on the basis of sex, age and generation.

Societies differ greatly, however, in the degree to which and in the ways in which they assign rôles on the basis of more extended kinship.   At one extreme on the scale of extension of institutionalised kinship are those societies in which nearly every aspect of the social system is structured in kinship terms—societies of which it might almost be said that kinship is co-extensive with the social system at large.   It is preoccupation with such societies which sometimes leads anthropologists to speak unguardedly as if "social structure" or "social organisation" were kinship and nothing else.[3] At the opposite pole, in urban areas of the modern West as well as among people inhabiting very difficult environments which preclude the formation of stable groups larger than the nuclear family, the institutionalisation of extended kinship is little emphasised.   However, this should be noted with respect to kinship systems: just as kinship systems are universal, so also is membership in some kinship unit nearly universal for members of any given society.   With the exception of orphans not reared in families, everyone is for some period a member of a family of orientation. And if a society is to persist, most of its members who reach adulthood must become members of families of procreation.[4]   It may

---

[1] Hooton summarises the available data concerning non-human primate families.   (See Hooton, E. A., *Up from the Ape*, 1949.)

[2] Murdock claims universality for the nuclear family.   (See Murdock, G. P., *Social Structure*, 1949, p. 2.)

[3] Eggan does not make this equation, but he notes, with regard to the Pueblo Indians, that "In many societies the kinship system represents practically the entire social structure . . . ." (Eggan, Frederick, *Social Organisation of the Western Pueblos*, 1950, p. 10.)

[4] Warner uses the terms "family of orientation" and "family of procreation" to refer respectively to the family in which an individual is born and reared and that in which he in turn produces and rears offspring.   This is a uesful distinction because it separates analytically elements which in concrete situations may be either fused (the extended family) or distinct (the isolated nuclear family).   (See Warner, W. L., Meeker, M., and Eells, K., *Social Class in America*, 1949, p. 96.)

therefore be said that in no society is kinship "unimportant." Most rôles in the society may be assigned on other than kinship bases, but since it may be assumed that the various rôles an individual plays are not entirely unrelated to one another, the kinship system will inevitably have pervasive consequences for the rest of the social system.[1] Therefore, when we look for the part played by kinship in social systems, we shall have to look for at least two major types of "importance": (1) the direct assignment of rôles on a kinship basis; and (2) the consequences of the circumstance that persons who fill rôles of other kinds also fill kinship rôles.

The direct assignment of rôles on a kinship basis is perhaps carried furthest in those "segmentary" societies in which most of the enduring social groups are formed of persons sharing common unilineal descent. Interest in unilineal descent has had a long history in anthropological writings, but the development of modern notions concerning its functions in societies conceived of as systems may perhaps be said to stem from the work of Radcliffe-Brown, beginning with his work in Australia.[2] In a subsequent series of papers, Radcliffe-Brown formulated the notion of the "lineage principle" as the structural basis for the division of a society's members into discrete corporate groups of kinsmen.[3] Evans-Pritchard, Eggan, Fortes, Leach and Warner, among many others, have since analysed the functions of such systems in North American, Asian and African societies.[4] The corporate unilineal descent group has thus come to be recognised as a type structural feature common in societies of the middle range of complexity.

In segmentary societies, the lineage principle and its corollary, the corporate lineage group, find their fullest expression. Territorial

[1] Parsons has demonstrated this for modern American society, where kinship structuring of rôles outside the nuclear family is minimal. (See Parsons, Talcott, "The Kinship System of the Modern United States," *American Anthropologist*, Vol. XLV, No. 1, 1943, pp. 22–38). My assumption that the various rôles an individual plays have consequences for one another is based upon the common psychological assumption that personality is in some sense a system of inter-related elements. The degree and kind of inter-relatedness among these elements is, I assume, subject to great variation.

[2] Radcliffe-Brown, A. R., "Social Organisation of Australian Tribes," *Oceania Monographs*, No. 1, 1931. There had, of course, been much earlier discussion of unilineal descent. For a summary of earlier work and some hypotheses, see Lowie, R., *Primitive Society*, 1921.

[3] Radcliffe-Brown, A. R., "Patrilineal and Matrilineal Succession," *Iowa Law Review*, Vol. XX, No. 2, 1935, pp. 286–303; "The Study of Kinship Systems," *Journal of The Royal Anthropological Institute*, Vol. LXXI, 1941, pp. 1–18.

[4] Evans-Pritchard, E. E., *The Nuer*, 1940; Eggan, Frederick, *Social Organisation of the Western Pueblos*, 1950; Fortes, Meyer, *The Dynamics of Clanship Among the Tallensi*, 1945; Leach, Edmund, *Political Systems of Highland Burma*, 1954; Warner, W. L., *A Black Civilisation*, 1937. These are, of course, only a few of the studies now available.

residence, authority, property rights and religion are often cast
in a unilinear genealogical mould; social rôle is in most contexts
the rôle of corporate lineage member. Anthropological studies
of the Nuer and the Tallensi supply well-known instances of this.
But unilineal descent and corporate lineage membership as determinants of social rôle are not confined to segmentary societies. In
many African societies, for example, corporate lineages and unilineal descent are found together with other major institutions in
which rôles are assigned on non-kinship bases. Many African
kingdoms combine corporate lineages with other political institutions in which authority relations depend upon territorial residence
and individual patron-client ties. In Busoga, lineage membership
structures inheritance and succession and, in part, marriage.
Traditionally, it was the structural basis for an important aspect
of religion—the ancestor cult. But paramount authority in
Busoga traditionally resided not in lineages but in the hierarchical
organisation of the state, in which many rôles were assigned not
on the basis of kinship but rather on the basis of territorial residence
and individual achievement.

Here my remarks above concerning the dual importance of
kinship in the total social system become relevant. In those
sectors of Soga society where rôles are assigned on the basis of
lineage membership, the importance of kinship is clear enough. But,
as I hope my analysis will show, the kinship system also has consequences for those institutions (here primarily the state organisation) where kinship does not directly determine social relations.
It seems to me that this is particularly true where the kinship
system is a unilineal one involving corporate lineages. Kinship
rôles inevitably influence the other rôles an individual plays, but
where kinship is extended and becomes the basis for corporate
group membership, it will drastically limit the degree to which
major rôles may be successfully assigned on non-kinship bases.
And, conversely, the assignment of major rôles on a non-kinship
basis will limit the effective assignment of rôles on the basis of
corporate lineage membership.

This is not, I think, as trite a statement as it may appear. Of
course, the same rôles cannot be assigned simultaneously on both
kinship and non-kinship bases, but I am saying something more than
this. It might be thought possible for both kinship and non-
kinship rôle assignment to be prominent in the same social system
so long as the contexts in which they operate be kept separate.
Surely this sort of situation is very common; it is prominent in
modern Western societies where families continue to exist while
most rôles outside the nuclear family are distributed on non-kinship

bases.   But this is only possible without the development of serious strains, I would argue, where the range of effective kinship is short, as is the case in the modern urban West.   For it appears to be in the nature of kinship relations that they embrace total persons.   It is difficult to treat a person as a kinsman in one context and as a non-kinsman in another.   In our society we recognise this difficulty by forbidding a person to sit as a juror at the trial of his kinsman and by institutionally frowning upon the employment of kinsmen in the same business or other occupational unit.   We solve the problem by so arranging matters that kinsmen do not meet in non-family contexts.[1]   Where the range of effective kinship is wide, however, and particularly where extended kinship is the basis for membership in large corporate groups, such separation of contexts is much less easily arranged.   Situations are likely to arise in which both membership in corporate kinship groups and rôle assignment on non-kinship bases appear to be relevant and where the two tend to conflict.   An individual who finds himself in such a situation cannot satisfy the requirements of both sets of norms.

It would appear then that the hierarchical, centralised Soga state and the corporate lineage organisation were structurally antagonistic. In the state structure, the key rôles were filled by persons who as individuals had distinguished themselves in the personal service of a superior.   Recruitment to such rôles was explicitly based upon ability and personal loyalty to the superior.   Though the ruler himself was hereditary, the administrative organisation through which he governed the state was not his own corporate descent group but rather, almost exclusively, his staff of such personal functionaries chosen for ability and loyalty.   On the other hand, however, *every* member of the society, whatever else he might be, was also a member of a corporate lineage.   In terms of lineage values, authority relations within the corporate group took little or no account of a person's social position outside it.   Furthermore, though there were positions of greater and lesser authority within the lineage, the emphasis was upon the *corporate unity* of the group as a whole and not upon authority relations between particular individuals.   It was inevitable, therefore, that state and lineage frequently collided, so to speak.   In fact, a person's position within the state was liable to distort his position within the lineage and thus disrupt the

---

[1] Parsons speaks of the "particularistic" and "functionally diffuse" character of kinship rôles.   (See Parsons, Talcott, *The Social System*, 1951, pp. 154–155.)   At earlier periods in the West, of course, kinship was very prominent in structuring relations outside the nuclear family.   Even to-day the limitation of kinship structuring to family contexts is more prominent in urban middle-class groups than elsewhere.

operation of the lineage in terms of its own rules.   And conversely, lineage ties tended to intrude into the state system and to make for instability within it.   One consequence of this instability, as we shall see, was a particular type of vulnerability to Western penetration.

Not, of course, that such situations are uncommon.   On the contrary, societies which combine lineage organisation with political institutions of the state type are quite common, both in Africa and elsewhere.   I therefore see this part of the analysis of Soga society as suggestive for similar situations elsewhere and particularly for other Bantu states in the Lake Victoria area.   Let me put it in the form of a general hypothesis: The co-existence in a society of corporate lineages with political institutions of the state type makes for strain and instability.   In the last chapter, I will try to qualify this hypothesis and make it more precise by more clearly defining "instability" and "strain."   It may, of course, be an incorrect hypothesis, but it is, I think, a good one in that it is capable of being tested.[1]

MODERN BUSOGA: THE INTRODUCTION OF MODERN WESTERN LOCAL GOVERNMENT.

Although, as I have already suggested, the traditional Soga political system was not entirely a harmoniously integrated one, its component institutions did have some important common features.   In both the corporate lineage and the hierarchically-organised state, authority relations were highly personal.   An individual's role *vis-à-vis* his lineage mate and his rôle *vis-à-vis* his superior or subordinate in the patron-client system were governed less by the position of each in the system at large than by the particular relationship between them as individual persons.   Thus a person's authority relations pertain essentially only to his own lineage head and not to just any lineage head.   In the state system, they pertain to his own superiors and subordinates and not to superiors and subordinates in general in the system at large. Furthermore, as I have already noted with regard to kinship relations, such persons tend to be related as total social persons, not merely in certain limited contexts.[2]

This point will perhaps become clearer if we contrast the type of authority system most characteristic of the modern West, that is,

---

[1] Fortes has recently noted, with regard to societies having both corporate lineages and centralised state systems, that: "The political structure of these societies was always unstable . . . ."   (See Fortes, Meyer, "The Structure of Unilineal Descent Groups," *American Anthropologist*, Vol. LV, No. 1, 1953, p. 26.)

[2] Parsons, Talcott, *The Social System*, 1951, pp. 154–155.

the bureaucratic type of system. It is the hallmark of all that modern Western peoples see as progress in government that authority relations should not be personal. Authority should pertain to the office, not the person. An official should treat everyone the same and not, as we say, "play favourites." As Max Weber, in his classical study of modern bureaucracy has put it, the rule is ". . . straightforward duty without regard to personal considerations . . . Everyone in the same empirical situation . . . is subject to formal equality of treatment."[1] And an official's relations with others are strictly limited to the relatively restricted area within which he has jurisdiction. "Private affairs" are none of his business. To this end, modern Western countries have instituted civil service systems in which the rules and conditions of service are designed to maximise disinterestedness and impersonality. Civil servants are paid on fixed and graded scales; their jurisdictions are clearly defined and limited, frequently in terms of written rules; they are subject to transfer from one post to another; their personal property is strictly separated from the financial and other resources of the office. Within the bureaucracy and in relations between the bureaucracy and the public, authority relations hold between offices or positions, not between the persons who hold them.[2]

This contrast between the authority system of traditional Busoga and that of the modern bureaucracy is of more than definitional interest to this study because, beginning with the establishment of the British Protectorate in the eighteen-nineties, administrative policy has emphasised the alteration of the Soga system in the direction of modern Western local government. British administration was established by more or less peaceful penetration. The state organisation was recognised and became the organisational machinery through which the first administrators governed Busoga. At first, little was changed aside from the abolition of inter-state warfare and the imposition of a tax. The formerly autonomous states were unified and the rulers were brought together to form a council. But gradually, over the following six decades, the administrators have attempted to modify the indigenous political institutions in the direction of a bureaucratic civil service so as to conform more closely to their conceptions of "natural justice" and "good government." The process, however, has been gradual. At no point has there been a sharp break with the past. The result has been that to-day Busoga is governed through an institutional

---

[1] Weber, Max, *The Theory of Social and Economic Organisation*, 1947, p. 340.
[2] Parsons refers to such rôles as "universalistic" and "functionally specific." (See Parsons, Talcott, *The Social System*, 1951, pp. 58–67.)

complex known as the "Busoga African Local Government," a structure which clearly bears the marks of its derivation from the old states and which receives much of the legitimacy which the Soga once accorded the rulers and chiefs, but which is radically different from the traditional system in its functioning.

Although the African Local Government is to-day a firmly established institution in that it represents and mobilises values which have come to be widely shared, it is not, within itself, an harmoniously integrated system and it is still less harmoniously integrated with other institutions in Busoga.   This is so because, to a substantial degree, the traditional authority system based upon kinship and personal loyalty between superiors and subordinates has survived, and it stands in direct conflict with the new civil service bureaucracy.   Behaviour which in the traditional system constituted laudable personal loyalty becomes, in terms of the civil service system, "nepotism" and "corruption."

However, the interesting, and I believe somewhat unusual aspect of the situation in Busoga (and in Uganda as a whole), is that the two types of authority system to-day stand side by side in the same society, both institutionalised and both in large measure treated as legitimate by the same persons.   It is common enough in non-Western areas under Western influence for new and old institutions to clash, but most commonly, it seems, the clash involves conflict between different groups of persons committed to conflicting institutions.   In Busoga, because the process of change has been gradual and because it has occurred under circumstances which made it rewarding to many of those concerned, it has come about (through processes which I shall describe in later chapters) that the new institutions have quietly come to be institutionalised alongside the old.   There has been no drastic and sudden transfer of power from one group to another.   The clash is literally a clash between institutions, and not between persons, since in large measure the same persons are involved in, and accept as legitimate, both sets of institutions.   The conflict does, however, have an impact upon individuals—often a quite disastrous impact.   However, instead of persons being divided one from another by conflicting institutional commitments, many individuals are divided against themselves.

It may be stated, then, as a second general hypothesis for purposes of this study, that the institutionalisation of these two kinds of authority—that based upon personal loyalty and solidarity between superior and subordinate and that based upon the impersonal, disinterested conception of bureaucratic "office"—within the same society again results in instability and strain, and that integration within the political system of such a society can come only through one of these types of authority giving way to the other.

This study, then, is concerned with the Soga political system over nearly a century of gradual but steady change. Its aim is the analysis of the system and in particular of the rather different kinds of internal conflict which have occurred within it under traditional and modern conditions.

Chapter II

HISTORICAL PROLOGUE

1862: The Historical Base-Line.

Written history begins for the Soga in the year 1862. On 28th July of that year, John Hanning Speke, an explorer for the Royal Geographical Society, arrived at Ripon Falls near the site of the modern town of Jinja, where the Victoria Nile spills out of Lake Victoria and begins its descent to Egypt (see Map 1). Since Speke's route inland from the East African coast had taken him around the southern end of the Lake, he approached Busoga from the west through the country of Buganda. Having reached his goal—the source of the Nile—he turned northward and followed the river down stream without further exploring Busoga. He records, however, being told that "Usoga" (the Kiswahili form of the name) was an "island," which indicates that the term meant to surrounding peoples essentially what it means to-day. The present-day Busoga District is bounded on the north by the swampy Lake Kyoga, on the west by the Victoria Nile, on the south by Lake Victoria and on the east by the Mpologoma River.[1]

The bases for Busoga's unity in the eyes of her neighbours, apart from this insular character of her geographical setting, are not immediately apparent. Linguistically, the Soga are among the northernmost members of the vast block of closely-related Bantu-speaking peoples which stretches westward across the Belgian Congo and southward toward the Cape of Good Hope. Differences between neighbouring languages are often slight, particularly among the Bantu languages of the Lake Victoria region. Politically distinct peoples often speak mutually intelligible dialects. The Soga as a whole, however, do not even share a single distinct dialect. The country is divided, north and south, into two quite clearly-marked linguistic zones. In the north and north-west, the people speak a dialect known locally as "Lupakoyo," which differs in certain sound patterns and to some degree in lexicon from the "Lutenga" spoken throughout the remainder of the area. Both are quite distinct from the present-day "standard" (written) forms of Luganda and Lunyoro, the languages spoken by the peoples who border Busoga on the west and north-west respectively. However, I have been told by many Soga (though I have not confirmed this

[1] Speke, John Hanning, *Journal of the Discovery of the Source of the Nile*, 1863, p. 370.

myself) that the Victoria Nile does not sharply separate Ganda and Nyoro speakers from speakers of the Soga dialects, but that these major dialect blocks run together at their margins. The

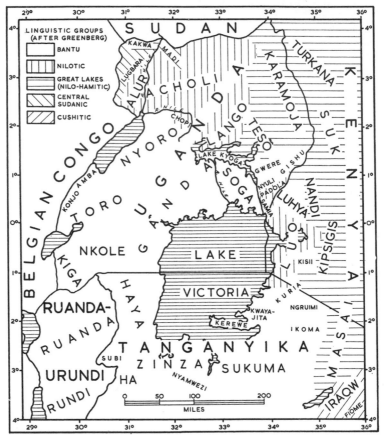

MAP 1.   Peoples of the Lake Victoria Area.

same is said to occur on Busoga's eastern boundary.   The Gwere, Nyuli and other small Bantu-speaking groups to the east are said to speak dialects similar to those of their immediate Soga neighbours.[1]

[1] Prior to 1900, the northern portion of the territory marked "Ganda" on Map 1 was part of Bunyoro.   Busoga and Bunyoro thus had a common boundary along the Nile between Lakes Victoria and Kyoga.   On the eastern side, Gwere is most similar to Soga (Professor A. N. Tucker, private communication).

Where Busoga borders upon non-Bantu-speaking areas, linguistic boundaries are of course much sharper. Across Lake Kyoga to the north and beyond into the Anglo-Egyptian Sudan, live such Nilotic-speaking peoples as the Lango, Acholi and Alur, while other members of the same linguistic group, the Luo and the Padola, are found along the Kenya-Uganda border on the north-eastern shores of Lake Victoria. To the east, the Soga and their Bantu neighbours are separated from such Bantu-speaking peoples of central and southern Kenya as the Kikuyu and Kamba by the Great Lakes ("Nilo-Hamitic") group.[1] Of these, the best-known to the Soga are the Teso, across Lake Kyoga to the north-east. Other members of the group—the Turkana, Karamoja, Suk, Nandi and Masai—are known only to those Soga who have travelled widely. All, however, are clearly distinguished by the Soga from the Bantu-speaking peoples, whom they recognise as close linguistic and cultural kinsmen. Following a common human tendency, they often enough look down upon the non-Bantu peoples as cultural inferiors, an attitude which the non-Bantu fully reciprocate.

Such tendencies are reinforced by the cultural position of the Soga among the Bantu peoples around Lake Victoria. Corresponding closely, though not exactly, with the linguistic groupings among the peoples of the Lake Victoria area are distinctions of social structure and value system. Most of the Bantu peoples of Uganda, northern Tanganyika and Ruanda-Urandi traditionally had political systems of the centralised state type. Ethnographically most famous among these Bantu states are Buganda, Bunyoro and Ankole, but the complex is much wider, extending south-west around Lake Victoria to include the Toro of Uganda (a nineteenth-century off-shoot of the Nyoro), the Ruanda and Rundi of Ruanda-Urundi and the Haya, Zinza, Ha, Nyamwezi and other peoples of north-western Tanganyika.

The core feature of the complex is the institution of rulership. At the head of each state was a paramount ruler who held his position within a royal partilineal descent group—sometimes a clan, sometimes a lineage within a clan—but who wielded authority over a territorial unit and its inhabitants without regard to kinship. Subordinate to the ruler was an administrative staff of chiefs who administered territorial sub-divisions in the name of the ruler. Within this broad pattern, there were variations in structural detail. Among the Nkole, Ruanda and Rundi, apparently, the royal group was part of an endogamous, aristocratic caste

[1] Here and elsewhere in this study I follow Greenberg's classification of African languages. (See Greenberg, J. H., "Studies in African Linguistic Classification," *Southwestern Journal of Anthropology*, Vol. V, Nos. 2, 3 and 4; Vol. VI, Nos. 1, 2, 3 and 4, 1949–50.)

which controlled not only the rulership itself but also many of the subordinate chiefships.[1] Among the Haya, Toro, Ganda, Nyoro and Soga, the royal group was not, at any rate in recent times, an endogamous group and commoners of ability were able to marry into the royal group and to achieve positions of great authority under the ruler.[2] Everywhere, however, there was rulership, a substantial degree of social stratification, and, among those higher in the social scale, a degree of the aristocratic courtliness and *politesse* which so often accompanies these structural features elsewhere in the world. Though among persons at the same level of society unilineal kinship groups played an important structural rôle, such structures were over-ridden, on the level of the total society, by hierarchical structures of authority and status. A man was a peasant, a chief or a ruler as well as a member of a clan or a lineage.

In general, all this was absent among the non-Bantu peoples of the area. Among the Nilotic peoples, social relations were very largely structured in terms of unilineal descent.[3] Among the Great Lakes ("Nilo-Hamitic") group, age-grading as well as unilineal descent played a central structural rôle.[4] Accompanying these structural differences were differences in value and attitude. Though there were differences of seniority within the unilineal kinship group, the entire group represented, in a quite real sense, a political "company of equals."[5] Even more could this be said of

[1] Oberg, K., "The Kingdom of Ankole in Uganda," in Fortes, M. and Evans-Pritchard, E. E. (eds.), *African Political Systems*, 1940, pp. 121–164; Roscoe, John, *The Banyankole*, 1923; Maquet, Jacques, "Le problème de la domination Tutsi," *Zäire*, Vol. VI, No. 10, 1952, pp. 1011–1016; Maquet, Jacques, "Kinship Groups in Old Ruanda," *Africa*, Vol. XXIII, No. 1, 1953, pp. 25–28.

[2] Roscoe, John, *The Baganda*, 1911; Roscoe, John, *The Bakitara*, 1923; Cory, Hans and Hartnoll, M. M., *Customary Law of the Haya Tribe of Tanganyika Territory*, 1945; Robertson, D. W., *The Historical Considerations Contributing to the Soga System of Land Tenure*, Government Printer, Entebbe, 1940.

[3] Evans-Pritchard, E. E., *The Nuer*, 1940; Evans-Pritchard, E. E., "Luo Tribes and Clans," *Rhodes-Livingstone Journal*, No. 7, 1949, pp. 24–40; Southall, A., "Lineage Formation Among the Luo," *International African Institute Memorandum XXVI*, 1952; Driberg, J. H., *The Lango*, 1923; Butt, Audrey, "The Nilotes of the Anglo-Egyptian Sudan and Uganda," *Ethnographic Survey of Africa, East Central Africa*, Part IV, 1952.

[4] Huntingford, G. W. B., "The Northern Nilo-Hamites," *Ethnographic Survey of Africa, East Central Africa*, Part VI, 1953; Gulliver, P. and P. H., "The Central Nilo-Hamites," *Ethnographic Survey of Africa, East Central Africa*, Part VII, 1953; Huntingford, G. W. B., "The Southern Nilo-Hamites," *Ethnographic Survey of Africa, East Central Africa*, Part VIII, 1953; Bernardi, B., "The Age-System of the Nilo-Hamitic Peoples," *Africa*, Vol. XXII, No. 4, 1952, pp. 316–332.

[5] The relatively egalitarian character of these Nilotic societies is illustrated by Evans-Pritchard's famous conversation with one of his Nuer informants. (See Evans-Pritchard, E. E., *The Nuer*, pp. 12–13.)

the age-set.[1] The great differences in power and status which cut across the Bantu states were absent.

All this goes far to explain the sharp distinction which the Bantu and non-Bantu peoples of the area drew, and still draw, between themselves. To Bantu, the egalitarian Lango or Teso is uncultivated and crude; to the latter, the Bantu are obsessed with distinctions of rank and somewhat effeminate. The dividing line is not, of course, as sharp as the stereotypes suggest. In the extreme north-west corner of Uganda, the Nilotic Alur had created a centralized state system not unlike those of the Bantu further south.[2] And on the margins of the Bantu states, such small Bantu groups as the Konjo, Amba, Kiga and Gishu had segmentary societies not greatly unlike those of the Nilotes.[3] It is an index of the strength of the stereotype, however, that the Soga have difficulty in classifying the segmentary Bantu tribes. All Nilotic and Great Lakes peoples (the Alur are too distant to be significant) are *bakedi*— "naked savages." A Soga's first impulse is to so classify the Bantu Gishu, because they behave like Nilotics, but when reminded that the Gishu are Bantu, he shrugs and tries to change the subject. To him, the world is divided among Europeans, Asians, "civilised" Bantu Africans and "uncivilised" non-Bantu Africans.

The Soga are, then, members of the Bantu group around Lake Victoria with centralised, state-type political systems. Not until the recent colonial period, however, did they belong to a single political unit. Within the boundaries of the present District were, at the time of Speke's arrival, a number of small states, broadly similar in structure, though they varied widely in population and in territorial extent. Within each state, the peasant-commoner population was divided among a number of dispersed patrilineal clans and lineages, while set apart from the peasant clans was a royal clan within which one lineage held the rulership of the state. Subordinate to the ruler was an administrative staff consisting of territorial chiefs and palace functionaries.

The states which comprised roughly the northern and eastern

---

[1] I do not, of course, mean that there are no distinctions of status in such societies. There are distinctions based upon age, genealogical seniority and individual achievement. I mean simply that these societies are egalitarian relative to the near-by Bantu states.

[2] Southall, Aidan, *Alur Society* (in press).

[3] Roscoe, John, *The Bagesu and Other Tribes of the Uganda Protectorate*, 1923; Edel, M. M., "The Bachiga of East Africa," in Mead, M. (ed.), *Co-operation and Competition Among Primitive Peoples*, 1937; Winter, Edward, *The Baamba: A Structural-Functional Analysis of a Patrilineal Society* (in press).

I am, of course, lumping together here many different types of "segmentary" societies in contrasting them with the Bantu states.

two-thirds of Busoga have survived in much their traditional form as "Counties" in the modern District Administration (see Map 2). The boundaries of the present-day Counties of Bugabula, Luuka, Bulamogi, Bugweri, and Bukoli correspond essentially with those

COUNTY BOUNDARY
TOWNSHIP
RAILWAY
1ST CLASS ROAD
2ND CLASS ROAD
3RD CLASS ROAD

0   5   10   15
MILES

MAP 2.   Busoga District, 1952.

of the traditional states which bore the same names.   The present-day Counties of Busiki and Kigulu represent the traditional states of Busiki and Kigulu plus the territories of smaller states amalgamated with them during the colonial period.   The modern County of Butembe-Bunya, is more artificial.   It represents an amalgamation of perhaps a dozen tiny states, though the traditional structure of this southern area is much less easy to reconstruct with confidence than that of the rest of Busoga. Lying across the caravan route which linked Uganda with the coast, it was subjected more than were areas further north to disruptive influences during the early contact period; earlier still it had been a popular raiding-ground for the expanding Ganda. Finally, during the years 1901–06 much of the area along the Lake Victoria shore was depopulated by sleeping sickness. In so far, however, as one can reconstruct, the larger of these southern states appear to have been Butembe, in the area around the present-day town of Jinja; Bunya, in the central portion of the County; and Bunyuli, in the south-eastern portion of the County.

Busoga, then, was not, in pre-administration times, a single society; it was divided both linguistically and politically. Its unity consisted in a repetition in numerous political sub-divisions of an essentially common pattern of social structure—a pattern which will become clearer as this account progresses.

PRE-HISTORY.

Although the rapidity and extent of social change in Busoga over the past century has rendered the reconstruction of the pre-history of the country very difficult, some discussion of the subject is in order because formerly accepted interpretations of general northern Bantu pre-history seem at present to be changing rather rapidly. The Bantu states of the Lake Victoria area have in the past been looked upon by ethnologists as classic examples of the "conquest state." According to the popular hypothesis, the states which European and Arab explorers discovered when they reached the area in the nineteenth century are the result of conquest and subsequent domination of indigenous Bantu-speaking agri-culturalists by cattle-keeping "Hamitic" immigrants from the north-east. For reasons which would themselves be interesting objects for study, late nineteenth and early twentieth century ethnographers were extremely fond of tracing Hamitic influences in Negro Africa. "Hamitic" is, of course, primarily a linguistic term, but it came to be identified as well with certain physical features (light skin, tallness, caucasoid facial features, etc.) and certain cultural traits (the "cattle complex," centralised political organisation, etc.). Any deviation from the stereotype of the short, black-skinned, thick-lipped, flat-nosed negro agriculturalist with a simple political system was ascribed to Hamitic influence.

The father of the "Hamitic hypothesis" as applied to the Lake Victoria area appears to have been Speke himself, who decided, on the basis of what he saw during his explorations, that the dynasties which ruled over the Bantu states of the area must have been the descendants of Galla invaders.[1] Subsequent ethnologists such as Roscoe, Seligman and Oberg adopted this interpretation and it was reinforced by the view of such linguists as Meinhof that the languages of the nearby "Nilo-Hamitic" (Great Lakes) peoples were just that—half Hamitic and half Nilotic.[2] With demonstrable Hamitic linguistic influence so near at hand, the ethnological hypothesis was strengthened.

Within recent years, the Hamitic hypothesis, at any rate in its simple form, has tended to become less and less satisfactory as an explanation for pre-history in the Lake Victoria area. Greenberg has shown that the Nilo-Hamitic languages are in fact, along with the Nilotic languages, members of the southern branch of his Eastern Sudanic language family and show no more than superficial word-borrowing from the Cushitic (branch of Hamito-Semitic, or Greenberg's "Afro-Asiatic") languages of north-eastern Africa.[3] Substantial Hamitic linguistic influence is thus pushed further away from the Bantu states.

The evidence of ethnography and tribal tradition as revealed by recent research also casts doubt on the Hamitic hypothesis. For one group of Bantu states—including Nyoro, Toro, Haya and the northern states of Busoga, tradition links the historical dynasties, not with Hamites, but with the Nilotic peoples. Father Crazzolara, after extensive investigation of tribal tradition among the Nilotic peoples of northern Uganda, came to this conclusion, and so have social anthropologists who have recently carried out field research in the area.[4] It would be improper to include here an extensive account of the results of this recent research prior to its publication. In brief, however, there appears to be a clear tradition among both Bantu and Nilotic peoples of the area that the *Babito*, the royal group in Bunyoro and Toro, are of rather recent Nilotic origin. At least some of the ruling dynasties in Buhaya appear to derive in turn from the Nyoro *Babito* and so also do the *Baisengobi*, the royal clan in the northern Soga states. In Buganda, too, there are

[1] Speke, John Hanning, *Journal of the Discovery of the Source of the Nile,* 1863, pp. 201–214.
[2] Roscoe, John, *Twenty-Five Years in East Africa,* 1921, pp. 80–82; Seligman, C. G., *Races of Africa,* 1930; Oberg, K., "The Kingdom of Ankole in Uganda," in Fortes, M. and Evans-Pritchard, E. E. (eds.), *African Political Systems,* 1940, pp. 121–164.
[3] Greenberg, J. H., "Studies in African Linguistic Classification," *Southwestern Journal of Anthropology,* Vol. V, Nos. 2, 3 and 4; Vol. VI, Nos. 1, 2, 3 and 4, 1949–50.
[4] Crazzolara, J. P., "The Lwoo: Part, I, Lwoo Migrations," *Museum Combonianum,* No. 3, 1950; Crazzolara, J. P., "The Lwoo: Part II, Lwoo Traditions," *Museum Combonianum,* No. 6, 1951; Southall, Aidan, *Alur Society* (in press).

vague traditions of Nyoro association for the royal group, though these traditions are less clear than in the case of Busoga and Buhaya.[1] In part, the view that these were Hamitic conquest states has rested upon the association of Hamitic influence with the cattle-herding people, variously known as "Hima" or "Huma," who occur throughout the area, sometimes scattered among the agricultural population and sometimes inhabiting separate communities of their own. The Hima are, in fact, physically quite distinct—being strikingly taller and thinner than most of their agricultural neighbours—and their economic and religious life is strongly dominated by cattle. It is of course possible that these people are in some sense genetically related to the Cushitic-speaking peoples of the East Horn of Africa, though to-day they universally speak Bantu languages. In the states discussed above, however, the Hima are quite clearly not the political aristocracy. Being cattle people, they frequently were, and are to-day, closely associated with cattle-wealthy rulers and chiefs, who employ them as herdsmen, and they often keep themselves socially apart from the agriculturalists. There is no evidence, however, that they were ever politically dominant. Such traditions as the royal groups in these states have regarding non-indigenous origin relate, not to the Hima, but to the Nilotic-speaking peoples to the north.

The situation is somewhat different in a second group of Bantu states—that consisting of the Nkole, Ruanda and Rundi. In those areas, apparently, the politically dominant group does consist of a distinctly taller and thinner cattle-herding aristocracy which holds an endogamous, caste-like position *vis-à-vis* the agricultural population. Such are the royal group in Ankole and the Tussi aristocracy of Ruanda and Urundi, who may indeed be related to the Hima living in the other areas. The problem remains, however, as to whether these tall cattle-people are in any sense Hamitic. To-day they, like Hima living in other areas, speak the same Bantu languages which their agricultural underlings speak.

Common sense would seem to dictate an agnostic view of the whole matter until more evidence is forthcoming and until existing evidence has been more carefully sifted, for modern techniques for the reconstruction of pre-history, such as Sapir summarised in his *Time Perspectives in Aboriginal American Culture*, have as yet been little applied in East Africa.[2] The archaeological record, particularly for proto-historic periods, is as yet very incomplete

[1] Kaggwa, Sir A., *Basekabaka be Buganda*, 1901.
[2] Sapir, Edward, "Time Perspectives in Aboriginal American Culture: A Study in Method," *Canadian Geological Survey Memoirs*, No. 90, 1916.

and no agreed racial classification has thus far emerged.[1] On present evidence one might equally well argue that the Bantu-speaking peoples are among the most recent immigrants into the Lake Victoria area! Though no one has thus far ventured to put a date to the entry of Bantu languages into the area, Greenberg's work would indicate that it occurred quite recently. Sonia Cole speaks, on the basis of paleontological evidence, of "Negroid" peoples being the most recent racial group to enter East Africa.[2]

It is important to note, however, that the Lake Victoria area is a linguistic, cultural and racial "shatter-belt." Within a radius of a few hundred miles of the Lake, one finds five major linguistic families (Niger-Congo (Bantu), Eastern Sudanic, Central Sudanic, Cushitic and, in central Tanganyika, Click), a variety of physical types ranging from very tall (Tussi) to pygmoid (Twa) and from relatively light to relatively dark pigmentation, and a wide variety of social and economic systems (pure agriculturalists and pure pastoralists, large centralised states, segmentary societies and autonomous villages). The successor to the Hamitic hypothesis will almost certainly be, not another simple formula, but a complex reconstruction based upon the painstaking evaluation of many types of evidence.

But let us leave the pre-history of the area as a whole and return to Busoga. Within a delimited area, it is possible to be somewhat more definite. I have already referred to the tradition which derives the ruling dynasties in several of the northern Soga states from the ruling *Babito* (bush buck) clan of Bunyoro. The *Baisengobi*, as the bush buck people are known in Busoga, provided the ruling dynasties in the traditional states of Bugabula, Bulamogi, Luuka, Kigulu, Bukoli and Bukono. Although the *Baisengobi* of all these areas see themselves as being closely related—indeed, as members of a single clan sharing exogamy and a single clan name—their traditions of origin, taken together, do not form an entirely coherent picture. All retain the tradition of Nyoro derivation, but different groups claim to have arrived in Busoga at different times and by different routes.

The *Baisengobi* of Bulamogi and Bukono appear to be closely linked. Both believe that they are descended from sons of Mukama

---

[1] But see Seligman, C. G., *Races of Africa*, 1930; Hooton, E. A., *Up from the Ape*, 1949; Lehmann, H. and Raper, A. B., "The Distribution of the Sickle-Cell Trait in Uganda and Its Ethnological Significance," *Uganda Journal*, Vol. XV, No. 1, 1951, pp. 41–43.

[2] Cole, Sonia, *The Prehistory of East Africa*, 1954, pp. 114–116. Dart ventures the opinion that: "A distribution map of the African races would have presented a very different picture 2,000 years ago. Few, if any, Negroes occupied the eastern half of the continent" (in Schapera, I. (ed.), *The Bantu-Speaking Tribes of South Africa*, 1937, p. 7.

PLATE II. The Relics of Lamogi. Foreground: Lamogi's shield. Standing (left to right): spear of Mukama, spear of Lamogi, the staff *nabbi*, spear of Mukama, two fetishes *watambogwe* and *walinaibi*, spear of Lamogi.

PLATE III. The Royal Stools of Bulamogi. The *nnamulondo katitiizi* on the right.

[*face p.* 30

PLATE IV. Sacred Grove for Rain-Making near the
Palace of the First Lamogi.

PLATE V. The Grave of Ngambani, Twelfth Successor
to Lamogi. The modern concrete grave-
stone lies within a circle of trees (background), said to have been planted around
the walls of Ngambani's chief wife's house.

Lukedi, a ruler of Bunyoro, whom they say was a blacksmith by trade. Tradition relates that Mukama Lukedi passed eastward to the north of Lake Kyoga to Mount Elgon, in the country of the present-day Gishu, and that he bore two sons, Nkono Wunyi (or Unyi) and Lamogi. Lamogi moved into what is to-day Gwere country and built his first palace (*mbuga*), later crossing the Mpologoma river into Bulamogi, where he established himself as ruler. Nkono Wunyi took possession of Bukono and their father, Mukama Lukedi, "returned to Bunyoro to take up his work as a blacksmith." The present hereditary ruler of Bukono is believed to be the eighteenth after Nkono Wunyi, while the present ruler of Bulamogi is believed to be the nineteenth following Lamogi.

The origin traditions of the *Baisengobi* of Kigulu and Luuka would appear to indicate a similar time depth (the present claimant to the rulership of Kigulu is believed to be the twenty-first successor to the founding ancestor) but the story of the first ancestor is somewhat different and suggests a relationship with Buganda as well as Bunyoro. The founder of both the Kigulu and the Luuka lines is said to have been Kintu, who "fell from heaven" near the present town of Tororo in what is now Padola country. Kintu then journeyed to Buswikira, in southern Busoga, where he bore a son, Wunyi. Later Kintu went to Buganda, where he became the first Kabaka (ruler), and Wunyi (or his son, Mukama) went to Bunyoro and became ruler there. Before leaving for Bunyoro, however, Wunyi (or Mukama) bore a son, Ngobi Lugwiriri. Ngobi Lugwiriri in turn had two sons, Obbo, who became the ruler of Kigulu, and Nyiro, who became ruler of Luuka.

The earliest arrivals among the *Baisengobi* would appear to be the Bukoli group, who say that the present ruler is the thirty-second successor to Okali, the first Wakoli, who is also linked in tradition with both Kintu and Mukama. The *Baisengobi* of Bukoli, though they share the bush buck totem, are thought of by most Soga as the most distantly related of the *Baisengobi* groups and are often referred to by a separate clan name, *Baisewakoli*. The group with the shortest tradition of settlement in Busoga are the *Baisengobi* of Bugabula, who are said to be descended from one Kitimbo, a son of the ruler of Bunyoro, who was sent via Lake Kyoga with many followers to found a daughter state in Bugabula. The present Gabula is said to be the twelfth successor to Kitimbo. The story itself and the shortness of the genealogical line suggests that Bugabula may represent a quite recent budding-off from Bunyoro after the *Babito* clan had already become well-established as the ruling group there. Such an interpretation is also supported by the apparently close political ties which were maintained between

Bugabula and Bunyoro down to historical times. As Speke was making his way down the Nile from Ripon Falls in 1862, he found that the portion of the river which forms the eastern boundary of Bugabula was controlled along both its banks by one Namuyonjo, a chief tributary to Kamrasi, then ruler of Bunyoro.[1] Somewhat later, shortly after Busoga had come under British administration, an Administrative Officer reported that the then heir to the rulership of Bugabula had spent much time at the court of Kamrasi's successor, Kabarega.[2] To this day, Soga of other areas often speak of Bugabula as "Bunyoro."

A final group, though they are not *Baisengobi*, should be mentioned in the same connection. The *Baisemenya*, who are the rulers of the traditional state of Bugweri, are said to be descended from Kakaire, who came from Bunyoro with the *Baisengobi* (possibly with Kitimbo, founder of Bugabula) as a servant. By one account, the *Baisemenya* once were *Baisengobi* but one of their ancestors committed incest and a separate clan was therefore founded. Like the *Baisengobi* of Bugabula, their tradition of residence in Busoga is a short one. The present ruler is believed to be the eleventh successor to Kakaire.

The precise nature of the long-term connection of these groups with Bunyoro is, of course, difficult to determine. It may, in fact, consist in common patrilineal descent, as tradition relates, or it may represent a series of genealogical fictions legitimating Nyoro political influence, which is known to have been strong in northern Busoga during the nineteenth century. Certainly there is a tendency in present-day Busoga (as in many societies where kinship is politically significant) for genealogies to be re-arranged in support of claims to legitimate authority. The geographical position of the *Baisengobi*-dominated areas *vis-à-vis* Bunyoro would equally support either of the above interpretations. They are the areas of Busoga nearest to Bunyoro, which during the nineteenth century extended across what is to-day northern Buganda to the banks of the Victoria Nile. This could equally well mean, however, either that these areas were conquered by immigrant Nyoro or that local ruling families fell under Nyoro domination and then fabricated genealogical links with the Nyoro royal clan.

It is also not clear, assuming that the *Baisengobi* were immigrants (which they clearly must have been at some point), to what degree they came as conquerors, imposing their authority upon a pre-

[1] Speke, John Hanning, *Journal of the Discovery of the Source of the Nile*, 1863, pp. 376–379.
[2] Uganda Government Archives, "Staff and Miscellaneous," 1894–II, 17th October, 1894.

existing population. Tradition in the *Baisengobi*-dominated areas is rather strikingly lacking in the conquest theme. By some accounts, the *Baisengobi* found the country empty or inhabited only by a few scattered members of a race unrelated to the present Soga. Of Kitimbo's arrival at Ingo, a part on Lake Kyoga, the Bugabula tradition says:

> When Kitimbo arrived, he did not fight because people feared (or respected) him and in that way he really became the prince of that area. When the people heard that he was the child of the ruler of Bunyoro, they made him prince and ruler of the area.

The *Baisemenya* in Bugweri relate that Kakaire arrived with an army and had to fight for possession of the country, but say that of the clans at present living in Bugweri only one, the *Baisemagumbo*, was in the area at that time. The Bulamogi and Bukono traditions do not mention any inhabitants of those areas prior to the *Baisengobi* immigration, though one or two commoner clans themselves claim to have arrived earlier. It should be noted here that most commoner clans also have rather clear traditions of migration into Busoga from other areas and of migration within Busoga from one area to another. Many have traditional origin-places along the Lake Victoria littoral or on islands in the Lake, while others are believed to have come from Buganda or from the countries of Bunyuli and Bugwere to the north-east of Busoga. Since everyone seems to have come from somewhere else, the question of priority of settlement becomes a most difficult one.

A number of factors in the situation make tradition difficult to evaluate. It is a major principle, which, as we shall see in Chapter VII, runs right through Soga theories of land-holding, that priority of settlement confers legitimate authority over land and its inhabitants. The interests of the royal groups thus run counter to their seeing themselves as conquering invaders. Rather, they like to think of themselves as the "original" inhabitants of the land who, by the benevolence of their administration, drew about them groups of followers to form the present-day population. Commoner clans often enough dispute the royals' claim to priority of settlement, but they are at a disadvantage here because royal genealogies are, for obvious reasons, better remembered. The tombs of past rulers are apt to be more clearly marked. On one occasion, I was taken around to see eight of the tombs of past rulers of Bulamogi. It was the custom, when a ruler died, to bury him in his palace compound—often in the hut of his chief wife—and to plant trees around the walls of the hut. (See Plates IV and V.) With such visual aids to the preservation of tradition, royal genealogies are much better preserved. Commoners' graves, if marked at all, are

usually marked only by a small pile of stones. And since commoners more often migrated to new areas, their graves may often
have been forgotten. Again, royal tradition tends to be preserved
by the bands of musicians and ballad-singers who were in the past,
and to a degree still are to-day, attached to courts of rulers. Thus
the whole pattern of courtly life which surrounded rulers would
have contributed to a greater preservation of their traditions.

More recent developments have contributed to the distortion of
tradition. On the one hand, royal genealogies tend to be frankly
fabricated for consumption by European officials. As we shall see,
the traditional rulers have to-day been divested of their authority,
but for them their traditional claims to rulership are often still a
living issue. The notion has spread that longer genealogies are
more like to impress the administration with the legitimacy of these
claims. Again, conflicting claims to rulership, which in the past
would have been settled by war, but which to-day simply tend to
accumulate and to remain unresolved, often result in genealogical
fabrication. At the same time, many persons in Busoga tend
more and more to think of tradition as no longer a really serious
matter. The vast changes which the past century has brought to
Busoga have rendered rather unreal to many a world in which there
were no bicycles, no schools, no cash-crop cultivation of cotton and
"no religion" (*ddini*, by which is meant Christianity or Islam).
On one occasion, I heard the following conversation take place at
a beer party:

> GEORGE (a member of the royal clan): "We found this place empty
> and made something of it. You fellows later came around begging
> for land, so we were generous and gave you some. Naturally you're
> now our slaves."
> HENRY (a commoner): "Oho! What a lie! We were here *long*
> before you. You took your power by trickery. You Princes have
> always been scoundrels!" (General laughter.)

For such persons, the origin myths have become simply tall tales
of a remote past, much as ordinary, non-scholarly Europeans regard
stories of the Middle Ages. Recent change has been too exciting
and too rewarding for many to look back with real nostalgia to a
golden age.

Finally, present uncertainty about the traditional mode of inheritance of rulership makes it difficult to estimate the time periods
represented by genealogies. Many Soga believe that in the past
succession was from brother to brother and that in quite recent
times there has been a shift to father-son succession. Of the eighteen
instances in the genealogy of the rulers of Kigulu where the mode

of succession is remembered, seven were cases of succession by full brothers or paternal half-brothers, four were cases of father-son succession, and four were cases of succession by brothers' sons. Of the remaining three instances, two represented succession by fathers' brothers and one by a grandson. The cases of father-son succession are clustered at the beginning and the end of the genealogy, while the cases of collateral succession occur through the intervening period. It is difficult even to guess at the time period represented by the full genealogy.

The dialect differences noted above between northern and southern Busoga are of little help in evaluating the traditions of *Baisengobi* immigration from Bunyoro. I am assured by Professor A. N. Tucker that the northern dialect is more similar to Lunyoro than is the southern dialect, but of course, the similarities need not relate to migration and conquest.[1] In any case, the correspondence between the northern dialect and the area dominated by *Baisengobi* dynasties is very imperfect indeed. Only Bulamogi and Bukono, of the *Baisengobi* states, are wholly within the northern dialect area. Luuka and Bugabula are divided between the two dialects, while Kigulu, Bukoli and Bugweri (the *Baisemenya* state) lie within the southern dialect area. Busiki, on the other hand, where the ruling clan, the *Baiseigaga*, have no apparent association with the *Baisengobi*, Bunyoro, or the bush buck totem, lies within the northern dialect area.

It thus appears to me to be difficult, on the basis of present knowledge, to determine with any certainty the truth or untruth of the conquest interpretation of the Soga states. Robertson, who worked in Busoga during the nineteen-thirties, is more sanguine. He feels with some certainty that at some point in the past Busoga was occupied by localised clan communities which later were conquered, or at any rate became dominated, by Nyoro immigrants.[2] I have indicated the types of traditional and linguistic evidence available which bear upon the problem, but I prefer to remain sceptical, in part because this evidence seems to me inconclusive and in part because, given proper historical research, it should prove possible in the future to throw much more light upon the proto-history of Busoga and neighbouring Bantu states. The careful collation of traditional clan histories, which in such a complex and large area would be a full research task in itself, would be very helpful. Still more useful would be the excavation, by professional archaeologists, of the tombs of rulers and other types

---

[1] Private communication.
[2] Robertson, D. W., *The Historical Considerations Contributing to the Soga System of Land Tenure*, Government Printer, Entebbe, 1940.

of sites which abound in Busoga and surrounding areas. Finally, the detailed linguistic history of the area remains to be disentangled. Another line of investigation also seems to me promising. While the empirical testing of historical hypotheses requires the skills of specialists of other kinds, such as linguists and archaeologists, a student of social systems can more properly contribute to historical thinking by suggesting hypotheses which seem to him consistent with social structure as he finds it "in the live." On the basis of my own research, which I shall describe in later chapters, it has appeared to me that in a sense the question of whether the *Baisengobi* were ultimately conquering invaders is beside the point. Soga political structure took the form of a hierarchy of patrons and clients, which extended from the ruler at the apex of the state system, with his staff of personal client-chiefs, down to the village headman, with his peasant villagers, who in many ways stood to him in a similar relationship of personal dependence. One of the results of this system was a substantial and relatively constant degree of population movement. A man would set out to "seek his fortune" in the service of a ruler or a chief and if he were successful he would be given control over a territorial unit. This unit he would then attempt to populate with his own kinsmen and dependents, if necessary driving away the existing population. In consequence, on the level of the local community at any rate, occupation by the ancestors of the present population, both royal and commoner, tends not to go back more than a few generations. If the *Baisengobi* were ultimately intrusive into Busoga as a whole, population movement since that time has been such that the present-day structure represents not so much a conquest of indigenes by immigrants as a coalescence of groups and communities around rulers and chiefs.

Comparative analysis of related societies should also contribute hypotheses concerning the political history of the area. Although most of the Bantu-speaking peoples around Lake Victoria had developed centralised political systems at the time when the first European explorers arrived, still there were on the margins of these states societies of the "segmentary" type in which specialised political institutions were absent or weakly-developed. Among the Gishu and some of the "Luhya" groups of the Kavirondo area, a more or less classical segmentary system appears to be the rule.[1] However, among one of the Luhya groups—the Wanga—and in at least one of the Kisii tribes, there were at least the beginnings of specialised political institutions of the state type.[2] In addition,

[1] Wagner, Günter, *The Bantu of North Kavirondo*, 1949.
[2] Wagner, *op. cit.*; Mayer, Philip, "The Lineage Principle in Gusii Society," *International African Institute Memorandum*, XXIV, 1949.

certain others of the peripheral segmentary Bantu societies have in historic times come under the sway of established states. The Amba and Konjo, for example, have over the past half-century been incorporated into the state of Toro.[1] Comparative analysis of these different types of political situation within a series of culturally closely related societies should yield hypotheses concerning the growth and functioning of state systems which can be related to archaeological and other historical research. One or two such hypotheses will be suggested in the final chapter of this book.

It should be noted, finally, that the problem of the rise of state systems in Busoga is not limited to the areas dominated by the *Baisengobi* or other apparent immigrants from Bunyoro. Busiki and the smaller states of south Busoga, though mostly much smaller in scale than the *Baisengobi* states, were very similar in structure. I know of no evidence, however, to indicate that these states were other than indigenous growths. For example, the *Baiseigaga*, who form the royal group in Busiki and in the small state of Busambira (to-day amalgamated with Kigulu to form the southernmost sub-county of Kigulu County) claim indigenous origin. The Busambira group believe that their first ancestor, Igaga, was created on Nhenda Hill, a prominent rocky out-crop within the present territory of Busambira. Without doubt migration played a part in the formation of these small southern states, but one finds no tradition of "conquering invaders." Perhaps it is not too much to suggest that, in view of the rather striking similarity in structure between the northern and southern states (which will be documented in later chapters) and in view of the absence of clear-cut evidence of difference in their processes of formation, the two groups of states may be regarded as posing essentially the same type of sociological problem.

BUSOGA ENTERS WORLD HISTORY.

East and Central Africa were among the last of the great non-Western areas to come under European domination and consequently the progression from exploration to colonial administration and hence to Westernisation in the modern sense has been much more rapid. The Europe which entered the New World in the sixteenth and India in the seventeenth century was still essentially a peasant Europe in which science and learning were the preoccupation of a few and the application of science to the affairs of daily life was essentially still a dream for the future. The Europe

[1] Winter, E. H., *The Baamba: A Structural-Functional Analysis of a Patrilineal Society* (in press).

which entered East and Central Africa was the Europe of the late nineteenth century—a Europe throbbing with industrialisation and self-conscious progress. The pace of events in the Lake Victoria area may be judged from the fact that by 1901—four decades after Speke's discovery of the source of the Nile—a railway from Mombasa had reached Lake Victoria, opening the whole region to substantial overseas trade. By the middle of the twentieth century, the Nile had been dammed at its source to provide electric power for industrialisation and there was serious talk of Uganda as a self-governing state in the modern Western sense. A more detailed consideration of the impact of European administration upon Busoga, and particularly upon its political structure, must have a chapter to itself later in this book, but a brief account here of the circumstances under which Busoga and her neighbours came into contact with Europe and European influences will perhaps provide background for an understanding of what follows.[1]

In the events which led from Speke's visit in 1862 to the establishment of the British Protectorate in Uganda in 1894, the Soga were seldom prominent. Important as Speke's discovery of the Nile's source was for the extension of geographical knowledge, the most significant result of his explorations politically was the establishment of contact between Europe and the state of Buganda. The Ganda state, of which Speke provides an excellent description, was at that time becoming the political centre of gravity for the whole region around Lake Victoria. It was more highly centralised than the other Bantu states of the area and was in the process of extending its influence over neighbouring territories, to a great extent at the expense of its primary rival, Bunyoro. Upon Buganda and Bunyoro, therefore, Europeans with missionary, commercial or imperial interests centred their attention. It appears that in the middle of the nineteenth century, the rulers of the south Busoga states had become in effect tributary possessions of Buganda, while in north Busoga, Nyoro influence was stronger. Thus Busoga, instead of taking a direct hand in the events which resulted in European domination of the area, tended merely to reflect and to follow in processes which centred in the more powerful neighbouring states. In quite a real sense, Busoga entered world history in the shadow of Buganda.

Another factor helped to reduce Busoga's part in the process of European expansion in the area and also, incidentally, to impoverish

---

[1] For fuller historical background see Thomas, H. B. and Scott, Robert, *Uganda*, 1935; Coupland, R., *East Africa and Its Invaders*, 1938; Coupland, R., *The Exploitation of East Africa*, 1939; Hill, M. F., *Permanent Way: The Story of the Kenya and Uganda Railway*, 1949; Oliver, Roland, *The Missionary Factor in East Africa*, 1952.

the historical record of how these processes reacted upon Busoga. Until the late eighteen-eighties, the route followed by caravans from the coast to Buganda led around the southern margin of Lake Victoria, thus avoiding the territory of the hostile Masai. Travellers thus entered Buganda from the south-west instead of by the more direct route through Busoga and consequently early written accounts of Busoga tend to concern only the area bordering upon Buganda and the coastal strip accessible by canoe from the lake.

But if Busoga was only indirectly involved in the events which followed upon Speke's visit, these events were full of consequences for her future and they must now be briefly described. The first attempt to apply external administration to the area which was to become modern Uganda came from Egypt and was stimulated, at least in part, by the campaign against the slave trade which was so prominent as a humanitarian cause all through the nineteenth century. Beginning some few decades before Speke's arrival, Arab, Swahili and Sudanese slave and ivory traders had penetrated inland to the lake regions, both from the north and from the east coast, where Arab communities had been established for centuries. According to Thomas and Scott, the Khedive Ismail, in response to anti-slavery opinion in Europe, undertook to occupy and administer the southern Sudan and adjoining areas of Uganda.[1] This area became known as the Province of Equatoria and in 1869 an Englishman, Sir Samuel Baker, was appointed Governor-General. Egyptian administration never in fact became a reality outside a relatively small area in north-west Uganda, though the officers in charge included such colourful figures as Colonel Charles Gordon, who was killed in the Mahdist revolt in the Sudan in 1885, and the German-Mohammedan naturalist, Eduard Schnitzer ("Emin Pasha"). Administrative posts were ultimately established for brief periods in what is now the Northern Province of Uganda and in Bunyoro, but "administration" seldom meant more than rather unsuccessful attempts to halt the slave traffic. Neither Bunyoro nor Buganda, to which the Egyptian administration sent emmissaries, was ever subdued in any sense and there was much friction, frequently due to the tendency of the Sudanese garrisons to live rather freely off the land. With the success of the Mahdist rebellion in the Sudan in 1885, the garrisons in Uganda were cut off and such administration as had been established tended to wither on the vine.

Though little was accomplished in an administrative sense, the brief Egyptian episode in Uganda's history did leave a definite

<hr />

[1] Thomas, H. B. and Scott, Robert, *Uganda*, 1935, pp. 11–12.

mark on the social structure of the country by contributing to the development of a substantial Islamic community. Together with the Arab traders of the East African coast, the Sudanese troops formed a nucleus around which local communities of African Moslems could develop. Both groups remained, the former as traders, the latter as troops under the subsequent British Administration and later as settlers. Although no administrative post was ever established in Busoga during the period of nominal Egyptian control, companies of Sudanese troops left over from this period were, at a later date, stationed in the District and both through proselytisation and through inter-marriage with Soga families they contributed substantially to what is to-day a large Moslem minority in Busoga.

The campaign against the slave trade and the accounts of the highly-organised Bantu states of the area which had reached Europe through the writings of Speke, Stanley (who further explored the region in 1875–76) and others also stimulated the interest of Christian missionary groups.[1] In 1877, a group from the Anglican Church Missionary Society, and in 1879, a party of Roman Catholic White Fathers of Algiers, arrived in Uganda and began work. Again, the centre of activity was Buganda, since the missionaries believed, quite correctly, that success in Buganda was the key to success in the whole surrounding area. So far as I have been able to discover, no attempt was made to establish permanent missions in Busoga until the eighteen-nineties.

The pace of events now began to quicken. Mutesa, the ruler of Buganda, had accepted both Mohammedan and Christian missionaries at his court, perhaps in part out of curiosity and in part in order to secure his political position, both internally and with respect to Buganda's traditional rival, Bunyoro. But during the latter years of his reign, and in that of his son, Mwanga, who succeeded him in 1884, politico-religious rivalry began to develop around the three intrusive religious groups and between their adherents and the pagans. As I shall describe in a later chapter, the structure of the Bantu states of the area contained serious sources of strain and instability, centring upon succession within the royal group. To these traditional potentialities for faction were added the divisive influences of the new religions, and Buganda entered upon a period of intermittent conflict which not infrequently broke into open warfare. Between 1888 and 1890, the rulership of Buganda

---

[1] For example, H. M. Stanley's famous letter to the London *Daily Telegraph* (15th November, 1875) appealing for a mission to the area stimulated a flood financial contributions to the Church Missionary Society. (See Oliver, Roland, *The Missionary Factor in East Africa*, 1952, pp. 39–40.)

changed hands three times as one or another of the conflicting factions became dominant.

At this point, European governments began to take a greater interest in East Africa. In 1885, at the Conference of Berlin, spheres of influence were negotiated and in agreements signed in 1886 and 1890, East Africa was divided among Great Britain, Germany and the Sultan of Zanzibar (under British Protectorate). Great Britain thus acquired a sphere of interest in the area later to become the Uganda Protectorate and Kenya Colony, Germany became dominant in what is now Tanganyika Territory, while the Sultan of Zanzibar's sphere was confined to a coastal strip ten miles in width.

In 1888, a Charter was granted to the Imperial British East Africa company. The first Company expedition, during 1889 and 1890, arrived to find Buganda a confusion of competing factions and soon withdrew. In 1890, however, a second party under Captain F. D. (later Lord) Lugard made contact with Mwanga, now restored as ruler, with whom he signed a treaty giving the Company the right to intervene in Ganda affairs. Lugard succeeded in uniting the two Christian factions and, with the help of the Sudanese troops remaining from the Egyptian garrisons, defeated both the Ganda Mohammedan faction and Kabarega, the ruler of Bunyoro, who had taken the opportunity of dissension in Buganda to renew his attacks. In 1894, Great Britain assumed a Protectorate over the area and in the following year the charter of the short-lived Company was revoked.

The remaining years of the century saw the consolidation of British administration and its extension over the areas peripheral to Buganda. In Busoga, which had been relatively little affected by the politico-religious struggles in Buganda, Company posts were established in 1892 in Bukoli and in 1893 in Bunya. In 1893, also, Christian missionary effort was begun by the Anglicans in Bukoli and by the Roman Catholics in Luuka. District headquarters were established at Iganga in 1900 and were moved to Jinja in 1901.

One further outbreak of warfare occurred during this period. In 1897, there developed a general mutiny of the Sudanese garrisons and the mutineers were soon joined by both Kabarega, ruler of Bunyoro, and Mwanga, ruler of Buganda, in a final ineffectual effort to free themselves from European domination. The rebellion, however, was soon defeated, and in 1899 both Kabarega and Mwanga, who had taken refuge in Lango country, were captured and exiled. In this brief, final outbreak, Busoga was more directly, though only locally, involved. The Sudanese soldiers stationed in Bunya mutinied, threw back the British force sent against them, and escaped across the Nile into northern Buganda. However, only a few Soga Moslems were involved; it was essentially an affair of foreigners.

In spite of the recent years of dissension and warfare, Buganda was still regarded by the British administration as the most advanced area of the Protectorate and the centre from which European administrative influence might spread. (It is thus appropriate, though somewhat confusing, that the Protectorate as a whole came to be known by the Kiswahili term "Uganda," though actually Ganda territory constituted only a small part of the total area). Under the Uganda Agreement, negotiated by Sir Harry Johnston as Special Commissioner in 1900, the infant son of the deposed Mwanga was recognised, under a regency, as ruler of Buganda and the authority of the Buganda Government, consisting of the ruler and his ministers and chiefs, was confirmed, subject to the "over rule" of Her Majesty's representatives. The territory of the Ganda state was extended to the west and north, largely at the expense of Bunyoro. Though direct Ganda control over other surrounding areas came to an end (Busoga was made an administrative District directly under the Protectorate Government in 1895), indirectly Ganda influence continued to be pervasive over wide areas of the Protectorate. Buganda had been the centre of European missionary and political effort and was therefore able to provide a body of men already familiar with Europeans and European ways. In the years following 1900, Ganda chiefs were widely utilised in the administration of surrounding areas and Ganda clergymen and teachers often staffed new mission stations. In Busoga, one of the consequences was the development of Luganda as the official written language in schools, churches and government affairs.

Over the past half-century, Uganda has developed her own unique variation on the general East and Central African pattern of multi-racial society. Indeed, in economic development, Uganda has followed a pattern more common in West Africa. Though during the early years of British administration there were plans for extensive European settlement, in the event economic development in Uganda has largely proceeded on the basis of peasant cash-crop cultivation. Many of the European plantations which were established during the early years became uneconomic during the First World War and others were abandoned during the subsequent depression period. To-day Uganda's economy rests heavily upon the export of peasant-grown cotton and coffee, with plantation crops contributing only a relatively minor share of the national income. An important consequence has been that the European population in Uganda has been dominantly missionary, commercial and governmental and there has not developed that conflict-producing competition for land which has embittered race relations in many other African territories. Europeans are regarded, and on the whole regard themselves, not as settlers, but as administrator-tutors with the task of preparing the indigenous population for economic and political self-determination in the modern world. Often enough there is disagreement—even rather bitter disagreement—over timing and method, but the basic aim is seldom questioned on either side. It is consistent with this aim that not only is there no official "colour bar," but that on the contrary Government policy expressly opposes discrimination on the basis of race. "In-group" attitudes based on race exist and play a large rôle in the private "sociability" activities of both Africans and Europeans, but the public expression of such attitudes is discouraged by both public policy and public mores. Race prejudice is "not nice" in Uganda.

In some ways it is not strictly correct to speak of relations between Africans and Europeans in terms of race relations, for the differences which divide the two groups are in large part cultural differences. Though to-day there are growing numbers of Western-educated Africans, most such persons are oriented rather more toward a modernised or Westernised Uganda than towards social relations with Europeans as such. In part this is due to the rapidity with which the frontier period passed in Uganda. Within a few decades of the discovery of the area by European explorers, the European community, dominated by civil servants and missionaries, had become a community of families with a social life of its own. The pioneer adventurer, who so frequently fathered mixed-blood families in other non-Western areas of the world, was obsolete in Uganda almost before he arrived. In consequence, the number of persons who, like the coloured population of South Africa, are European in culture and non-European in biology is very small. In part, also, the lack of a detribalised European-oriented African group is due to the largely transient character of the European community. Most of its members—civil servants, missionaries or representatives of commercial firms—spend only part of their working lives in Uganda and remain primarily oriented to England as "home." Thus there is little in the way of a stable European social life to which a truly "marginal" African could orient himself. On the whole, I think it is true to say that most Westernised Africans in Uganda remain primarily oriented to African communities and that they see themselves as the advance guard of a new African society which will equip itself with Western skills and Western political arrangements but will remain distinctly African in cultural flavour.

For all these reasons, the test case, in race relations theory, of persons culturally similar but biologically different seldom arises. Europeans and educated Africans patronise the same shops, stay at the same hotels and, particularly on official and semi-official occasions, drink, eat, chat and dance together—all with little strain, perhaps, because members of both groups see the relationship as a temporary one, both in terms of their own lives and in terms of the future of Uganda.

There is a third element in the multi-racial complex of contemporary Uganda society: the Indian community. Increasingly after 1900, immigrants from British India and Goa entered Uganda to work as artisans, to engage in business, and to fill the lower ranks of the Protectorate civil service. Historically, they filled a vacuum in a country where there were few European settlers and as yet few Africans with the requisite skills to engage in non-agricultural and non-administrative occupations. Indian traders carried commerce to the countryside and, in a few cases, built up substantial fortunes in the more sophisticated and highly-organised forms of business enterprise. To-day, however, they pose a political problem of the first magnitude for the future of Uganda. Unlike most Europeans, they are not transients. Many Indian families have been established in the country for three generations and see themselves as permanent residents. But as more and more Africans acquire education and technical skill, they tend to find Indians already established in the economic activities into which they aspire to move. Relations between the two groups are further strained by the lack of any substantial cultural *rapprochement*. Neither Hindu nor Mohammedan Indians have attempted to proselytise extensively among Africans and few have taken African spouses. With the increasing emphasis within recent years upon African economic development and African self-government (Uganda is often spoken of in British Government policy statements as developing into "a primarily African state"), the Indian community feels itself more and more insecure. Its future is perhaps Uganda's foremost long-term problem.

In this chapter, I have tried to sketch in sufficient historical background so that Soga society and the changes which it has undergone might be described without undue digression. To sum up: pre-administration Busoga was divided among a number of small kingdom-states, broadly similar in structure to the other Inter-Lacustrine Bantu states of the area. Within the area as a whole, there is evidence of considerable population shift and considerable fluidity of political boundaries. During the last century, Busoga was subjected to substantial Ganda influence and toward the end of the century this influence was strengthened by European support for Ganda expansionism. Over the past half-century, the country has been unified and integrated with its neighbours through the British Protectorate; the resulting new political entity—Uganda—is developing, under British tutelage, into a modern Western-type nation-state.

Let us now turn to Busoga itself and examine, first of all, the economic and technological foundations of contemporary Soga society.

Chapter III

ECOLOGY, ECONOMY, COMMUNICATIONS

Natural Environment and Population.

Topographically, Busoga resembles a cluster of overturned saucers on a tray. Low, flat-topped hills, one to three miles across, alternate with swampy valleys in a constant, undulating pattern. Occasional hills are topped with much-weathered granite outcrops, but most are covered with heavy red earth and support vegetation from the margin of one swamp to the next. Between the hills, sluggish streams, frequently dry during January and February, percolate through heavy growths of grasses and papyrus to join the larger rivers which flow northward into Lake Kyoga. Elevation above sea level varies from 4,400 feet at the hills along the Lake Victoria shore to 3,400 feet at Lake Kyoga.

Climatic differences divide Busoga into two zones.[1] Mean annual rainfall is relatively constant throughout the District, varying from forty to fifty-five inches per year, but variations in the distribution of precipitation throughout the year are great enough to produce marked differences in natural vegetation and agricultural potential. In the southern and central sections, where there is less monthly variation in rainfall, effective fertility is much greater. Where human occupation does not interfere, as in the area along the shore of Lake Victoria depopulated by sleeping sickness, a dense growth of elephant grass (*Pennisetum Purpuretum*), brush and trees appears. Throughout the settled areas of the southern zone, however, a dense agricultural population has suppressed the natural vegetation. The staple food crop is the plantain, supplemented by millet, cassava and sweet potatoes, while cotton, maize, ground-nuts and recently coffee are grown for sale. Flocks of chickens, small herds of sheep and goats, and, in areas not affected by sleeping sickness, a few cattle are kept, but the intensive use of land for agriculture leaves little scope for extensive grazing.

In the northern zone and in the extreme south-east, a less favour-able monthly rainfall distribution and a lighter, sandier soil produce a natural vegetation of the short grass-savanna type and a sparser human population. Millet and sweet potatoes tend to replace

---

[1] An account of Soga agriculture and the climatic factors influencing it may be found in Tothill, J. D., *Agriculture in Uganda*, 1940.

plantains as basic food crops and cattle become of greater importance
in most areas.   As in the southern and central zones, cotton and
groundnuts are the principal cash crops.

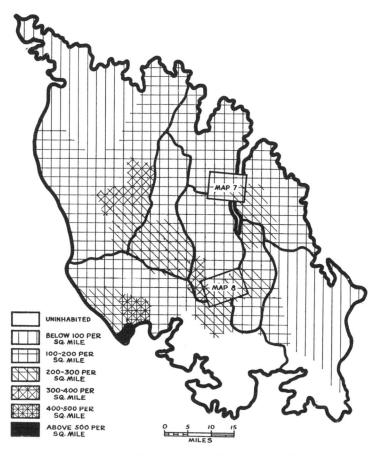

UNINHABITED

BELOW 100 PER
SQ. MILE

100-200 PER
SQ. MILE

200-300 PER
SQ. MILE

300-400 PER
SQ. MILE

400-500 PER
SQ. MILE

ABOVE 500 PER
SQ. MILE

0   5   10   15
MILES

MAP 3.   The Distribution of Population, 1952.

The two zones are not sharply delimited, but rather shade into one
another through a series of intermediate stages.   Maps 3, 4 and 5
indicate some principal variations in agricultural pattern and in the
distribution of population.[1]   The highest population densities are

[1] Permission to publish tracings of Maps 3, 4, 5 and 6, which were prepared
for the *Busoga District Plan*, was kindly granted by the District Commissioner,
Busoga.

found in a belt extending across the District from south-west to
north-east.   This belt is essentially co-extensive with the area of
greatest dependence upon the plantain as the basic food crop.

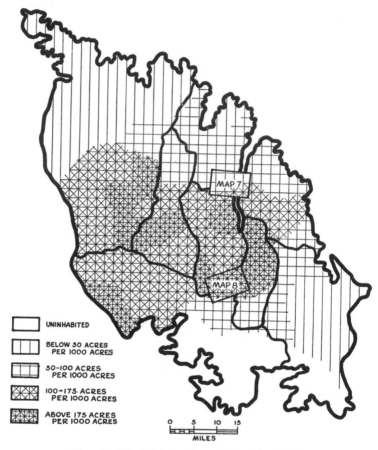

MAP 4.   The Distribution of Plantains, 1952.

The greatest densities of cattle, on the other hand, are found in the
north of the District, where plantains are more difficult to grow and
where consequently human population is sparser.   An indication
of the degree of concentration of population in the relatively densely-
populated, plantain-growing central belt is provided by Table I.
    Some six-sevenths of the Soga, therefore, live in areas where
plantain cultivation is substantial—areas with more than 50 acres

of plantains per 1,000 acres—while nearly three-fifths live in areas with more than 100 acres of plantains per 1,000 acres and where, I should judge from observation, nearly every family draws the major portion of its staple food from plantain gardens. This information—rather tedious in itself—is of some importance as one measure of the typicality of the village communities to be described at later points in this book. Most of my knowledge of

TABLE I

DISTRIBUTION OF POPULATION BY AREAS OF GREATER AND LESSER
PLANTAIN PRODUCTION[1]

In areas with less than 50 acres of plantains per 1,000 acres..	74,757
In areas with 50 to 100 acres of plantains per 1,000 acres ..	129,294
In areas with more than 100 acres of plantains per 1,000 acres	301,944
Total Busoga population	505,995

[1] These figures were arrived at by combining the populations of sub-counties lying largely within areas of varying concentration of plantain cultivation as given on Map 4. The Sub-Counties of Mumyuka, Ssabagabo, Mutuba IV Mutuba V, Mutuba VIII and Mutuba IX of Bugabula; Ssabaddu of Bulamogi; and Ssabaddu and Ssabawaali of Bukoli lie largely within the "below 50 acres per 1,000 acres" area. The Sub-Counties of Mutuba III of Bugabula; Ssabawaali of Luuka; Mumyuka, Ssabagabo, Ssabawaali and Musaale of Bulamogi; Mumyuka, Musaale and Mutuba I of Busiki; Mumyuka and Ssabagabo of Bukoli; Ssabawaali of Bugweri; and Mumyuka and Musaale of Butembe-Bunya lie largely within the "50 to 100 acres per 1,000 acres" area. The remainder of Busoga consists of areas with more than 100 acres per 1,000 acres. The population figures were taken from *African Population of Uganda Protectorate: Geographical and Tribal Studies*, East African Statistical Department, 1950, pp. 20–21.

village life is drawn from the two local areas indicated by insets on Maps 2, 3, 4, 5 and 6. The northern of the two areas, the villages in the vicinity of Kaliro Township in southern Bulamogi County, lies in the less densely-populated section with relatively more cattle and fewer plantains, while the southernmost part of Kigulu County represents the more densely-populated section, heavily dependent upon plantains and with very few cattle. The very sparsely-populated, extensively cattle-hearding areas with few plantains in the extreme north-west and south-east of the district are not represented among the communities of which I have close knowledge and therefore, in so far as ecological factors influence the pattern of social life, the contents of this book cannot be said to apply to them.

THE PEASANT ECONOMY.

Aboriginal Soga agriculture, like its present-day counterpart, was of the sedentary variety. In contrast to much of central and southern Africa, where rapid depletion of soil fertility requires frequent movement in search of new land, Busoga is endowed with soil of sufficient fertility and with a sufficiently beneficent climate to allow a more or less complete and permanent appropriation of cultivable land and the permanent occupation of dwelling sites.

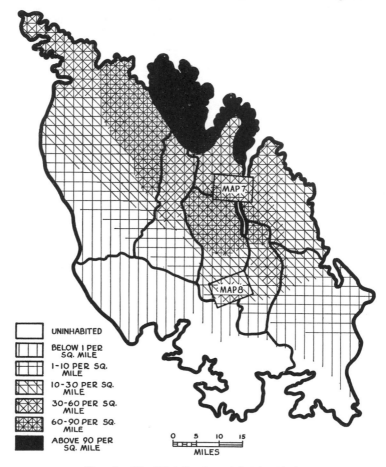

MAP 5.　The Distribution of Cattle, 1952.

Crop rotation and short-term fallowing, both of which were established in traditional Soga agricultural practice, sufficed to rejuvenate soil fertility. The dependence upon plantains as a basic food crop is both a characteristic of sedentary agriculture and at the same time one of the factors which make a sedentary life possible. A carefully-cultivated plantain garden may remain productive for more than fifty years.[1] Plantains thus occupy a permanent section of the holding, while the remainder is rotated among food crops, cash crops and fallow.

The Soga village is therefore a spatially stable community. Each homestead, with its dwelling huts, its plantain garden and its cultivated and fallow plots, is a fixed unit around which powerful sentiments of attachment may develop. This pattern of stability is important to an understanding of Soga life because it underlies the fierce attachment to a particular bit of soil characteristic of the Soga cultivator and gives him a bond of kinship with peasant farmers the world over.

Post-contact economic development has been such as to allow the Soga to participate in and receive the benefits of external trade with a minimum of readjustment in the village way of life. The introduction of cotton cultivation before the first World War provided the basis for a cash economy which could develop as a supplement to the aboriginal subsistence economy. This was early recognised by the Uganda Government and formed one of the bases of its policy against the alienation of land to non-natives.[2] Although in the early days of the Protectorate a small amount of European settlement took place, the major emphasis in Uganda's economic development has been on the cultivation of cash crops on peasant small holdings.[3] To-day, the only non-native agricultural enterprise of any consequence in Busoga is a single sugar-cane plantation operated by Indians.

The mainspring of Busoga's economy is therefore the village of peasant cultivators. The village (*mutala*) is not a cluster of dwellings but rather a stretch of land, usually co-extensive with an area of high land between swamps, over which homesteads are scattered in a more or less uniform distribution, each homestead set in among its own cultivated plots. Maps 7 and 8, showing the village communities in which intensive investigation was carried out, illustrate the pattern of alternating hill-villages and swampy valleys. All cultivable land is fully appropriated in the sense of being included in someone's holding and integrated into a cycle of crop rotation,

---

[1] Tothill, *op. cit.*, p. 114.

[2] An account of the development of the Uganda Government's land policy in relation to economic development is given in Thomas, H. B., and Spencer, A. E., *A History of Uganda Land and Surveys and of the Uganda Land and Surveys Department*, 1938.

[3] Lord Hailey, in his *Native Administration in the British African Territories*, Vol. I, 1950, provides a summary of the relative contributions to Uganda's economy of African peasant agriculture as against European and Indian plantation agriculture. In 1946, the values of produce from these sources were estimated at £6,152,281 and £1,742,739 respectively (p. 3).

although no more than half the cultivable land of a village may be under crops at a given moment. Intra-District variations in population density have been indicated on Map 3. The densities indicated there, however, are based upon total land area, which includes forests, rocky hilltops, areas along the borders of swamps rendered unsuitable for cultivation by periodic flooding, and areas given over to roads and other non-agricultural uses. Agricultural surveys of two villages carried out in 1938 by the Uganda Department of Agriculture provide a somewhat clearer picture of effective population density and land

TABLE II

Size and Utilisation of Land Holdings in Two Sample Villages[1]

	Village A	Village B
Population density per square mile of cultivable land	349	373
Average population per homestead	4·8	4·4
Average acreage of cultivable land per homestead	8·7	7·5
Average acreage per homestead under various crops		
Plantains	2·27	1·73
Cotton	2·05	1·91
Groundnuts	0·22	0·25
Millet	0·59	0·61
Sweet potatoes	0·13	0·38
Maize	0·04	0·22
Other crops	0·20	0·42
Average total acreage under cultivation per homestead	5·50	5·52

[1] Tothill, J. D., et al., A Report on Nineteen Surveys Done in Small Agricultural Areas in Uganda with a view to Determining the Position with Regard to Soil Deterioration, Uganda Protectorate, Department of Agriculture, 1938, pp. 74–87.

utilisation. Both villages lie within the central belt, one in Sub-County Ssabaddu in Bugweri County and the other in Sub-County Ssabagabo in Kigulu County. Table II provides an indication of the size and utilisation of land holdings for these two villages, which may be considered in general typical of the central belt.

Thus actual population densities in relation to cultivable land may range considerably above the overall densities indicated on Map 3. It is of interest to note that in 1938, when these surveys were carried out, Village B was considered to be somewhat over-populated. That in spite of a subsequent period of population growth serious problems of soil deterioration have not developed in the central belt is largely attributable to the fact that areas formerly depopulated by sleeping sickness have been available for gradual resettlement and have thus served as safety-valves for over-population. Village A in the above survey and the villages of southern Kigulu County in which I worked were areas of this sort. Although ultimately, of course, this source of new land will be exhausted, it will continue to be available for some years to come since much of the area immediately adjoining the Lake Victoria shore remains to be re-populated.

Table II also provides some measure of the division of peasant holdings for cash-crop and subsistence cultivation. Plantains, millet and sweet potatoes are grown for consumption by members of the homestead, while cotton and maize are sold to provide cash income. The groundnut crop is divided, a portion being sold while the rest is reserved for consumption. The peasant holding is therefore devoted in roughly equal proportions to the market economy and to the subsistence economy.

Throughout most of Busoga, the principal focus of the subsistence economy is the plantain garden and each variety of plantain contributes in its own way to the diet of the homestead. The varieties known as *bitooke*, whose fruit forms the bulk of nearly every Soga meal, are of greatest importance. Gathered while green, the fruit is peeled and boiled to form a mash which is then garnished with sauces prepared from groundnuts or other vegetables or, less commonly, since meat is not plentiful enough to form part of the daily diet, with meat gravy. Other varieties, the *gonja* and *mbidde*, form the main constituent of beer, which is the indispensable accompaniment of sociability in Busoga. The usefulness of the plantain is not limited to its fruit; nearly every part of the plant is utilised in one way or another. The stems provide fibres for building and mat-making, while the leaves are used for wrapping bundles and as makeshift umbrellas in case of rain. Leaves and stems not used for other purposes are spread about the roots of the growing plants to form a mulch and thus contribute to the renewal of soil fertility.

The peasant holding also provides many of the materials for house-building. Double lines of poles are placed upright in the ground to form a rectangular or circular pattern. Tough, bamboo-like elephant grass stems are then tied to the poles with fibres in horizontal lines and the spaces between the two resulting walls filled with mud. Walls and floors are completed by the application of a plaster made of mud, cow-dung and sand. Nowadays, the more affluent peasants roof their houses with flattened gasoline or kerosene tins or with corrugated iron sheets, but most make do with a heavy thatch of *lusenke* grass (*Imperata cylindrica*) which is plentiful throughout the country (see Plate VI).

Where a homestead contains a number of dwelling huts or out-buildings, these are arranged in a roughly circular pattern around a courtyard of bare earth which is swept daily and kept free of plant growth (Plate VII).   The homestead complex may include grain stores, a shed for young calves and, among those most receptive to Government public health campaigns, a covered pit latrine.   Often a rack made of elephant grass stems is provided for drying dishes and kitchen utensils in the sun.

TABLE III

OCCUPATIONAL SPECIALISTS IN BUYODI, BULAMOGI
IN 1952

Sub-village headmen	5
Sawyers	5
Traders	4
Basket makers	4
Smiths	3
African Local Government Policemen	3
Carpenters	3
Potters	2
Herdsmen	2
Automobile mechanics	2
Weaver of millet stores	1
African Local Government road headman	1
Shopkeeper	1
Teacher in Primary Vernacular School	1
Bricklayer	1
Milk seller	1
Parish Chief	1
Village Headman	1
Brickmaker	1
Bicycle mechanic	1
Total	43

The land also provides the materials for a number of village crafts carried on by part-time specialists who sell their products in the weekly village markets.   Clay for pottery-making is found in swamp-bottoms and in the large hills built by the white *nswa* termites.   Village carpenters produce simple chairs, tables and bedsteads.   *Mituba* trees (*Ficus spp.*), frequently interplanted with plaintains to give shade, provide the bark from which barkcloth is made.   Although now almost entirely superseded by cotton cloth for clothing purposes, barkcloth is still in considerable demand as a traditional burial wrapping and as a material for the temporary partitioning of houses.   Baskets and bags are made from various local grasses or from the papyrus which grows in great profusion in the larger swamps.   Even blacksmithing continues to thrive as a village craft in the face of competition from imported goods.   Although the heavy iron hoes, which are the primary agricultural

PLATE VI. Peasant's Thatched Hut: simple folding
chairs are produced by village carpenters.

PLATE VII. A Peasant's Courtyard: dwelling hut, grain
stores and drying rack for dishes.

[face p. 54

PLATE VIII. Picking Cotton. A bag is made by tucking
up the long white Arab-introduced gown
(*kkanzu*).

PLATE IX. Muhima Herdsman with a Chief's Cattle.

implement, are now mostly imported from abroad, other implements, such as axes, adzes and the knives used for felling and peeling plantains are locally produced by peasant-smiths working with the traditional hand-operated bellows and stone forge (see Plate XI).

The occupational specialists living in Buyodi, a village of 546 inhabitants in Bulamogi County, at the time of my visit in 1952 are set out in Table III.

Of these forty-three specialists, only the Local Government employees (the policemen, the road headman and the parish chief)

TABLE IV

INCOME OF AVERAGE SOGA TAXPAYER FROM SALE OF PRODUCE DURING 1952

Type of produce	Value in East African shillings
Cotton	317·62
Groundnuts	44.90
Maize	9·12
Coffee	0·11
Simsim (oilseed)	0·08
Cattle	0·92
Goats	0·26
Hides	3·65
Skins	9·79
Total	386·45

and the teacher have full-time jobs, and even these occupy peasant holdings on which they and their families grow both food and cash crops. The two herdsmen are Hima from the Western Province of Uganda who herd cattle for chiefs and other wealthy persons in exchange for a share in the milk and calves produced by the herds under their care. None, therefore, are full-time specialists in the sense that they are entirely dependent upon non-agricultural specialist occupations for their livelihood. For village dwellers, peasant agriculture is a universal pattern.

Although many of the fundamental needs of the Soga homestead are met by the land itself and by local village craftsmen, three-quarters of a century of contact with the outside world have resulted in the addition to the peasant's style of life of many items obtainable only from abroad in exchange for money. It is to the acquisition of such goods and services that cash crop cultivation is devoted. Table IV shows the quantities of marketed produce, expressed in terms of their value to the peasant, which were produced by the Musoga taxpayer in 1952.[1]

Since the staple foodstuffs are produced by each homestead for its own use, this money income is very largely available for expenditure on such imported goods and services as bicycles, sugar, tea, clothing, utensils, tools, school fees and for the payment of taxes.

Buying and selling centres around the little *"duka"* (shop) towns which are scattered about Busoga at intervals of from ten to fifteen miles (see Plate XII). The largest of these towns appear on Map 2 as "townships," but there are many smaller ones which are not recognised as townships. These centres contain no substantial "urban" populations; their *raison d'être* is trade and they consist almost exclusively of Indian- and Arab-owned shops offering goods for sale to peasants from near-by villages. Cotton ginneries and buying stores, again operated largely by Indians, where the peasant sells his crop, are frequently located in the vicinity of such towns. During the cotton- and groundnut-buying seasons, the *duka* towns are hives of activity. Lorries heavily laden with produce race along the roads and peasants crowd into the shops to buy at inflated prices. Old debts are repaid and new ones contracted, while the chiefs and their agents hurry to collect taxes before the money has been dissipated.

As so often elsewhere in the world, these trading institutions are regarded by the peasants with mixed suspicion and dependence. They are the places of foreigners where the medium of communication is often Kiswahili, the East African *lingua franca*. Peasants and Indian traders look upon each other as fair game in any financial transaction and carry out their business in an atmosphere of mutual hostility and rudeness. Indian traders sometimes cheat illiterate Soga and Soga sometimes thieve from the traders' shops. Nevertheless, the towns are an integral part of peasant life. The goods and services which they bring have so completely passed into the pattern of village existence that the visitor finds it difficult to imagine Soga villages without bicycles, tea, cotton cloth, or, indeed, without the towns themselves which, though in one sense foci for conflict, are also places of excitement and sociability. In any case, their existence is a measure of the degree to which Busoga has passed from the isolation of subsistence cultivation into the world-wide network of trade.

The combination of subsistence and cash economy which the Soga have achieved has allowed them to adjust gradually and selectively to new influences. It has kept them out of wage labour

---

[1] *Busoga District Plan*, District Commissioner, Busoga, p. 2. "Taxpayers" include all able-bodied males above the age of eighteen years.

and permitted them to meet the conditions imposed by colonial status in the familiar context of the village community. The lack of extensive European settlement has meant that opportunities for wage labour have been few, but such opportunities as have presented themselves have failed to attract large numbers of the Soga away from peasant agriculture.

TABLE V

RISE IN THE PRODUCTION OF UNGINNED COTTON,
1908–15

Year					Pounds of unginned cotton
1908–9 ..	..	..	..	..	149,436
1909–10..	..	..	..	..	823,684
1910–11..	..	..	..	..	2,919,653
1911–12..	..	..	..	..	2,921,907
1912–13..	..	..	..	..	2,565,278
1913–14..	..	..	..	..	2,216,704
1914–15..	..	..	..	..	2,504,096

The effect of cash-crop cotton cultivation upon the readiness of the Soga to work for wages where the opportunity has arisen may be seen in the monthly and annual reports of Provincial and District Commissioners.[1] Although differences in methods of reporting cotton planting make difficult the accurate plotting of increase over the years, these reports do provide runs of figures for short periods which indicate the general trend. Table V shows the increase in the production of unginned cotton in the District between 1908, shortly after the crop was introduced, and 1915.

Table VI provides a later series of figures, calculated in terms of acreage of cotton planted in the District.

TABLE VI

RISE IN THE ACREAGE OF COTTON PLANTED: 1925–31

Year					Acreage of cotton planted
1925	..	..	..	..	..	87,333
1926	..	..	..	..	..	88,503
1927	..	..	..	..	..	77,654
1928	..	..	..	..	..	114,803
1929	..	..	..	..	..	129,090
1930	..	..	..	..	..	133,904
1931	..	..	..	..	..	137,868

[1] On file in the Central Offices, Jinja.

During the early years of this century, many Soga worked as head porters and during the First World War the "Basoga Carriers" were organised to supply the troops campaigning in German East Africa.[1] In 1920 "more than 23,000 porters were supplied to Government and over 4,000 to private employers."[2] By 1923, however, the Provincial Commissioner, Eastern Province, reported:

> The supply of labour in (Busoga) District has been very unsatisfactory. The Basoga . . . prefer . . . to live in idleness on the work of their women and children and reap the benefits produced by their sales of cotton. Can this state of affairs tend to anything but a general decline? . . .[3]

And in 1924:

> The fact must be faced that under the present Labour Regulations natives who can meet all their requirements from the proceeds of their crops cannot be expected to work in addition as casual labourers. In these highly productive areas labour must either be obtained from elsewhere, or carried out by odd casual labourers who drift about the country.[4]

By 1931, cotton was being planted at the rate of 1·76 acres per taxpayer and immigrants from other Districts had largely replaced Soga in unskilled labour. The Provincial Commissioner reported that: "Practically all of the 2,500 natives employed on the Kakira Sugar Estate are recruited from the West Nile (District). The Basoga do not appear to have the aptitude . . . for this kind of work."[5]

To-day, most hired labour in Busoga District is provided by immigrant Africans of other tribes. According to information gathered by the East African Statistical Department, in March, 1951, 34,523 Africans in the District were working for employers of five or more employees.[6] Of these, only 9,934 were Soga. Furthermore, although no figures are available showing the tribal representation in various types of employment, according to the writer's observation, such Soga as take employment outside the villages are

---

[1] "Report of the Provincial Commissioner for the Month of August, 1915," Central Offices, Jinja.

[2] "Report of the Provincial Commissioner for the Year Ended 31st March, 1920," Central Offices, Jinja.

[3] "Report of the Provincial Commissioner for the Year Ended 31st December, 1923," Central Offices, Jinja.

[4] "Report of the Provincial Commissioner for the Year Ended 31st December, 1924," Central Offices, Jinja.

[5] "Report of the Provincial Commissioner for the Year Ended 31st December, 1931," Central Offices, Jinja.

[6] Report on the Enumeration of African Employees in Uganda in March, 1951. East African Statistical Department, 1952, Appendix III.

more likely to be found in white collar jobs, requiring some education, than in unskilled labour. Soga probably constitute the bulk
of the 4,412 persons employed by Protectorate and African Local
Governments. Other major employers, including agricultural
enterprises (7,007, consisting largely of employees of the single cane
plantation), ginning (4,213), food processing (2,667), tobacco
processing (1,128) and construction (8,645) employ Soga mainly as
clerks and depend for unskilled labour upon immigrants from other
parts of Uganda or from Belgian Ruanda-Urundi. At the same
time, only 1,402 Soga have left the District to find employment.
It is evident that peasant agriculture has been sufficiently more
profitable and, perhaps more importantly, sufficiently more "comfortable" in a social sense to offset the lure of wage labour.

THE OUTSIDE WORLD.

The Soga village was never an isolated, self-sufficient community.
The political organisation of the traditional states bound villages
together and directed their loyalty toward the rulers as the central
foci of unity and authority. Trade and communication routes
connected the states with each other and with the more powerful
states of Buganda and Bunyoro. For an unknown period before
the arrival of European explorers, Arab and "Swahili" traders
moved up and down the Lake Victoria region trading guns and
cloth for slaves and ivory. All available evidence indicates that
aboriginal East Africa was a cosmopolitan area where isolation was
the exception and inter-ethnic contact and mixture the rule.

Modern conditions have intensified these tendencies. The
Kampala line of the East African Railway, which was built during
the 'twenties and 'thirties to bring trade goods and to carry the
cotton crop down to the port of Mombasa for export, now carries
large numbers of Soga passengers across their own country and into
neighbouring Districts and Territories. A network of good roads
brings every village in Busoga to within a few hours' journey of
every other. Though as yet few Soga own automobiles, almost
everyone either owns a bicycle or can borrow one from his neighbour.
For longer journeys, there are buses which travel all the main roads
and connect all the *duka* towns with one another. Posts and
telegraph offices located in the larger *duka* towns provide facilities
for rapid communication which are widely used by Soga as well as
by Indians and Europeans.

Although located in the extreme south-western corner of the
District, the political and communications centre of the country is
Jinja, the headquarters of the District Administration and Busoga's

largest town.[1] In one of its aspects, Jinja is an overgrown *duka* town. Its three main commercial streets are lined with Indian-owned shops catering mainly to the peasants who find there a greater range of goods and services than is offered by the smaller trading centres. But where the *duka* town only brings the peasant into economic relations with Indian traders, Jinja is also his link with the political system of the Uganda Government and the British Commonwealth. In Jinja live the European civil servants and their families, a community for whom Busoga is a career and not a home. To the peasant, the European is a phenomenon essentially different from the Indian. The Indian, who comes out into the *duka* towns to trade with him, he knows well. Although relations may be hostile and lacking in mutual trust, they are intimate. The European, however, is inscrutable. The peasant meets him only in the context of formal authority relations, carried on across a desk in the Central Offices in Jinja or at formal meetings held by officers on tour. The European as a person outside such situations is unknown to him. He seldom ventures into the European quarter of Jinja, which contains the residences of the civil servants and the European Club. The social life which goes on there is, to the peasant, mysterious and unknown.

A few miles to the north-east of Jinja, on a hill overlooking Lake Victoria, lies Bugembe, the headquarters of the Busoga African Local Government. The African Local Government is the successor to the political organisation of the traditional states and is the institutional complex with which the British Administration in Jinja deals directly in its governing of Busoga. Bugembe is the apex of the African Local Government organisational pyramid. From the offices of the senior officials located there radiate lines of authority which run out through the County, Sub-County and Parish chiefs to the peasant villages. At Bugembe also are the Busoga District Council to which the peasant, through a system of indirect election, sends his representatives, and the Busoga District Court, where he may appeal a law case if he fails to receive satis-faction in the courts of the Sub-County and County chiefs. Where Jinja represents the authority of the respected but little understood European government, Bugembe represents an authority system which the peasant understands. Although the African Local Government is vastly different, both in its formal constitution and in the dynamics of its functioning, from the political organisation

---

[1] Jinja also contains Busoga's only substantial urbanised African population. Since at the same time that my work was being done Jinja was being studied by other members of the Institute staff, I make no attempt to deal with conditions there. See Sofer, Cyril, and Ross, Rhona, "Jinja Transformed," *East African Studies* (forthcoming).

PLATE X. An Early Stage in Beer-Brewing. Ripe
mbidde are placed in a pit lined with
plantain leaves and squeezed with elephant
grass to produce juice for fermenting.

PLATE XI. Village Smith with Bellows and Forge.
Finished blades are stacked against the wall
in the background.

[*face p.* 60

PLATE XII. *"Duka* Town." Iron-roofed shops along a single wide, dusty street.

PLATE XIII. A Vernacular Primary School.

of the traditional states, still it is an authority system in which distinctly Soga beliefs and values have great influence.

The Soga peasant is aware that events occur outside Busoga which influence his life in the village, sometimes very profoundly. He may on occasion have journeyed to Kampala, the metropolis of Uganda, or to Entebbe, the Protectorate capital. During the second World War, his son may have been among the thousands of Soga men who served with British forces in North Africa and Burma, bringing back tales of European military might and of the strange race of little yellow men against whom it was directed. But for the most part, his knowledge of events outside Busoga comes from rumour and from the Luganda press.

TABLE VII

LITERACY AMONG ADULT MALES AND THEIR WIVES

		Southern Bulamogi villages		Southern Kigulu villages		
		Buyodi	Budini	Wairama	Bunyama	Bukwaya
		Adult Males				
Per cent. literate	..	49	54	19	39	30
		Wives				
Per cent. literate	..	16	17	4	17	14

The influence of the press upon communication in Busoga is of course a function of the frequency of literacy among the people of the District. No District-wide literacy rate figures are available, but data which I gathered in five villages in 1951–52 may provide some conception of the numbers who are at least potential readers of written communications. Table VII shows the frequency of literacy, measured by ability to read the survey questionnaire reproduced in Appendix I, among adult males and their wives in these five villages.

As Table VII indicates, the distribution of literacy throughout the District is rather uneven. In villages like Budini, in Southern Bulamogi, where there is a large mission school, somewhat more than half of the adult males and one-sixth of their wives are literate, while in Wairama, which is relatively remote from the nearest school, the literacy rate is much lower. The proximity of schools is important both because schools teach literacy directly to children and because the teachers who live in the vicinity of schools bring books and other printed matter into the community and thus stimulate reading among adults.   Map 6 shows the distribution of schools

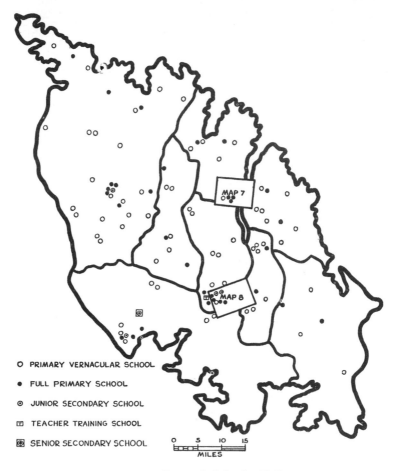

MAP 6.   Busoga's Schools, 1952.

throughout the District.   Their number is constantly growing and hence the number of literate adults increases with each generation. It is my impression, however, that many people learn to read without ever having attended school.   Literacy being very highly valued, many adults learn from one another.

Of course not all those persons classed as "literate" in Table VII regularly read newspapers and many would undoubtedly find difficulty in doing so, though most have occasion to read notices, make simple paper-and-pencil calculations, and send or receive letters. However, several Luganda newspapers published in Kampala have substantial readerships in Busoga, particularly among chiefs and other persons with formal education, who in turn pass on the news to less literate villagers. In this way a rudimentary and somewhat distorted knowledge of such features of the international scene as the atomic bomb and the "cold war" is diffused among the peasant population.

In this chapter, I have tried to summarise the economic life of Busoga and its consequences for the distribution and standard of life of the Soga peasant. From pre-Administration times the peasant has inherited a pattern of settlement in dispersed but permanent villages, making for stability of local community units, and a pattern of subsistence agriculture which gives him a relatively sure and adequate food supply. The rise of cash-crop cultivation has provided him in addition with a source of money for the acquisition of Western goods and services within the village context and without the necessity for the socially more disruptive wage labour. Under these conditions, many Western goods and services (including, for a substantial section of the population, education) have been thoroughly absorbed and have become part of the Soga way of life. As we shall see in Chapter VI, money from cash-crop cultivation has also provided the basis for a new kind of élite style of life for the few. First, however, let us examine the structure of kinship groups and village communities among peasants.

CHAPTER IV

KINSHIP AND CLANSHIP

FORMAL CATEGORIES OF KINSHIP.

In Soga society, both traditional and modern, the structuring of social relations around consanguineal and affinal relatedness has formed one of the major institutional complexes relevant to the distribution of authority. For reasons which I touched upon in Chapter I, the consequences of a society's kinship system for other institutions in that society tend to be particularly pervasive, whether or not those institutions are directly structured in kinship terms. Authority is, in part, directly structured around kinship in Soga society, but even in sectors of the society where this is not so, kinship intrudes. In this and the following chapter, I shall therefore describe in some detail the Soga kinship system as it operates at the peasant level of society. This material may then be enlarged upon in later chapters when the structure of the state is considered.

One further introductory remark. Both because Soga society is quite highly differentiated (there are local patterns and "national" patterns, élite patterns and "common man" patterns) and because it has recently undergone extensive change, the analysis of Soga kinship must of necessity be rather complex. I must digress to talk about "before and after" and about contemporary variation. This, however, is inevitable in any attempt to analyse the structure of a modern African society. I can only ask the reader to bear with me.

All Soga are divided among a number of exogamous, totemic patriclans (bika, singular: kika) whose members recognise a common descent in the patrilineal line but are unable to trace the exact geneaological relations among them. The notion of descent from a common ancestor is recognised in the way in which patriclans are named. Clan names are formed by the combination of the human noun-class prefix Mu- (singular) or Ba- (plural) with the form ise (father) and the name of the common ancestor. Thus the clan whose common ancestor is Igaga call themselves Baiseigaga, literally "they of the father Igaga." A single member calls himself a mwiseigaga. The precise number of these patriclans has not been determined, but they are surely very numerous. I counted more than 150 among the populations of a handful of villages. Many of the patriclans appear to be widely dispersed over Busoga. At any rate, in those areas of Busoga of which I have some detailed knowledge, the patriclan is never a localised unit. Villages are never made up solely or even mainly of clan-mates and their families, nor is the membership of a clan ever confined to a village or cluster of contiguous villages.

The large number and wide dispersion of the clans suggest that the present situation is the result of an extended period of growth, fission and movement of clan populations. Traditional histories of clans support this conclusion. A large proportion of the Soga clans think of themselves as having originated outside Busoga or at any rate in parts of the country now inhabited by few of their members. Some, like the *Baisengobi*, who were the rulers of several of the traditional states, say they came from Bunyoro where their ancestors were descended from the royal *Babito* clan. Others, like the *Baisegabanya*, trace their origin to Bunyuli in the present Mbale District, or, like the *Baiseibira*, to islands in Lake Victoria. Sometimes it is possible to follow the process by which dispersion has taken place. The *Baisemusubo* who live in Butongole village in the northern County of Bulamogi say that they are the descendants of a colony who left the main body of their clan-mates at Kalalu, in the County of Bugweri some twenty miles to the south, to migrate in search of new land. Since Bugweri is one of the most fertile and most densely populated areas of Busoga, this story sounds quite plausible. It suggests that the pressure of population on the land has been one of the sources of clan dispersal. A second source is indicated by the example of another group of *Baisemusubo* now living in the north-eastern County of Bugabula. The Bugabula group, it is said, are the descendants of a man from Kalalu who became a servant of the ruler of Bugabula and later was made a chief. Since chiefs were noted for having many wives and many children, an event of this kind could easily account for the growth of a substantial group of clan-mates in the new area. Evidently both ecological and social factors have had a hand in the dispersal of Soga clans.

It is also clear that the ultimate result of such processes was often the splitting of original clans to form new ones. Occasionally, this has occurred within the memory of persons still living. The *Baisemukuve*, for example, are said to have split within recent times to form two distinct patriclans, one retaining the original clan name and the other adopting the name *Baisekyema*. Both groups continue to recognise the guinea fowl as their totem. It is the common totem and not the common clan name which defines the limits of exogamy. Since, as a result of such processes of fission, there may be several clans with the same totem, the number of patriclans in Busoga is considerably larger than the number of exogamous units.

The lines along which patriclans grow and divide are best seen in terms of the lineages (*nda*) of which they are constituted. The lineage is made up of persons related in the patrilineal line who can trace the genealogical links which relate them to each other and to a common ancestor. Soga make a clear distinction between clan and lineage. Whereas an individual, in speaking of his clan, says "I am one of the father Igaga," in speaking of his lineage he says, "I am of the lineage of Idhoba" (*nda ya Idhoba*). Both units share the feature of putative descent from a common ancestor, but it is clearly recognised that in the case of the lineage the genealogical links are known, while in the case of the clan they are merely assumed to exist because of the common totem and clan name.

As in any society in which unilineal kinship is an important structural feature, new lineages constantly arise while others die out. Partly this is caused by the natural biological unevenness of population growth. Some marriages produce many offspring while others produce none. In a community which is spatially stable and socially undifferentiated, such non-social factors may in large part account for the growth, fission and decline of lineages. But, in Busoga at least, such factors are modified and supplemented by the social system. The founding ancestor of a new lineage is commonly a man of some importance. He may have been the leader of a group of kinsmen who migrated to a new area or he may have achieved prominence in the community by virtue of his outstanding personal characteristics. Subsequent chapters will show that Soga society has always accorded recognition to individual achievement, particularly in the political sphere. An individual might be given control over a village or other unit and upon assuming office might be accompanied by a body of kinsmen. Individuals who thus achieve prominence outside the framework of the lineage system influence that system by becoming the points at which lineages grow and divide. Ultimately, a new lineage, arising in this way, may grow to the point where it divides from the main body and becomes a new patriclan, as occurred in the case of the *Baisemukuve* mentioned above.

The emphasis upon patrilineal kinship is reflected in the terms which Soga use to denote kinsmen of various types. The kinship terminology, shown in Table VIII, is of the "Omaha" type analysed by Radcliffe-Brown in his classic paper "The Study of Kinship Systems."[1] The application of the terms in illustrated in Figs. 1,

---

[1] Radcliff-Brown, A. R., "The Study of Kinship Systems," *Journal of The Royal Anthropological Institute*, Vol. LXXI, 1941, pp. 1–18.

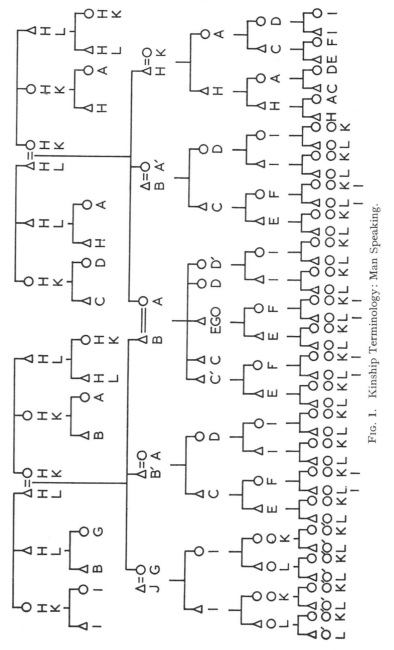

FIG. 1. Kinship Terminology: Man Speaking.

2, 3, 4 and 5.[1] In an individual's own lineage, kinsmen are stratified
by generation into "grandparents," "fathers" and "fathers' sisters,"
"siblings," "children" and "grandchildren." These terms are
extended out through all collateral lines within the lineage and to
clan-mates of the appropriate ages with whom precise genealogical
relations are unknown. The collateral extension suggests the sociological equivalence of members of the lineage within each generation,

TABLE VIII

SOGA KINSHIP TERMS OF REFERENCE

Symbol	Lusoga term	English translation
A'	*mukaire*	mother
B	*lata* or *ise*	father
A'	*mukaire omuto*	little mother
B'	*lata omuto*	little father
C	*muganda*	sibling, same sex
D	*mwanhina*	sibling, opposite sex
C'	*muganda mukulu*	older sibling, same sex
D'	*mwanhina mukulu*	older sibling, opposite sex
E	*mutabani*	son
F	*mughala*	daughter
G	*songa*	father's sister
H	*dhadha*	grandparent or male of mother's lineage
I	*mwiwa*	female clan-mate's child (male speaking)
J	*mukoirume*	in-law
K	*mukazi* or *mukyala*	wife
L	*musangi*	husband of wife's sister
M	*mughalikwa*	co-wife
N	*iba*	husband
O	*mwidhukulu*	grandchild
O'	*mwidhukulu ow'okubiri*	second degree grandchild

while the stratification by generation reflects relations of super- and
subordination within it. In contrast, the lineages to which an
individual's own lineage is linked by marriage tend to be internally
differentiated only by sex and not by generation. Thus, in an
individual's mother's lineage, all males are "grandparents" (or
mothers' brothers) and all females are "mothers," while in his wife's
lineage, all males are "in-laws" and all females are "wives," regard-
less of generational position. Kinship terminology thus tends to
define the relations between an individual and his kinsmen in
lineage terms.

Kinship terminology, of course, never reflects perfectly all the
differences in patterned behaviour between kinsmen of different

---

[1] In order to save space and to avoid the confusion which results from the
use of vernacular terms, the key to the symbols used in Figs. 1, 2, 3, 4 and
5 is given separately in Table VIII.

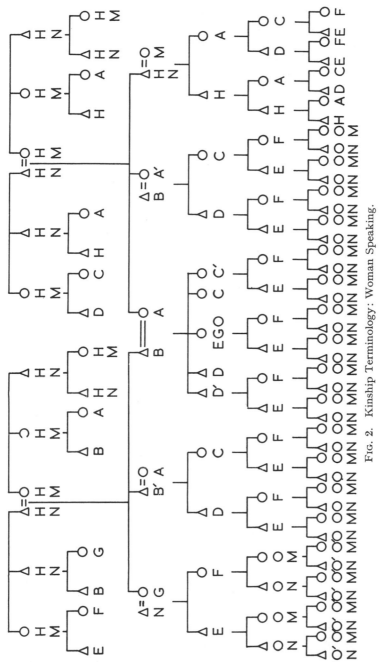

Fig. 2. Kinship Terminology: Woman Speaking.

types. For whatever reason, terminological usage always classifies more crudely than does the subtler and more variable idiom of social structure.   The Soga system of terminology suggests no more than a general emphasis upon patrilineal descent; it does not describe the precise patterns of behaviour carried out between

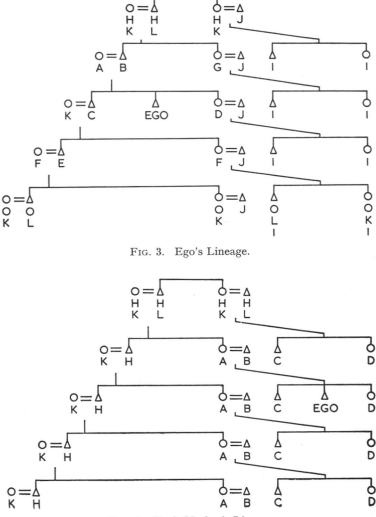

FIG. 3.   Ego's Lineage.

FIG. 4.   Ego's Mother's Lineage.

kinsmen of different types and it does not define precisely which patrilineal groups are of functional importance.[1] In the following sections, I shall describe the behaviour patterns institutionally enjoined upon kinsmen and the functional groups to which patrilineal descent gives rise. I shall deal first with the peasant homestead and the relationships which most commonly occur within it, then proceed to the other and wider groups formed upon the basis of more extended kinship. Since Soga society is relatively highly

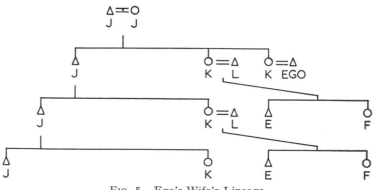

FIG. 5. Ego's Wife's Lineage.

differentiated, this account of kinship relations at the peasant level cannot exhaust the kinship structuring of social relations in Busoga as a whole. At the level of the state in traditional Busoga and among the "national élite" in modern Busoga, patterns occur which, though they are variations on a common Soga theme, nonetheless differ somewhat in functional significance from the peasant village pattern. These variations, however, will be treated in later chapters; for the moment I shall focus upon kinship among peasant villagers.

THE STRUCTURE OF THE HOMESTEAD.

Elderly Soga sometimes speak as if in former times the typical homestead were an extended family unit. When warfare was common, they say, larger homestead populations provided greater security against attack. However this may be, to-day the typical

---

[1] The term "lineage" is similarly ambiguous. Fundamentally, it means merely a group of persons related by some rule of descent. Such groups may vary widely in size and in the degrees and types of social functions allocated to them by institutions. As I show later, the functionally most prominent unit of this kind in Busoga is the "succession lineage," a lineage of some five to seven generations in depth whose members form a council with authority over succession and inheritance.

Soga homestead houses a single family consisting of the male homestead head, his wives and children, and perhaps an odd kinsman or two from outside the simple family circle. It rarely contains more than one married male. This pattern emerges quite clearly from the data which I collected in a survey of all homesteads in five villages: Buyodi and Budini in southern Bulamogi County and Bunyama, Wairama and Bukwaya in southern Kigulu County.

TABLE IX

HOMESTEAD HEADS CLASSIFIED BY AGE AND SEX

	16–45 years		Over 45 years	
	Number	Per cent.	Number	Per cent.
Budini and Buyodi				
Male with dependents ..	151	57	101	38
Male living alone	9	3	5	2
Female with dependents ..	—	—	1	*
Female living alone	—	—	—	—
Total			267	100
Bunyama, Wairama and Bukwaya				
Male with dependents ..	111	46	94	39
Male living alone	9	4	12	5
Female with dependents ..	—	—	4	2
Female living alone	—	—	9	4
Total			239	100

* Less than one per cent.

These data are presented in Table IX, where homestead heads are classified by age and sex, and in Table X, where homestead populations are tabulated in terms of relationship to the homestead head. For the moment, the differences between the two areas may be ignored since these differences will be taken up in the discussion of village communities in the following chapter. Here I wish to deal with broad general patterns.

Table IX shows that in these five villages, most homesteads (between 85 and 95 per cent.) are headed by males and contain dependents. Only between 5 and 9 per cent. represent males living alone and very few indeed are headed by women, either living alone or with dependents. Table X shows the kinship composition of the homesteads in the five villages.[1] In every village except Budini, where

[1] This method of analysing the kinship composition of homesteads was suggested by Fortes, Meyer, "Time and Social Structure: An Ashanti Case Study," in Fortes, Meyer (ed.) *Social Structure: Studies Presented to A. R. Radcliffe-Brown*, 1949, pp. 54–84.

there is a mission school and where consequently there are many children temporarily resident with relatives or friends, wives and children of homestead heads constitute at least three-quarters of the homestead populations. This tendency towards the small, single-family homestead may be expressed in another way in terms

TABLE X

HOMESTEAD POPULATIONS CLASSIFIED BY RELATIONSHIP TO HOMESTEAD HEAD

Relationship to Homestead head	Buyodi		Budini		Bunyama, Wairama and Bukwaya	
	Homestead head 16–45 years	Homestead head over 45 years	Homestead head 16–45 years	Homestead head over 45 years	Homestead head 16–45 years	Homestead head over 45 years
Homestead heads' wives and children	183	206	142	206	304	323
Per cent. of total ..	86	94	61	85	75	75
Patrilineal kin						
Brothers and families ..	11	1	22	9	26	9
Sons' families	—	9	2	12	1	32
Fathers and fathers' brothers	1	—	1	1	—	—
Fathers' sisters ..	1	—	1	—	1	1
Mothers and mothers' sisters	8	—	16	4	26	6
Sisters	2	1	8	2	11	6
Male clansmen	—	—	—	—	8	3
Female clansmen ..	—	—	—	—	—	1
Wives' sisters	3	1	2	1	3	6
Total	26	12	52	29	76	64
Per cent. of total ..	12	6	22	12	19	15
Non-patrilineal kin						
Daughters' families ..	—	—	1	1	3	10
Sisters' families	1	—	6	2	6	8
Fathers' sisters' families	—	—	1	—	—	—
Mothers' brothers ..	—	—	—	—	1	—
Other mothers' kin ..	—	—	3	—	1	—
Wives' kin	2	—	11	2	7	16
Total	3	—	22	5	18	34
Per cent. of total ..	1	—	10	2	4	8
Non-kin	—	—	16	3	10	11
Per cent. of total ..	—	—	7	1	21	3
Total population ..	212	218	232	243	408	432

of the average size of homesteads. In Budini and Buyodi combined, the average homestead contains 4·4 members; in Bunyama, Wairama and Bukwaya, the average homestead group is 4·5.

I should repeat here that I am speaking only of the *peasant* homestead. As we shall see in Chapters VII and VIII, headmen and chiefs, not to mention rulers in traditional Busoga, had and have much larger homesteads.

The "single family" which typically inhabits a Soga homestead is, however, very frequently a polygynous family. Polygyny is

very much the approved pattern and a realtively high proportion
of Soga men achieve it.   Table XI shows the frequency of polygyny
in the five villages, expressed both in terms of the numbers and
percentages of men polygynous and in terms of numbers and per
centages of marriages polygynous.   Again, Budini is a special case
since, particularly among men under forty-five, there is a high
concentration of teachers and other employees and close associates
of the Catholic mission who are under strong pressure to adhere to
the Christian rule of monogamy.   Leaving Budini aside, between
14 and 30 per cent. of all men are polygynous, while beteen 37 and
59 per cent. of all marriages are polygynous.   Again, inter-village
differences may be neglected for the time being.   These are very high
polygyny rates, perhaps approaching the maximum possible given
the roughly equal sex ratio and given that all men are expected
ultimately to marry.   Most men do ultimately marry (only 4 men
in Buyodi, 9 in Budini and 9 in Buyama, Wairama and Bukwaya
combined in the "over 45" age group have never married), but
this is achieved by a substantial difference in age at marriage
among men as against women and by a rather high divorce rate,
making it possible for most men to be married for some period,
though at any given time many must be single.   Men are considered
adult and ready to marry at the age of sixteen, though many must,
under the circumstances, wait longer.

It is difficult to generalise about the small portion of the homestead populations which consists of persons other than the male
head's wives and children.   The institutional expectation concerning the homestead is that it shall be occupied by a man, his wives
and children.   Other persons are included only under special circumstances, usually the break-up of another homestead to which the
head is related.   Where such circumstances do arise, however, there
are definite expectations as to what kinds of kinsmen should join
an already established homestead.   The homestead head's younger
brothers or brothers' children, unmarried sisters, and elderly
patrilineal kinsmen of both sexes may properly join the homestead.
So also may the widows of the head's father or brothers, real or
classificatory, and the sisters of his mother or wives, who are classificatory mothers and wives.   All these are the homestead head's
patrilineal kinsmen or their wives and, as Table X indicates, they
constitute the bulk of the homestead members who are not heads'
wives or children.   Concerning the presence in the homestead of
totally unrelated persons, institutional expectations may be said to
be neutral; such persons are present whenever mutual convenience
suggests such arrangements.   Most such persons are either hired
agricultural labourers (chiefly immigrants from other tribes) or, as

TABLE XI

FREQUENCY OF POLYGYNY

	Buyodi				Budini				Bunyama, Wairama and Bukwaya			
	Men		Wives		Men		Wives		Men		Wives	
	16–45	Over 45	of men 16–45	of men over 45	16–45	Over 45	of men 16–45	of men over 45	16–45	Over 45	of men 16–45	of men over 45
Never married	23	4			42	9			81	9		
Previously married now single	5	2			5	1			13	15		
Married, with one or more wives												
1	54	32	54	32	79	37	79	37	77	57	77	57
2	9	13	18	26	7	8	14	16	31	14	62	28
3	3	2	9	6	—	2	—	6	12	10	36	30
4	—	—	—	—	—	1	—	4	—	1	—	4
5	1	—	5	—	—	—	—	—	—	1	—	5
6	—	—	—	—	—	1	—	6	—	—	—	—
7	—	—	—	—	—	—	—	—	—	1	—	7
8	—	1	—	8	—	—	—	—	—	—	—	—
9	—	—	—	—	—	—	—	—	—	1	—	9
Total men	95	54			133	59			214	109		
Men polygynous	13	16			7	12			43	28		
Per cent. of men polygynous	14	30			5	20			20	26		
Total marriages			86	72			93	69			175	140
Marriages polygynous			32	40			14	32			98	83
Per cent. of marriages polygynous			37	56			15	46			56	59

in the case of Budini village, children of the homestead head's friends who live with him in order to be near a school. The presence of matrilineal or affinal kinsmen (those listed as "non-patrilineal kin" in Table X), however, is regarded with disapproval. Such persons, if the homesteads to which they properly belong have been broken up, should live with their own patrilineal relatives.

However, the structural significance of the presence in the homestead of persons other than the head's wives and children can be discussed more conveniently later in this chapter when extra-homestead kinship relations are considered. For the present it is sufficient to note that the dominant relationships within the homestead, both statistically and normatively, are those between husband and wife, parents and children, between siblings and between co-wives.

HUSBAND AND WIFE.

In the homestead division of labour, the wife is primarily responsible for the care of small children and for the tidiness of the homestead. She is also responsible for the basic food supply, plantains, in all stages of production and preparation. The plantain grove is thought of as the woman's sphere. She cultivates about the roots of the plants and mulches the soil with fallen leaves and stems, only calling in male assistance for initial planting and the heavier pruning operations. Each day, the woman is expected to "dig" (*kulima*) in the plantain garden and to gather and prepare the fruit for the day's meals. Men say that they know nothing about plantains and pretend not to know the distinctions between the different varieties suitable for boiling, roasting, beer-making and eating uncooked.

N.K. was showing me around his homestead. After looking at the dwelling huts and out-buildings, we walked out into a large, well-kept plantain garden and I asked about methods of cultivation and the different varieties of fruit. N.K. laughed and beckoned to one of his three wives who was working nearby. "Oh, one of the wives will tell you about that," he said. "The wives rule the plantain garden."

I was then shown around the garden by the wife, who pointed out the differences, invisible to my untrained eye, between the different varieties and rather proudly showed me how to handle the knives used for felling and peeling plantains. All the while, N.K. followed along, looking interested and expressing surprise as if each bit of information were new to him. This seemed partly a pose, but it clearly indicated to me that in the plantain garden N.K. felt on unfamiliar ground.

The wife's responsibility for and control over the basic food supply is recognised and respected by her husband. Often the garden is divided into sections which the wife cultivates primarily for the homestead, i.e. for her husband and children and her husband's guests, and those which she cultivates more for herself and from which therefore she may take fruit for feeding her own kinsmen when they come to visit. One homestead head, drawing an analogy between the homestead and the traditional political structure, told me that one section of the garden was *butongole* and one *bwesengeze*. In the political system, *butongole* was territory which a chief ruled on behalf of his superior, while *bwesengeze* was his personal estate from which he might take tribute for himself.[1] This division of the plantain garden has no status in law; in the customary land law, the entire holding belongs to the husband. But it is felt to be a sound principle of homestead management thus to allocate sections of the garden and to respect the special rights of the wife to one section. Similarly, in a polygynous homestead each wife should have her own hut and her own plantain garden. The boundaries seem always to be clearly recognised, though there may be considerable sharing of the work of cultivation, particularly where co-wives are sisters.

The cultivation of cash crops and other annuals is primarily men's work. This is true particularly of the heavy clearing and initial breaking of the soil preparatory to planting and of the uprooting and burning of cotton plants after picking, though wives may assist in the weeding during the growing season. Men are also responsible for such house-building and repairing operations as are not carried out by specialists.

The marketing of cash-crops is also predominantly in male hands. Cotton and groundnuts which have been gathered and cleaned by members of the homestead are strapped on the carrier rack of a bicycle or thrown on to a lorry and taken by the homestead head to the ginnery or buying store. The control of money received for these crops would appear at present to be a matter of some variation and even dispute. Traditionally, one is told, the homestead head was in complete control of cash income, no matter whose labour produced it. Cash-cropping is of course quite recent, but such a pattern would have followed naturally from the male dominance which the present-day Soga homestead head sees to have been the traditional pattern. The male head controlled the homestead's resources and dispensed them in accord with his view of other members' needs. At the time of my visit, however, it appeared that wives were tending to claim, and in some cases to receive, greater control over homestead finances. To-day some wives sell such minor homestead products as eggs and chickens and use the money as they see fit. Others have their own cotton plots from which they themselves market the crop. Some husbands view such tendencies with alarm, feeling that "the wives are getting out of control."

On the whole, the woman's contribution to the support of the homestead in terms of working hours is considerably greater than the man's, while the man retains greater authority over the use of homestead resources. This inequality is consistent with the ideal pattern of distribution of authority between male and female rôles. The man is the centre of authority in the homestead and its representative in its dealings with the outside world. He must be free to travel to the trading centre and to sit around the beer pot with friends gossiping and discussing village affairs. The "good woman," on the other hand, is one who works hard around the house, bears children, and does not endanger her virtue by going about unescorted. She should kneel and address her husband as *ssebo* ("sir") or *mukama wange* ("my lord") and, particularly when visitors are present, should take her meals separately from him. In law, she is in many ways not a person. She may not hold real property and in court should be represented by her husband or (depending upon the circumstances) by her father. Her personal relations with her husband are, by Western standards, distant and formal.

Such is the ideal, at any rate in male eyes. There are, of course, variations. Some married couples, particularly if they have reached middle age and have been married for some years, approach the Western pattern of marital companionship. Long and intimate association in the homestead, which is also a joint economic enterprise, produces a relationship of easy give and take and deep affection. In other homesteads, there is open revolt. Wives feel unduly restricted and rebel by flouting their husbands' authority or by taking lovers. Again, elderly women past child-bearing age in any case cease in many ways to be social "women." My own relations with Soga women of varying ages provide an index to the change in the social position of women with advancing age. Women of child-bearing age were invariably shy and would seldom stop at my tent to chat. Friends warned me that I should avoid contact with such women and never give them lifts to the trading centre in my car lest I excite suspicions of adultery. Elderly women, however, often visited me and chatted quite freely. It is clear that the ideology of male dominance, which will be encountered again in the discussion of marriage, centres about the sexual and child-bearing potentialities of women and that once these disappear their subordination to males also declines. Those Soga men who feel most strongly that modern women are getting out of hand, constantly refer to extra-marital sex activity in citing examples. It is my impression that female deviations from the norm of submission and male anxieties about such deviation are not fundamentally new developments in the Soga social system. Soga marriage, I believe, has always been relatively unstable and the dominance of the husband rather tenuously maintained. What is new is greater opportunity for women to escape male authority by seeking employment in Jinja or Kampala and the general relaxation of sanctions brought by Administration supervision of the courts' handling of marital disputes. According to the East African Statistical Bureau, only 521 women were employed in Busoga District in September, 1952, but the possibility is there and Soga of both sexes are sharply aware of the fact.[1]

PARENT AND CHILD.

In any patrilineal kinship system, the father-son relationship is pivotal because it is the "growing point" for social groups based upon extended kinship and the link which binds the members of such groups together. To a boy, his father represents not only the focus of authority within the homestead, but also his tie with the wider authority system of the lineage. It is therefore not surprising that in Busoga the father-son relationship is both close, in that father and son are extremely important to one another, and distant, in that a son is markedly subordinate to his father and respectful in his behaviour towards him.

A homestead head is, first of all, most anxious to have a son. Without a son, a man has no proper heir and without an heir he is likely to be left helpless in his old age and to be quickly forgotten when he dies. As will be explained presently, this is more true to-day than in the past. It appears that in traditional Soga society, collateral links across the lineage were rather more emphasised and direct father-son links rather less. The difference, however, is relative. Having a son was and is vital to a man. It is in a sense a wife's duty to bear sons for her husband (though her failure to do so is not cause for divorce, as in some African societies). It was one of my commoner experiences in Busoga to be asked whether my wife had not yet given me a son. Having only daughters, I was an object of some pity.

For pagans, such sentiments are reinforced by the belief system of the ancestor cult. A man should be buried in his own *butaka*

---

[1] *Report on the Enumeration of African Employees in Uganda in September, 1952,"* East African Statistical Department, 1952.

(ancestral land) and his spirit (*muzimu*) should be tended by his descendants. A neglected spirit is both miserable and dangerous to others. Though Christians and Moslems may lack specific belief in the ancestral cult, the complex of sentiments associated with patrilineal continuity upon the land remain very strong even in them. Such sentiments are, it appeared to me, very near the heart of the Soga value-system.

A.B. took me to a small thicket near his house and pointed to several piles of stones. "Those are the graves of my ancestors," he said. "I do not build shrines (*masabo*) for them, but I respect them very much and I sometimes pray to them. When I die, I will be buried there and my son will respect me in the same way."

A.B., I had learned earlier, was a practising Roman Catholic and had gone to considerable trouble and expense to secure for his son an education in the Catholic schools. The son, who had accompanied us, looked very grave during the conversation and it was apparent that he shared his father's feelings.

In a later chapter, we will see how such sentiments have taken on a new prominence in conflicts over land.

Although a man desires sons, he is at some pains not to pamper them. The relationship is not one of companionship or easygoing affection. Towards his sons, a father is in fact rather stern and aloof. During the first three years of his life, a child of either sex spends most of his time with his mother or older sisters, relatively little with his father. Even during these early years, however, a man is apt to treat his sons rather differently from his daughters. An infant daughter is more often held on her father's lap and petted; a little boy is seldom treated with such obvious affection. As he grows older, he learns to stand or kneel respectfully in his father's presence and to address him as *ssebo* ("sir"). Traditionally, a boy learned his occupation—peasant cultivation plus perhaps a part-time craft—from his father and for most this is still true to-day. Small boys may be seen herding sheep, goats and cattle and, later on, helping with cultivation. To-day, an increasing number spend some period of years at school. Except for the few who attend boarding school, this does not take them out of the village setting, though it does introduce a new educative experience outside the home and to that extent the tutorial aspects of the father's rôle *vis-à-vis* his sons is reduced in importance. New opportunities for employment have a similar influence. For the vast majority of Soga sons, however, the father remains a stern and commanding figure.

This pattern changes as a man grows older. Although ultimately one son (or more than one if the family holding is unusually large) will inherit his father's land, those who reach maturity during his lifetime almost invariably set up independent homesteads. If possible, a married son takes up residence near his father's place, but it is a separate homestead on a separate holding. As is apparent in Table X, three generation extended family homesteads are quite uncommon. They occur most often in the case of village or sub-village headmen, who have additional authority beyond that of the ordinary peasant father. In the few extended family homesteads with which I became acquainted, relations between father and married son appeared to be somewhat strained. Young men feel that when they marry they should set up independent establishments where father's authority is less ever-present. This need for separation between the son's homestead and that of his father is expressed in the respect relationship, bordering upon avoidance, which obtains between a woman and her husband's father. A father should not share in his son's "homestead affairs" (*eby'omu ndu*). A man ought not to sleep with his wife when his father is in his house.

Soga society is thus not a gerontocracy. Though a father's authority over younger sons is great and though he retains this authority in some degree so long as he lives, in part, at any rate, because he controls the inheritance of land in an agrarian society, still young adult men are not in general dominated by the old. The period of "manhood" (*busadha*) proper, when a man receives the utmost respect in his homestead, is the period of early middle age when his sons are growing up.

The relationship of a son with his mother is of a very different order. Where the father is stern and rather cold, the mother is affectionate and comforting. A little boy, when frightened or unhappy, is swept into his mother's arms and elaborately soothed and reassured. Under similar circumstances, a father might well scold him or even laugh scornfully at his childishness. A boy soon comes to regard his mother as a never-failing source of affection, his father primarily as a disciplinarian. This centring of affection upon the mother tends to persist rather strongly throughout a man's life and is a focus of sentimentality in songs and stories. Older men, rather strikingly unsentimental in most respects, speak freely of their love for mother and of their loneliness for her. Though this is no more than a hunch, I have the feeling that, whereas in most Western societies the adult male normally transfers most of his heterosexual attachment to his wife, in Busoga a man's mother tends to remain the most important woman in his life. There is much folklore concerning the tendency of women to attract men younger than themselves and for wives to leave ageing husbands in favour of younger ones.

For the young girl, relations with the two parents are less sharply differentiated. The pattern of allocation of stern authority to the father and the care and comforting involved in child-rearing to the mother is to a large degree independent of the sex of the child. But just as a boy learns his sex rôle from his father, so a girl learns hers from her mother. After the age of four or five, the young girl begins to be given a share in women's work. She helps her mother in preparing food and is given increasing responsibility for the care of younger siblings. During the same period, she begins to be differentiated from her male siblings and learns to respect them as persons with superior authority. However, the girl's subordination to her father and her brothers is affectionate and protective in quality. Since her training is largely the responsibility of her mother, her father's control over her tends to be limited to protecting her (to-day, at any rate, often rather unsuccessfully) from the improper attentions of young men. When she marries, her father and brothers will be her refuge from ill-treatment by her husband, and her children, being closely related but outside the circle of the lineage, will be special objects of their affection.

SIBLINGS.

Relations between siblings, particularly between male siblings, are characterised by a patterned hostility. Young siblings are frequently said to be afflicted by a sickness known as *lyuse*. It first appears in a child when his mother becomes pregnant. He frets and whines because, it is said, his mother's milk has spoiled. Later on, the two siblings are said to "hate" each other. Until the age of four or five, *lyuse* may afflict boys or girls or mixed pairs of siblings. Thereafter, it persists only in boys. Unless their food is treated with certain herb medicines, brothers may continue to have *lyuse* throughout their lives. In later life, it manifests itself in disputes and lawsuits over inheritance of land since in most cases only one son can inherit. It is recognised that this "hate" between brothers is not the hate of real enemies, however. Outsiders are enjoined not to take sides in such disputes lest the brothers settle their differences and turn on their allies. A chief who has a *lyuse* lawsuit in his court should be understanding and tolerant and try to arbitrate the dispute so that brothers will not waste their time and money in litigation which is essentially without purpose.

This explicit and almost institutionalised sibling rivalry is in a sense a corollary to the stern subordination-superordination relationship which obtains between fathers and sons. Although the principle of the unity of siblings and of the patrilineage as a whole is an important feature of the kinship system, it is a unity based upon authority and not upon affection.   If in certain situations the lineage presents a united front in its dealings with the outside world, internally it is characterised by a barely-suppressed hostility between its members.

CO-WIVES.

Relations between co-wives vary from affection and constant mutual help to active resentment.   As has been so frequently noticed in patrilineal polygynous societies, sisters make the best co-wives.   Being of the same lineage, they mutually support each other in a homestead whose other members belong to the husband's lineage.   Harmonious co-wife relationships are not confined to sisters, however.   Often a wife will suggest that her husband marry again in order that she may have a companion and helper in her household duties.   Of course, sexual rivalry occurs, but Soga marriage is not a "soul-mate" relationship.   The loneliness which patrilocal residence and the rather distant husband-wife relationship involve for a wife mean that the companionship provided by a co-wife goes far to compensate for any rivalry over the husband's attentions.

Traditionally, the first wife was designated by a special term (*kairu lubaale*) and had special ritual duties in the household.   The pattern is carried over by Christians in the practice of terming the first wife, the one married by Christian rites, *mukyala ow'empeta*, the "wife of the ring."   In everyday speech, she is known as *mukyala*, "Mrs.," as distinguished from subsequent wives who are known simply as *bakazi*, "women."   This pattern of temporal priority, however, has little importance to-day.   There is a vague preference for inheritance by the senior son of the first wife, but this is not a strict rule which must be followed.   As I note below, Soga inheritance is extremely flexible, depending more upon the preferences of the testator and his lineage mates than upon birth order and marriage order.   In fact, it is often the youngest and prettiest wife who is favoured in the life of the homestead.   It is she who is most frequently on display when visitors are about and she may even be called *mukyala* in the presence of persons who are unaware of the true situation.

These are the relationships which most commonly occur within the homestead.   The homestead, however, is not isolated kinship-wise.   Through consanguineal and affinal ties, it is related to many persons outside in ways which are important in the fabric of peasant life.

MARRIAGE AND IN-LAWS.

One important group of relationships extending outside the homestead arises from marriage. Soga marriage, in its legal consequences, is a contract between the bridegroom and the father or guardian of the bride. For the bridegroom, the choice of a mate is a relatively free one within the limits set by exogamy. Arranged marriages are said to have been frequent in the past, but they do not appear to be so to-day. For a woman, the choice is much less free. Not only does the marriage contract itself depend upon the consent of her father, but, in addition, her opportunities for meeting young men are limited. It is part of the patriarchal pattern of Soga society that marriageable girls are jealously guarded and kept at their household duties. Opportunities to meet young men tend to be limited to those formal occasions, such as weddings and funerals, when girls may properly attend large gatherings.

Although it is the consent of the bride's father which seals the marriage contract, this almost invariably involves, in addition, the payment of bridewealth to him by the bridegroom. The sum paid may vary from as little as 20 shillings to more than 500 shillings plus a number of goats or cattle. Marriage also usually involves, for Christians or Moslems, a religious ceremony followed by a celebration feast. The expense and organisation of the ceremony and feast fall upon the bridegroom and upon such of his lineage mates (primarily his father, brothers and father's brothers) and his mother's lineage mates, as he can persuade to help him. He must provide new clothes for himself and the bride and after the ceremony at the church or mosque, should entertain a large gathering of his own and the bride's kinsmen as elaborately as possible. The feast commonly includes entertainment by bands of hired musicians and the serving of plantains, meat, tea and beer to the guests. If possible, a hired car or truck should be provided to carry the most important kinsmen on both sides to the church or mosque and back to the bridegroom's home for the celebration feast. The elaborateness of the arrangements varies, of course, with the means of the bridegroom, but the cost of the feast and ceremony commonly amounts to more than 100 shillings. In the case of wealthy persons, it may amount to more than 1,000 shillings. Elaboration and expense are greater in first marriages than in subsequent ones and among Christians and Moslems as compared with pagans.

That the bridegroom and his kinsmen should bear the expenses of the wedding in addition to the relatively large bridewealth payment is intelligible when the legal side of marriage is considered. A husband acquires rights in his wife which, short of extreme cruelty on his part, cannot be terminated without his consent. He acquires exclusive right to her sexual activity and even to her physical presence in his homestead and these rights are, with certain restrictions, inherited by his brother at his death. Although to-day, at any rate, widow inheritance cannot be forced upon a woman, if she fails to marry her husband's brother he may claim refund of the bridewealth originally paid for her.

The position of the wife is in many ways a point of strain in the kinship system. A member by birth of her own lineage, she must live in a homestead dominated by her husband's lineage and bear children for it. She is thus a connecting link between two lineages and is torn by dual loyalties. Once she has borne a son who has reached maturity, the tension eases. She becomes a mother of a member of the lineage with which she lives and has an honoured position. But during the early years of marriage her position is a difficult one. The rigid control over her behaviour which the customary law gives to her husband is perhaps an institutionalised means of counteracting her tendency to be drawn back to her own kinsmen.[1]

A wife may not leave her husband's homestead, even for short visits to her parents, without his permission. In fact, particularly during the early years of marriage, wives often do desert their husbands and return to their parents. A father who allows his daughter to do this is guilty of a serious offence called *kutuza omukazi*, "harbouring a wife." Not only must he not allow his daughter to remain in his homestead, but he is also responsible for her return to her husband if she deserts him for another man. Even if a wife has sufficient cause for divorce, she may not simply return to her father. Her father must offer to refund the marriage payment and then, if the husband refuses to accept it, her father may sue him for refusal, citing the wife's reasons for wanting a divorce.[2]

Another institutionalised means of controlling the latent tension involved in the marriage bond is the formalised respect relationship which obtains between a man and his *bakoirume*, as all males of the wife's lineage are called (see Fig. 5). A man is expected to pay frequent calls at the homestead of his wife's father. On such occasions, an atmosphere of great formality prevails and gifts are exchanged. When visiting his *bakoirume* a man should always dress correctly in the long white robe (*kkanzu*), which leaves no part of the

---

[1] A more detailed analysis of marriage and the determinants of separation in Soga society will be presented in another publication.

[2] Since a wife in Busoga cannot legally (and in fact almost never does) reside apart from her husband without the repayment of bridewealth, which constitutes divorce, I use the terms "separation" and "divorce" interchangeably.

body exposed, as a sign of respect. He must behave with the utmost politeness.

In spite of such institutional counter-measures, however, Soga marriage is quite unstable. In Table XII, all present and past marriages of the men in the five villages in the sample area are tabulated according to whether they remain intact or have ended in death or separation. Of these marriages, between 13 and 47 per cent. have ended in separation. (Again, Budini, being a mission-dominated village, is probably atypical.) Most such separations take place by mutual consent, without formal legal proceedings, but often the tensions arising out of marriage result in litigation. Of 446 cases heard in the court of Sub-County Ssabawaali, Bulamogi County in 1950, 48, or 10·8 per cent. arose out of marriage.[1] Soga marriage, it appears, is not a strong enough bond to resolve the conflict, present in any patrilineal society, between a woman's loyalty to the group into which she was born and of which she remains a member and her loyalty to the group into which she marries and for which she bears children.

The Lineage as a Corporate Group.

The marriage contract establishes for an individual a series of relationships with persons outside the homestead, his *bakoirume*. Except for the husband-wife relationship itself, however, affinal kinship is not the basis of membership in any corporate group, any group whose members see themselves as a unit and who act together toward common ends. Corporate kinship groups are formed only on the basis of common patrilineal descent.

For the peasant, the principal occasion upon which kinship mobilises joint action and common identification arises at death. When an individual dies, such members of his lineage (*nda*) as live near enough gather at his homestead to bury him in his plantain garden and to mourn his passing. The mourning period commonly lasts some two weeks, after which a feast and a formal council of the lineage mates are held. It is the task of the council to fill the gap in the kinship network created by death—to choose a successor to his kinship rôle and an heir to his property. These are commonly two different persons. The property heir is usually a son, while the successor to the kinship rôle should be a younger sibling, one who in the kinship terminology is the equivalent of the deceased (see Figs. 1 and 3). This person is called *musika ow'enkoba*, "the heir of the belt," because he takes the belt of the deceased which is

---

[1] These include civil actions for payment or repayment of bridewealth as well as criminal actions arising out of adultery or bigamy on the part of the wife.

TABLE XII

FREQUENCY OF SEPARATION

	Buyodi				Budini				Bunyama, Wairama and Bukwaya			
	Men		Wives		Men		Wives		Men		Wives	
	16–45	Over 45	of men 16–45	of men over 45	16–45	Over 45	of men 16–45	of men over 45	16–45	Over 45	of men 16–45	of men over 45
Present marriages												
1	54	32	54	32	80	37	80	37	77	57	77	57
2	9	13	18	26	6	8	12	16	31	14	62	28
3	3	2	9	6	—	2	—	6	12	10	36	30
4	—	—	—	—	—	1	—	4	—	1	—	4
5	1	—	5	—	—	—	—	—	—	1	—	5
6	—	—	—	—	—	1	—	6	—	—	—	—
7	—	—	—	—	—	—	—	—	—	1	—	7
8	—	1	—	8	—	—	—	—	—	—	—	—
9	—	—	—	—	—	—	—	—	—	1	—	9
Marriages separated												
1	33	24	33	24	20	7	20	7	34	21	34	21
2	5	5	10	10	1	1	2	2	28	11	56	22
3	1	—	3	—	—	1	—	3	13	16	39	48
4	—	1	—	4	—	—	—	—	5	7	20	28
5	2	1	10	5	—	—	—	—	3	2	15	10
6	—	—	—	—	—	—	—	—	—	3	—	18
7	—	—	—	—	—	—	—	—	—	—	—	—
8	—	—	—	—	—	—	—	—	—	1	—	8
14	—	—	—	—	—	—	—	—	—	1	—	14
Marriages broken by death of wife												
1	6	17	6	17	4	12	4	12	11	27	11	27
2	1	5	2	10	—	—	—	—	2	3	4	6
3	—	1	—	3	—	—	—	—	—	5	—	15
4	—	1	—	4	—	—	—	—	—	2	—	8
7	—	1	—	7	—	—	—	—	—	—	—	—
Total marriages	—	—	150	156	—	—	118	93	—	—	354	365
Total separations	—	—	56	43	—	—	22	12	—	—	164	169
Per cent. marriages broken by separation	—	—	37	28	—	—	19	13	—	—	46	46

the symbol of his kinship responsibilities.   The *musika ow'enkoba* becomes the legal guardian of the children of the deceased and should, if possible, marry his widow.   It is here, in the choice of the kinship successor, that the extension to adjoining collateral lines of the terminology for siblings becomes most meaningful, for the range of persons from which a successor may be chosen is not limited to an individual's immediate siblings.   A man is succeeded by his next junior "sibling" within whatever lineage acts corporately for succession purposes.   The entire generation of siblings within this group, which I shall call a succession lineage, succeed, one after the other, and the lineage is thereby united into a single body.   At any one point in time, sublineages within the succession lineage are, in

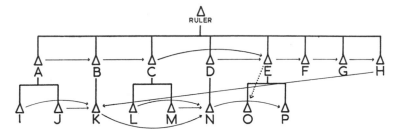

FIG. 6.   Succession Within a Ruler's Lineage.

a sense, ranked in order of temporal succession, but this ranking is quite ephemeral; classificatory brothers succeed one another until the generation runs out, at which time succession passes to the senior surviving member of the next generation.   Succession is often extended collaterally throughout a lineage as much as five generations in depth.   Ultimately, genealogical knowledge fails or component sub-lineages become too large or too distant from one another, socially or geographically, and fission occurs.

The system can perhaps best be understood with the help of illustrative cases.   Fig. 6 shows succession among the descendants of the ruler of the small traditional state of Busambira in southern Kigulu County.   Individuals are lettered according to birth order and hence according to seniority in succession.   Individuals do not, however, die in "proper" order.   In the first generation of the ruler's descendants, D died "out of place," so to speak, before C, whom he would have succeeded.   E thus succeeded both C and D. This also occurred in the following generation.   With the death of H, the first generation of the ruler's descendants was exhausted and so succession passed to their sons.   According to rule, I and J should then have succeeded, since they were sons of the senior member of the previous generation. Both I and J, however, predeceased H and so succession passed to K, the senior son of the next most senior member of the preceeding generation. Similarly, L and M died before K and O before N. Succession consequently passed from K to N and then to P, who at present is still living.

Fig. 7 illustrates the tendency of lineages to divide when the bonds of cohesion are no longer sufficient to maintain unity. In this case fission occurred in the fourth generation from the founding ancestor. The two lines descended from the great-great-grandfather of the

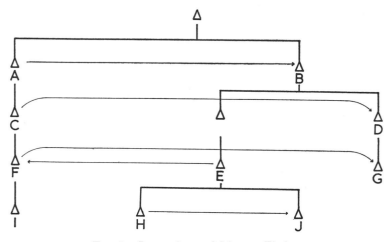

FIG. 7. Succession and Lineage Fission.

present generation continued to act as a single lineage for purposes of succession until the death of H, who was then succeeded by J, his full brother, instead of by I. I, being next in birth order to H, felt that he should succeed. However, he told me,

> They just kept their *busika* (succession) for themselves. We should have succeeded them because we are one lineage. We have always succeeded them. We think that they are just trying to hide the *busika* and to break up the lineage.

In Soga belief, the succession lineage should be maintained intact as long as possible and fission, when it does occur, is therefore frequently accompanied by ill feeling.

It is in such situations that the differences in scope which the word "lineage" (*nda*) may cover emerge. Where the obvious successor, the next junior sibling, is a near patrilineal kinsman, the problem is simple and clear-cut. The persons who gather at the funeral for the lineage council, and who therefore in that situation constitute the lineage, may be limited to a small group of close kinsmen. When, on the other hand, it is necessary to go out to a distant collateral line in order to find the appropriate successor, the pooled genealogical knowledge and authority of a wide range of patrilineal kinsmen may be required and the lineage which assembles will be larger. (It may be noted here that, though decisions concerning succession are in the hands of the adult males of the lineage, they very often must draw upon the genealogical knowledge of "wives" and "mothers." Women often remember genealogical complexities better than men). The word *nda*, however, is used whether the lineage which is mobilised is of narrow or wide range. On the other hand, to my knowledge, except possibly in the case of the *Baisengobi*, the royal clan in several of the northern states, the genealogical knowledge of living persons never extends to the clan as a whole. The largest "lineage" (that is, patrilineal group in which relationships may be more or less exactly traced and which therefore may act as a corporate group for succession purposes) always falls short of the whole clan.

The *musika ow'enkoba* does not inherit the property of the deceased. Property—land, livestock and money—pass to a son (*musika atwala ebintu*, "the heir who takes the things") who must also be chosen by the council of lineage-mates. Normally there is only one heir, both in Soga custom and because to-day most plots of land which are inherited would support only one homestead. Even the substantial Moslem community adhere to this pattern and do not apply the usual Islamic division of the inheritance. Although property passes downward from father to son and thus tends to divide the lineage into its component lines, the control which the lineage as a body exercises over inheritance counteracts this tendency. Wills are frequently made, either in writing or verbally before witnesses, but the lineage council is not bound by them. It may, and frequently does, respect the wishes of the deceased, but the council is free to break the will and to choose an heir whom it considers best fitted to take over his father's property.

I remarked earlier that there were indications that the father-son tie had recently received greater emphasis at the expense of collateral ties across the lineage. All Soga agree that the separation between the kinship successor and the heir to land and other property is a recent pattern, introduced in the later nineteenth century by the Ganda, who during that period dominated much of Busoga. The Ganda agree with this and add that a similar shift occurred in Buganda in the time of either Kabaka Suna or Kabaka Mutesa

(Mutesa succeeded Suna in 1857).[1] Although there is no documentary evidence to substantiate this story, the unanimity with which it is repeated gives it some claim to accuracy. Genealogies as given to-day clearly record the change. For example, in the lineage illustrated in Fig. 6, it occurred during the eighteen-nineties with the death of E. In this case, the inheritance in question was not a peasant's holding, but the rulership of Busambira. Until the death of E, rulership and kinship succeession had passed together from one brother to the next but now, though kinship succession passed to E's next junior brother, F, the rulership passed to his son, O. Similar shifts may be found in both peasants' and chiefs' genealogies during the 'eighties, 'nineties and early nineteen-hundreds.

The idea that such a change in fact occurred seems quite consistent with Soga kinship structure as it operates to-day. The kinship successor should marry the deceased's wife and becomes the guardian of his children; it would seem logical that he should also inherit the deceased's land and other property in order to support them. It would also seem quite possible that some of the tensions which I thought I observed, on the one hand between father and son and between brothers, and on the other between direct lineal descent and the collateral tie across lineages, are the result of such a change. If a son were not his father's potential heir, this would appear to eliminate much of what appear to-day to be the structural roots of sibling rivalry and father-son tension. And a shift from brother-brother to father-son inheritance would seem likely generally to weaken the solidarity of the corporate lineage and to produce greater tendencies toward the type of fission in succession lineages illustrated in Fig. 7.

Why did the change occur, if in fact it did? No firm answer can be given. The Soga attribute it to Ganda influence, but this hardly seems a satisfactory explanation, particularly since a similar change seems to have occurred only slightly earlier in Ganda society. A tempting hypothesis is that it was associated with the acquisition of new types of property. Though some trade existed, the aboriginal economy of the Lake Victoria area appears to have consisted largely of subsistence cultivation, with the surplus being consumed by the political hierarchy. Wealthy persons, which is to say chiefs, seem simply to have consumed more of the same types of agricultural produce and village craft products as were consumed by peasants. Before the middle of the last century, however, Arab slave and ivory traders are said to have penetrated to the

[1] Thomas, H. B., and Scott, Robert, *Uganda*, 1935, p. 1.

Lake Victoria region, bringing with them cloth, guns and other types of new trade goods.[1] Early historical accounts show chiefs accumulating substantial quantities of these goods through participation in the slave and ivory trade.[2] This trend continued to develop and, during the early decades of this century, cash-crop cultivation brought ordinary peasants within the sphere of the money economy. Perhaps in such situations individuals felt it desirable to preserve control of the new wealth within the direct line of descent rather than to see it dispersed throughout the wider lineage. Or perhaps there is a general latent tendency for the father-son tie to emerge into greater importance with any disturbance of such a society's equilibrium. The tendency of Western contact to bring out father-son inheritance in formerly matrilineal societies has often been noted[3]; perhaps patrilineal systems of the aboriginal Soga type which emphasise broad lineage solidarity are subject to similar dislocation under similar circumstances. All this, however, is largely speculation. Let us return to the functions of the lineage to-day.

Having chosen the *musika ow'enkoba* and the *musika atwala ebintu*, the council of lineage-mates comes to an end and a feast is held to celebrate the healing of the wound created by death. The feast is known as *kwabya olumbe*, "chasing away death." The mourning period is over; the deceased's kinship rôle has been filled and his property placed in the hands of his heir, and the life of the lineage may go on. Where traditional Soga belief has resisted the inroads of Christianity and Islam, this is not the end of the matter. The spirit (*muzimu*) of the deceased lives on to take a continuing interest in and to influence the earthly lives of surviving kinsmen. Of particular importance are the spirits of lineage-mates who, if angered by the neglect of living members of the lineage, may bring sickness or even death. A son builds a small thatched hut (*ssabo*) in the homestead courtyard where he leaves offerings of food and beer. More distant ancestors, particularly those who have given their names to distinct lineages, have more substantial shrines built for them and receive offerings from a wide range of patrilineal descendants. Even where formal adherence to Christianity or Islam has eliminated the ceremonial aspects of ancestor worship, the ancestors continue to be revered and the connection with them provided by continuity on the land and symbolised by their graves in the plantain grove continues to be highly valued. A peasant feels most secure when he occupies *butaka*, land to which he has a

---

[1] *Ibid.*, pp. 6–7.
[2] Speke, J. H., *Journal of the Discovery of the Source of the Nile*, 1863.
[3] Fortes, *op. cit.*

special claim through inheritance from a long line of patrilineal ancestors.

The corporate rights of the lineage in choosing the kinship successor and heir are firmly entrenched in Soga customary law as it operates to-day. The law courts recognise their decisions as binding where inheritance and legal guardianship are in question. The lineage is thus a group in which property and authority are always the major considerations. The solidarity which characterises it is not a "comfortable" solidarity in the affective sense. If siblings are equivalent in terms of their place in the lineage, relations between them are, to-day at any rate, often implicitly hostile because of the very structure of the lineage itself as a corporate group. The competition between brothers for a single inheritance is the adult counterpart of the sibling rivalry pattern described above. Older members of the lineage in the lineage council are often called upon to arbitrate between brothers, each pressing his claim to the inheritance. Unity is maintained by the authority of the older generation in so far as they are able to enforce their decisions. Thus the lineage, as the kinship terminology would suggest, is an extension of the relations which, within the homestead, obtain between father and son and between siblings.

I should not give the impression that corporate action in terms of patriliny ends at the limits of the succession lineage. Particularly among the larger clans, there tends to be an hierarchy of clan heads (*bakulu ab'ekika*) who lead and co-ordinate the activities of clansmen within delimited geographical areas. To-day the areas over which clan heads have jurisdiction correspond closely with present-day political units. Often, for example, there will be a head for the Parish (*muluka*), one for the Sub-County (*ggombolola*), one for the County (*ssaza*) and another for Busoga as a whole. How much this following by clans of the political divisions of the state is a recent pattern is hard to say. As I will point out in more detail in a later chapter, there has been some change and even more rationalisation of political units since the beginning of British administration. It seems quite clear that traditionally there were separate heads for sections of clans in the units which are to-day called Counties. Most of these were in the past independent states and as often as not were hostile to one another. The position at lower levels, however, is very difficult to reconstruct. Again, it is difficult to tell whether or not the units over which the clan heads had authority were in the past actual lineages (that is, patrilineal descent groups among whose members genealogical links were known). To-day, at any rate, this is most often not the case. The members of a clan within a village are likely, in areas of population stability, to constitute a lineage. But even in such areas there has been considerable population movement and hence all clan-mates within a Parish, Sub-County or County are very unlikely to constitute a true lineage. As we shall see in Chapter V, both recent events and traditional patterns of inheritance have contributed to population movement and hence to lineage dispersal.

Clan heads at the various levels may be chosen either by inheritance or by election. Both methods were frequently mentioned when I questioned members of various clans. In fact, however, the distinction between "election" and "inheritance" in clan or lineage affairs is not very sharp. In the case of an ordinary peasant, the heir to property may be chosen by testament and the kinship successor should be selected according to the rule of seniority, but in both cases the assembled lineage-mates as a corporate body have the right to choose within a certain range of eligible persons according to criteria of fitness. It is this discretionary right of the corporate group which underlies the uncertainty of informants when discussing the selection of clan heads. The Lusoga word *nsikirano* does not imply the rigidity which the English word "hereditary" conveys. The group which meets to choose a new clan head (usually at his predecessor's funeral) may consist, in the case of a Parish clan head, of representatives of other major succession lineages as well as the succession lineage of the late head. In the case of a higher clan head, it may consist of the latter plus the heads of subordinate territorial divisions. There is, however, real variation in the type of inheritance rule applied in so far as any inheritance pattern is followed. In some clans, the new head is the kinship successor of the old, while in other clans father-to-son inheritance is followed. In either case, however, the assembled council may exercise discretion.

The duties of a clan head include, as I have mentioned, participation in the council which chooses new clan heads. In addition, the hierarchy of heads constitutes a kind of appeal system against the decisions of succession lineages. Heirs or successors who are dissatisfied with the rulings of succession lineage councils may appeal to the territorial heads for reversal of such rulings. Other infractions of clan custom may also come under consideration by the clan heads. In one case which I observed, a son was tried and fined one goat for burying his deceased father without holding a *kwabya olumbe* ceremony and without notifying other members of the lineage. In another case, the assembly considered whether a certain marriage constituted a breach of exogamy. Incidents of the latter type are extremely rare and occur mainly by accident. The work of the assembly in such cases consists largely in more thorough genealogical investigation; the fault of the accused person consists in not having investigated more thoroughly before marriage. Though some territorial clan heads attempt to hold regular meetings, most of their activities are carried on at funeral feasts, when a good attendance by clan-mates may be expected. One man's funeral feast may be the occasion for adjudicating a dispute concerning persons of quite a different succession lineage.

As one might expect from the high value placed upon lineage unity and solidarity and from the general lack of rigid ranking within the lineage, the lineage and clan councils function in a broadly democratic way. The head acts as co-ordinator and chairman, but he has no authority to over-rule the wishes of the group. His influence depends largely upon his personal qualities of leadership. As is so often the case with assemblies of this kind elsewhere, the ideal is not rule by a numerical majority but rather the establishment of unanimity. Each member present may stand and give his opinion and such speech-making generally goes on until unanimity is reached even though this may require several days. I have never seen a council have recourse to formal voting. Proponents of a minority point of view, having seen which way the wind is blowing, generally yield as gracefully as possible so that the final decision, on the surface at least, is presented as the decision of the whole group.

MOTHER'S LINEAGE.

If an individual's place within his own patrilineage is an extension of his relations with his father, siblings and children, his relations with the patrilineage of his mother follow the pattern of intra-homestead relations between mother and son. In relations with the mother's lineage, no property is at stake and no authority is involved. The popular stereotype of these *bakaire* and *badhadha*, as all members of the mother's lineage are called (see Fig. 4), is one of warmth and indulgence. In his mother's brother's homestead, a child may misbehave more freely than at home without being punished. When a boy reaches adulthood, he goes to his mother's brother for help in accumulating bridewealth for his marriage. There are felt to be dangers in this pattern. Too much indulgence spoils a young person's character. He needs the severe discipline of a father and consequently it is felt to be unfortunate for a child to grow up in his mother's brother's homestead.

In the traditional system of belief and ritual, the special character of the mother's brother-sister's son relationship is utilised in the carrying out of ritually dangerous tasks. Before burial, the body of a deceased person must be brought to the burial place and wrapped in barkcloth. These preparations, however, are felt to be fraught with supernatural danger to the lineage-mates of the deceased and so they are delegated to the *mwiwa*, the sister's son who, while a close kinsman and hence intimately involved in the loss which death has brought, is outside the lineage group and so immune to the dangers of the situation.[1]

In later chapters, the considerable importance of the mother's brother-sister's son relationship in the larger political structure of the state, both traditionally and under modern conditions, will be discussed.

In this chapter, I have described the ways in which kinship and clanship structure authority relations for the Soga peasant. Within the homestead, the father is a strongly authoritarian figure, his position resting upon both his partial control of inheritance and his supernatural significance, after death, in terms of the ancestor cult. Among brothers, on the other hand, there is little in the way of clearly-defined relative status; inheritance rules are vague and brothers are rivals. These two axes of the social relations among the males of the homestead—the lineal and the collateral—are reproduced in wider patrilineal kin groups. The segregation of generations and the equivalence of collaterals are reproduced in the pattern of succession by brothers and classificatory brothers across the lineage. Like brothers, too, lineage mates of a generation are both solidary, having corporate functions with regard to succession, and subject to conflict over issues of fission and unity. Patrilineal kinship thus defines above all a sphere of authority and property and of competition for their possession. Affinal kinship gives rise to quite a different order of social relations. In a society whose members are divided into self-contained patrilineal groups, affinity provides links, albeit rather unstable ones, between such groups. From another point of view, affinity results, in succeeding generations, in maternal ties which, though not involving power and property, are characterised by great warmth of feeling.

In succeeding chapters, I shall show these various patterns of peasant kinship reproduced, with modifications, in the state system. But first I shall examine the ways in which they operate in the structure of village communities.

[1] A fuller account of the ritual of burial is given in Zibondo, Ezekeri, "Empisa Ezokuzika mu Busoga," *Uganda Journal*, Vol. II, No. 2, pp. 133–144.

CHAPTER V

VILLAGE COMMUNITIES

VARIATIONS ON A THEME.

In Chapter IV, I described those institutions in Soga peasant society which are structured about kinship and unilineal kin groups. It is significant that during this description I hardly had occasion to mention the village community, for the Soga village is not primarily a kinship unit. It is rather first and foremost a territorial unit—frequently a low hill bounded by swamps—under a village headman. When a Soga speaks of a village (*mutala*) or of one of the sub-villages (*bisoko*) into which villages are divided, he thinks primarily of such a territorial unit.

This is not to say, of course, that kinship institutions are irrelevant to village structure. On the contrary, kinship institutions are intimately bound up with village structure in two ways. First, the position of village or sub-village headmen is in most areas hereditary in the same way as a peasant's holding. It is inherited in the patrilineal line and is under the control of the succession lineage. Thus, as the Soga say, the village or sub-village is "owned" by a lineage group. Second, where the population of a village or sub-village has remained stable, all of its members tend to be related to one another by ties of near or extended kinship. The village or sub-village becomes a network of kinship relations, and relations among its members tend to be structured in kinship terms. It is important to reiterate, however, that the village or sub-village is not primarily, in terms of institutional definition, a kinship unit. It is never, to my knowledge, a lineage unit in the sense in which villages often are in African societies. It is never made up exclusively, or even largely, of a group of lineage-mates and, more importantly, relations between a headman and his people are not institutionally defined as lineage relations. As will be seen in Chapter VII, where the relationship of the headman to his people will be described in some detail, the headman is primarily a holder and distributor of certain rights in the land of his village or sub-village and a link between his people and the wider political system. A headman's kinship ties with his people may alter the tone of his relations with them, but they do not alter the basic definition of his position.

Within this broad pattern, villages and sub-villages vary considerably. First, they vary in terms of their position in the

traditional political system.   Although all headmen hold much the
same position in law to-day, traditionally there were headmen of at
least three different types holding different positions in the political
system.   In some areas, these differences are still significant.
Second, there have been great differences from area to area in the
stability of population over the past century and hence villages and
sub-villages to-day vary in the degree to which their populations are
inter-related by kinship ties.   Reference was made earlier to a
series of sleeping sickness epidemics which ravaged southern
Busoga during the early years of the present century.   A strip
along the Lake Victoria shore remains completely depopulated,
but a further belt several miles deep to the north of the depopulated
area was also, though less severely, affected.   An unknown, but
apparently substantial, part of its population either died or migrated
to other parts of the country, after which it was again resettled.[1]
The result was a thorough shaking-up of the population.   Although
some of those who returned were the original inhabitants or their
descendants, many were persons from other parts of Busoga.   The
area affected by the epidemic extended at least as far north as
Iganga, and probably somewhat beyond, and included what is
to-day one of the most densely populated areas of the country.
As a consequence, the populations of villages and sub-villages in
this southern area are much less inter-related kinship-wise than
are those further north and kinship institutions operate somewhat
differently in the two areas.

As I noted earlier, my detailed field research was confined mainly
to two areas: Busambira, in southern Kigulu County, and the area
around Kaliro, in southern Bulamogi County.   It is these two
areas from which the data on village and sub-village structure to be
presented in this chapter were drawn.   The two areas were chosen to
represent major variations, both in the social features noted above
and in the economic features described in Chapter III.   Further,
an effort was made to compare these two areas, on the basis of more
superficial observation, with other areas of Busoga.   I feel, therefore, that the major variations in Busoga as a whole are probably
represented in the data from these two areas, but it is only fair to
state that most of my information does come from two rather small
groups of villages.

Let me describe briefly the traditional and modern settings of the
two areas.   The villages of Budini and Buyodi were traditionally

---

[1] "The extent of the ravages of the disease may be gauged by the fact that
by 1905 the deaths from the infection reported in the Kingdom of Buganda
alone totalled 92,544 and this figure was probably exceeded in Busoga."
(Thomas, H. B., and Scott, Robert, *Uganda*, 1935, p. 300).

included in the state of Bulamogi, whose boundaries were essentially the same as those of the present-day Bulamogi County (see Maps 2 and 7). The combined population of the two villages in 1952 was 1,172.[1] Bulamogi was one of the larger states (the population of Bulamogi County in 1948 was 48,870)[2] and was ruled by a dynasty of the *Baisengobi* clan. Its political organisation was relatively complex. The ruler, whose title was Zibondo, commanded a large administrative staff of household and territorial officials, headed by the *katikkiro*, the "prime minister," who had direct control over the palace and its environs. The outlying area of the state was divided into a number of major subdivisions, each under the administration of a prince (*mulangira*) or a commoner chief (*mukungu*) appointed by the ruler. Subordinate to the chiefs and princes, were the headmen of the villages (*ab'emitala*) and the sub-villages (*ab'ebisoko*). In recent times, Kaliro, the residence of the present Zibondo and his predecessor, has become a trading centre for the surrounding area. The town contains many Indian- and Arab-owned shops as well as a posts and telegraphs office. Several bus routes and the railway line connect it with other major trading centres and with Jinja. Near the town is the Anglican church and primary school, presided over by Soga clergymen and teachers. A short distance to the north, in the village of Budini, is the large Roman Catholic centre, which includes a church and primary school operated by European priests as well as a maternity hospital and convent directed by European nuns. Budini village, being located near the town and having within its boundaries the European-manned Catholic centre, has been considerably affected by outside influences. Buyodi, on the other hand, lies at considerable distance from the town, is not crossed by a motorable road, and may be considered more or less typical of northern rural Busoga.

The three contiguous villages of Bunyama, Wairama and Bukwaya (combined population in 1952: 1,079) were traditionally part of the small state of Busambira, which in the early years of the British Administration was amalgamated with the larger state of Kigulu and to-day forms part of Sub-County Ssabawaali of Kigulu County (see Map 2). The remaining nine villages of Busambira were Izimba, Nakisenyi, Kakombo, Nawanzu, Kabira, Namirali, Buluza, Kiboyo and Bujwege (see Map 8). Busambira, though similar in structure, was in pre-Administration times a political unit much smaller in scale than Bulamogi (its 1948 population was

---

[1] According to my own survey figures.
[2] East African Statistical Department, *African Population of Uganda Protectorate: Geographical and Tribal Studies*, 1950, p. 20.

3,894)[1] and of less complex organisation. Paramount political authority was in the hands of a ruler of the *Baiseigaga* clan known as the Kisambira.   Unlike the Zibondo in Bulamogi, the Kisambira

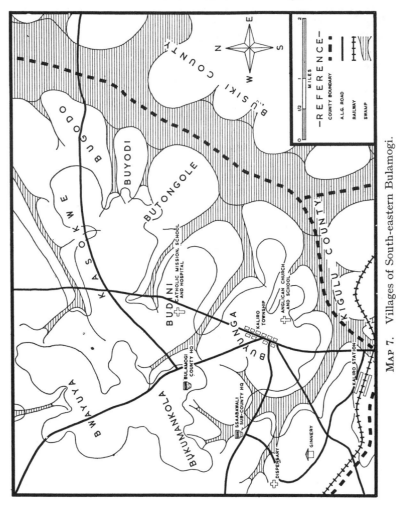

MAP 7.   Villages of South-eastern Bulamogi.

had no staff of chiefs interposed between himself and the village and sub-village headmen.   He or his *katikkiro* dealt directly with the headmen and he was in general much less remote from village

[1] Preliminary analysis by Parish units of the African population of Uganda, circulated by the East African Statistical Department in 1950.

life than was the Zibondo. Although Busambira, like many other small political units in southern Busoga, has lost its separate political identity, it remains a unit in the minds of its people.

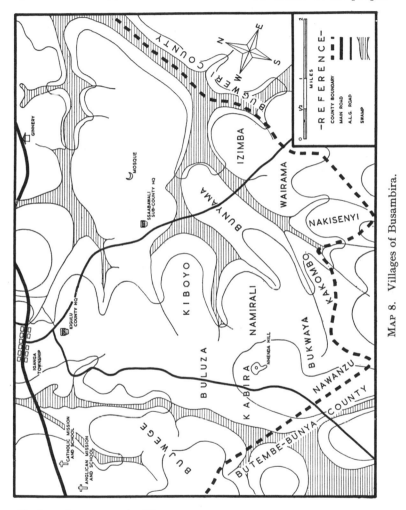

MAP 8. Villages of Busambira.

To-day, its economic life centres around the large *duka* town of Iganga, which has grown up around the capital of the old Kigulu state. The Catholic and Anglican missions and the headquarters of Kigulu County are also located near Iganga. However, although Iganga is a centre for the diffusion of new ideas and new material culture, Busambira is far enough removed from the town to be outside its immediate range of influence. The three villages of Wairama, Bunyama and Bukwaya may therefore be considered representative of that part of south Busoga which was largely depopulated by sleeping sickness and later resettled. These are the communities from which my data are drawn. Let us now examine some of the variations in pattern which they represent and the consequences of these variations for life in the peasant village.

POPULATION STABILITY AND KINSHIP STRUCTURE.

Before illustrating some of the commoner types of local community structure, it may be well to indicate more precisely the differences in population stability which exist to-day between the northern and southern parts of Busoga as a result of the sleeping sickness epidemics at the turn of the century. By "population stability" I mean simply the degree to which the present generation of adults were born and reared in the communities in which they now live. In one sense, of course, such a variable is sociologically uninteresting since, in this case at any rate, instability is the result of a particular, unique non-social event—the sleeping sickness epidemic. On the other hand, particularly in a society in which extended kinship institutions are of great moment, it does have substantial significance for local community structure. The ability of extended kinship institutions to operate in daily social intercourse depends, at least in part, upon spatial proximity between persons so related. Where the spatial pattern has been disrupted, it may be expected that extended kinship institutions will operate less effectively or in different ways. Furthermore, the sleeping sickness epidemics were widespread enough to affect a substantial area of Busoga and consequently communities lying within that area represent a major variation in present-day Soga society.

The much greater population stability of Budini and Buyodi, lying in the unaffected area, as compared with Bunyama, Wairama and Bukwaya, which were severely affected, emerges in Table XIII. Current marriages of men born in Busoga are classified according to the birth-places of both husband and wife. In Budini and Buyodi, 77 per cent. of the men and 7 per cent. of their wives were born in the sub-villages in which they now reside. In the Busambira villages, only 27 per cent. of the men and 1 per cent. of their wives were born in their present home sub-villages. In the Busambira villages, 27 per cent. of the men are immigrants from other counties, while in Budini and Buyodi this figure is only 5 per cent.

Population instability has a much greater impact upon the tendency of men to remain in their home areas than it does in the case of women. Institutionally, residence in Busoga is patrilocal, not within the father's homestead but nearby in the same sub-village. Women in any case move at marriage to the areas in which their husbands were born. Furthermore, the rules of exogamy make it difficult for a man to find a wife in his own village or sub-village,

TABLE XIII

BIRTHPLACES OF SPOUSES IN CURRENT MARRIAGES

Men born in	Women born in						
	Sub-village	Village	County	Busoga	Outside Busoga	Total	Per cent.
Budini and Buyodi							
Sub-village ..	18	19	137	65	8	247	77
Village.. ..	—	—	—	3	2	5	2
County ..	2	2	30	17	2	53	17
Busoga ..	2	—	6	6	1	15	5
Total	22	21	173	91	13	320	101
Per cent. ..	7	7	54	28	4	100	—
Bunyama, Wairama and Bukwaya							
Sub-village ..	2	2	42	34	4	84	27
Village.. ..	—	—	21	10	1	32	10
County ..	1	—	66	43	3	113	36
Busoga ..	—	1	29	50	6	86	27
Total	3	3	158	137	14	315	100
Per cent. ..	1	1	50	44	4	100	—

since he may not marry a woman belonging to any one of his parents' or grandparents' clans. As we shall see in a moment, the stable village or sub-village tends to become so intricately cross-cut by kinship ties that most of its young men must find wives from elsewhere. For the men, however, who would otherwise remain at home, population instability has a great impact. It means that among the male homestead heads kinship relations are much less pervasive and that relations between neighbours are to a much smaller degree structured about kinship.

One way of looking at the effect of population instability upon kinship institutions is in terms of its consequences for lineage localisation—the degree to which male household heads live in communities containing substantial numbers of their lineage-mates. Fig. 8 shows the percentages of married males with varying numbers of clan-mates, on the one hand in the Busambira villages and on the other in Budini and Buyodi. In the Busambira villages, 63 per cent. of the men belong to clans having from one to five married male members in the three villages. In Budini and Buyodi, only 29 per cent. belong to such small clans. In Budini and Buyodi, 57 per cent. of the men belong to clans having more than ten married male members, while in the Busambira villages, this figure is only 28 per cent. (Both of these differences are significant at less than the 5 per cent. level.)[1]

These differences are slightly exaggerated, since the combined married male population of Budini and Buyodi is 262, while that of the Busambira villages is only 233. This difference in population, however, is only 12 per cent., while the differences noted above in numbers of men belonging to clans of varying size are around 30 per cent.[2] On the other hand, the use of clan instead of lineage membership as an index tends to under-represent the patrilineal heterogeneity of the Busambira villages as compared with Budini and Buyodi. Clan was used instead of lineage because the data were gathered by means of a questionnaire, which required that questions be asked in such a way that simple and uniform answers could be given. Because of the tendency of lineages to split at different intervals, lineage names do not yield such simple and uniform information. If a lineage has divided within the lifetime of men still living, older persons may still speak of themselves as members of the higher order or "parent" lineage, while the children of the same persons may use the new lineage name in referring to themselves. The clan name, however, is much more stable. In fact, in a stable area, clan and lineage tend to converge, since all members of a clan living in the local area will tend to represent a lineage within the clan and will act as a single corporate succession lineage. For the Busambira villages, this is less true than for Budini and Buyodi. The fact that Busambira has received a substantial amount of immigration from other parts of Busoga means that persons living in the same village may be members of

[1] In calculating the significance of this and other percentage differences referred to in this book, I have made use of the "chi-square" test.
[2] The difference in number of cases between the two samples is 29. If one were to equalise the two populations by adding to Busambira 29 persons belonging to clans containing more than ten married male members, thus reducing the differences between the two populations by the greatest possible amount, the differences would still be significant at less than the 5 per cent. level.

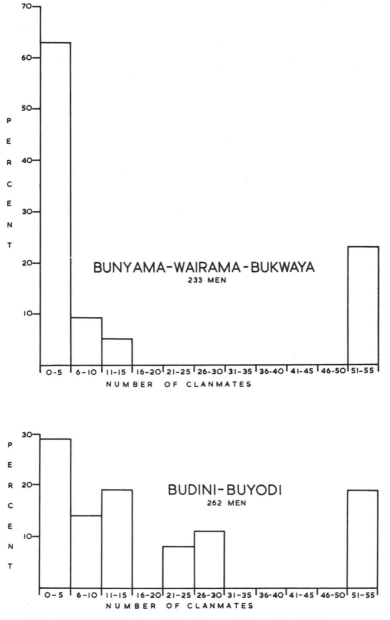

FIG. 8. Size of the Local Clan Group in Two Sample Areas.

completely separate lineages of the same clan.   In that case, they will not act as members of the same succession lineage.   The effect of using clan instead of lineage as the index of patrilineal group membership is, therefore, to under-estimate the difference between the two areas.   The effective lineage isolation of the average inhabitant of the Busambira area would be somewhat greater than these statistical data indicate.

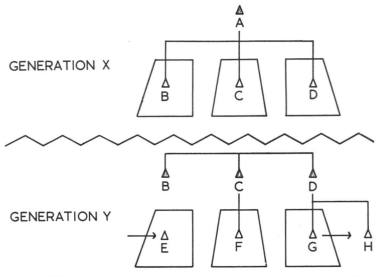

Fig. 9.   Dispersion of a Local Lineage Group under Conditions of High Population Density.

It is apparent that a resident of Budini or Buyodi is more likely to have lineage-mates among his neighbours than is a resident of one of the Busambira villages.   It has been suggested that the more heterogeneous clan composition of the Busambira villages is due, at least in part, to the effects of a series of sleeping sickness epidemics. It therefore might be considered a temporary phenomenon which would be erased by a subsequent period of population stability. It seems quite possible, however, that under prevailing conditions of population density, the "scrambling" of clans represents an irreversible change.   Fig. 9 illustrates a process which would become increasingly common with greater clan heterogeneity.

In generation X, each of three brothers holds a plot of land within a village area.   In the following generation, one of the three brothers (D) has left two sons, another (C) has left one son, while the third (B) has died without leaving an heir.   If all cultivable land in the village is taken up, then there is no room for the differential growth and decline of the different lines within the lineage. For the lineage to maintain its numbers within the village, B's plot must become available just at the time when H, the second son of D, reaches adulthood and is in need of land. Otherwise, a stranger, (E), will come in and take up the plot left by B. The likelihood of H's reaching adulthood just at the time of B's death is, of course, not great. Where the number of lineage-mates within the village is larger, the likelihood of such events occurring at the same time is increased since land will become available at greater intervals as a result of the dying out of some lines within the lineage. In the Busambira villages, however, three members of one lineage within a single village would not be an infrequently small number since, as we have seen, 63 per cent. of the married males there belong to clans with not more than five members in all of the three villages.

If land could be bought and sold, of course, the process described above might be counteracted by the extra sons in expanding lineages buying land from members of other lineages. In the Soga customary land law, however, the buying and selling of land is not possible. Peasant lineages control the disposition of land only through inheritance. When a peasant dies without leaving an heir, land reverts to the headman for re-allotment without regard to kinship. The customary rights of the headman also limit the ability of clans to keep aside land left by deceased members for the use of other members at a later date. It would appear, therefore, that the relatively greater lineage heterogeneity of local areas is likely to be a lasting feature of a large area of southern Busoga, of which the Busambira villages are more or less representative.

THREE STRUCTURAL TYPES.

Figs. 10, 11 and 12 illustrate diagramatically the genealogical relations among the adult populations of three sub-villages at the time when this study was being carried out. I have taken the sub-village as the unit for purposes of illustration merely because an entire village would be too large to be represented conveniently on a single genealogical chart. The sub-village, however, is essentially a microcosm of the village; it is a unit of the same kind and the kinship ties which bind its members are similar. Were I to draw a chart of any one of the villages from which these sub-villages are drawn, it would look much the same—would show essentially the same density of kinship relations—but would be several times as large. Kirumbi (Fig. 10) is one of six sub-villages making up Buyodi village; Gasemba (Fig. 11) is one of the six sub-villages of Budini while Bunyambale (Fig. 12) is one of five sub-villages in Bukwaya. In order to save space, I have shown only the adult population. All personal names shown on the charts are, of course, fictitious.

Kirumbi is a sub-village "owned" by a lineage of the *Baisengobi*, the royal clan of Bulamogi. The headman is Fred (homestead IV), whose married son, Adam, lives with him. Three other homesteads (I, II and III) are occupied by his full brother, Carl, and by his paternal parallel cousins, George and Henry. All speak of themselves as being of the lineage of their common patrilineal ancestor, the son of a ruler of the Bulamogi state. This ancestor, the great-grandfather of Fred, Carl, Henry and George, was placed in authority over some dozen villages by his father, the ruler. His grave, which lies within the borders of Kirumbi sub-village, is to-day marked, Western-fashion, by a large concrete slab upon which is inscribed:

"————, son of Zibondo ———— (the ruler), who was given all of the villages in the Sub-Counties of Musaale and Ssabawaali."[1]

Other descendants of this man to-day hold the headships of Buyodi and Budini villages and of most of their constituent sub-villages. However, such higher genealogical matters will be taken up in Chapters VI and VII. For the moment let us return to the internal structure of Kirumbi, remembering that it is a sub-village dominated by princes.

Princes are not numerically predominant among the heads of homesteads in Kirumbi, however. The largest lineage group, making up nine of the fifteen homestead heads (VI, VII, VIII, IX, X, XI, XII, XIII and XV) in the sub-village is a lineage of the *Baisemukubembe*, a commoner clan. All are sons or grandsons of Keith (XII) or his deceased brother. Keith is to-day a very old man, past eighty so far as I could judge, and is no longer the active leader of the local lineage. Strictly speaking, all the *Baisemuku-bembe* homestead heads in Kirumbi are of the lineage of Keith's father, but it is an index of Keith's advancing age that some members of the group now tend to speak of themselves as "the lineage of Keith." Ordinarily a lineage is not named after a living individual, but Keith is, socially speaking, gradually ceasing to be a living person. It is of interest that Paul and Mark (homestead XV) also tend to speak of themselves as members of Keith's lineage, in spite of the fact that they are descended, not from Keith, but from his deceased brother. The reason for this is that Keith's brother never

---

[1] The "Sub-County" (*ggombolola*) had not yet come into being as a type of political unit at the time when this man lived, but people to-day tend to equate traditional political units with their nearest modern counterparts. Recent changes in political units will be explained in Chapter VI.

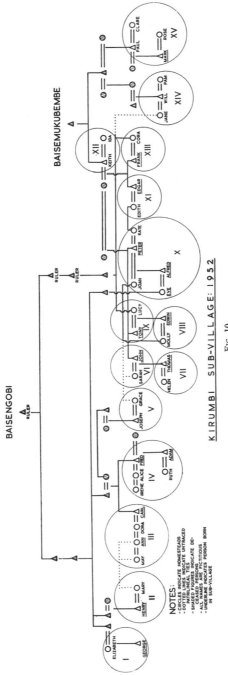

Fig. 10.

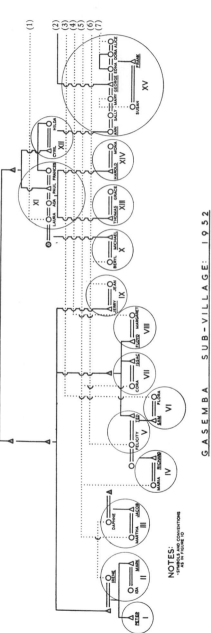

BAISENSAMBAIZA

GASEMBA SUB-VILLAGE: 1952

Fig. 11.

NOTES:
SYMBOLS AND CONVENTIONS
AS IN FIGURE 10

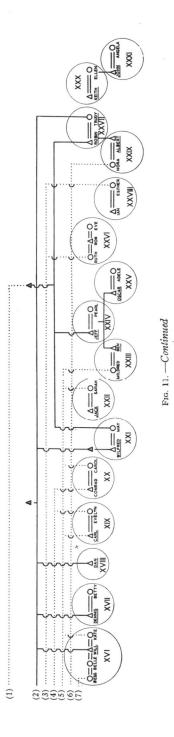

BAISEMUGAYA   BAISEMUHOYA

Fig. 11.—*Continued*

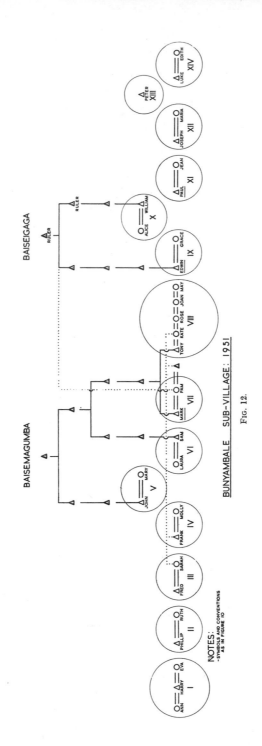

NOTES:
-SYMBOLS AND CONVENTIONS
 AS IN FIGURE 10

BUNYAMBALE   SUB-VILLAGE: 1951

Fig. 12.

lived in Kirumbi. He spent his life in Kigulu County and when he died Paul came to live near Keith and became amalgamated with Keith's line. This is a rather neat example of the fictionalising of lineage relationships which appears to be general in societies where unilineal kinship groups are institutionalised.[1] Through amalgamation of distinct collateral lines, the unity and solidarity of the group is maintained. It may be predicted with confidence that in some future generation the true position will be forgotten and that Paul will come to be considered a son of Keith.

Only two homestead heads are not members of either the *Baisengobi* or *Baisemukubembe* lineages. Joseph (homestead V) is a maternal cross-cousin of Fred, the sub-village headman. Joseph's father was a man of Bugabula County who became a "client" (a personal political servant, a position which will be explained at greater length in Chapters VI and VII) of the father of Carl and Fred, who was then village headman of Buyodi and a Parish chief.[2] The latter married Joseph's father's sister and was given land in Budini village, where Joseph was born. Joseph is thus a *dhadha* (classificatory mother's brother) to Fred, the sub-village headman, who gave him land in Kirumbi. By extension, Joseph is a "mother's brother" to all of the *Baisengobi* homestead heads in Kirumbi and his position in the sub-village is therefore secure. His case provides an example, at the lowest level, of the function of the mother's brother-sister's son tie in establishing political relationships.

Will (homestead XIV), the only other "stranger" homestead head in Kirumbi, illustrates the same principle in reverse. His father, a man of Kigulu County, married a brother's daughter (that is, a classificatory "daughter") of Keith. Will is thus a *mwiwa* ("sister's son") to all of the *Baisemukubembe* homestead heads in Kirumbi and when his father died he left Kigulu and settled near Keith, who helped him to get land in the sub-village. Keith, not being sub-village headman, could not himself give Will land, but he was able to use his influence as senior member of a large local lineage to act as Will's sponsor in his dealings with the headman.

This, then, is the "core" structure of Kirumbi: A lineage of the royal clan holding the headmanship; a larger commoner lineage making up the bulk of the homestead heads and two "stranger" homestead heads, one attached to each of the lineages. This does not, however, exhaust the network of kinship ties in Kirumbi. Affinal ties link the two local lineages. Tony (IX), Alfred (X) and

---

[1] Fortes has summarized much of the comparative data on this point. (See Fortes, Meyer, "The Structure of Unilineal Descent Groups," *American Anthropologist*, Vol. LV, No. 1, 1953, pp. 17–41).
[2] The position of the Parish chief will be explained in Chapters VI and VII.

Frank (XIII), among the *Baisemukubembe*, have married *Baisengobi* women.   So has Will (XIV), one of the "strangers." Alfred's wife, Eve, is a paternal parallel first cousin to the *Baisengobi* homestead heads and was born in Kirumbi.   Many of the other wives, though coming from other villages, are linked to one another by near or distant patrilineal kinship.   May, Ann (III) and Mary (II) form one group of patrilineally related wives; Grace (V), Sarah (VI), Molly (VIII) and Joan (X) form another; while Kate (X) and Edith (XI) form a third.   The more distant patrilineal ties between wives (indicated by dotted lines) are in most cases accidental; women marry into the sub-village and later discover that they have clan sisters there.   In other cases there is a conscious effort to create further ties.   Wives bring their younger sisters to live with them and they later marry the same or a neighbouring homestead head.   In either case, such ties increase the density of kinship relations and provide local kinship relations for wives, thus mitigating the kinship isolation which otherwise would be the lot of women under patrilocal residence.

The case of Kirumbi also throws some light upon the problem of whether the *Baisengobi*, the royal clan, came as conquerors imposing their authority upon indigenous peoples.   In this case, at any rate, the *Baisengobi* seem to have a longer history of settlement than do the *Baisemukubembe* who constitute the bulk of the male population. Judging from the evidence of graves in the sub-village, the *Baisengobi* have been there at least since the time of the great-grandfather of Fred, the present headman.   The *Baisemukubembe*, it is agreed by all parties, are more recent immigrants.   The father of Keith (XII) left his home in the small southern state of Butembe and became a servant of the great-great-grandfather of Fred, the earliest ruler shown in Fig. 10.   At this time, however, he lived in northern Bulamogi and Keith was born there.   It was not until somewhat later that Keith moved to Kirumbi and took up land.   Neither the *Baisengobi* nor the *Baisemukubembe*, however, have a really long history of residence in Kirumbi.   Neither group appears to be earlier than middle or early nineteenth century.   The *Baisengobi* of Bulamogi as a whole claim a considerably longer history, but the lineages which to-day control Kirumbi and surrounding villages and sub-villages are all descended from the ruler shown at the top of Fig. 10.   There is a tradition in the community that in the time of Fred's grandfather the headmanship of the sub-village was held by a commoner client of the *Baisekisige* clan.   It is said that he "became tired" (*yakoowa*), which may well be a euphemism for dismissal, and that Fred's grandfather took back the headmanship for himself and his son.   Of the *Baisekisige*, however, there is to-day not a single representative in the population of Kirumbi. It is for such reasons that I expressed doubt and puzzlement in Chapter II concerning the long-term history of the Soga states. As we shall see, other sub-villages have equally foggy histories. The large sub-village of Gasemba (Fig. 11) in the nearby village of Budini, illustrates another type of local community structure— one in which there are several substantial local lineage groups and in which the village headmanship is held in a commoner lineage. The headmanship is held by a lineage of the *Baisemugaya* clan and the headman is George (homestead XV). As in the case of Kirumbi, however, the headman's lineage has not been long established in the sub-village. George related to me how his father came to Gasemba:

"————, my father, was born in ————, a village well to the north of here. He was a client of Zibondo ———— (an earlier ruler of Bulamogi) and that Zibondo gave him this sub-village to rule over and to be his own. We were not always *Balamogi* (people of Bulamogi). Our clan originated in Bugaya, one of the islands of Lake Victoria. . . . I am the head of the *Baisemugaya* in Bulamogi, but the head for all of Busoga lives in Bugabula County. . . ."

Here again, we see relative newcomers controlling the headmanship and constituting a substantial part of the sub-village population. George is a second-generation immigrant in the community over which he has authority. He and his lineage-mates are not, however, newcomers to any greater degree than the *Baisensambaiza*, who form the largest lineage group in Gasemba. Paul (XI), their senior member, came to Gasemba from the nearby village of Kyani when his father died, leaving him, in his opinion, with insufficient land. He was preceded in Gasemba by his paternal parallel cousin, the father of Jerry (IX) and the grandfather of Peter (I), Mark (II), Ted (V), Isaac (VII) and Floyd (VIII). This cousin was *katikkiro* ("second in command") to George's father, who was then headman. When he died, Paul succeeded to his kinship rôle and became the senior member of what had become a substantial local succession lineage. Although the position of *katikkiro* to a sub-village headman no longer formally exists, Paul to-day acts as an assistant to George in many ways, helping in the collection of taxes, in the control of land, and acting as the representative of the other *Baisensambaiza* in their dealings with George. The two lineages are linked by George's marriage to Ann, a daughter of Paul's brother Cyril (XII).

The other major lineage group, the *Baisemuhoya*, is represented by the homesteads of Ben (XXIII), Jeff (XXIV), Oscar (XXV), Robin (XXVII) and Albert (XXIX). All are the sons of one man, an ordinary peasant, who came to Gasemba to settle and was given land by George's father. His lineage is linked to the *Baisemugaya* by the marriage of his sister May to Wilfred (XXI) and by that of his brother Robin (XXVII) to George's sister Trudy. In the next generation, these marriages will result in reciprocal mother's brother-sister's son relationships between the two lineages. The *Baisemuhoya* are linked to the *Baisensambaiza*, somewhat more distantly, by the marriage of their father's clan sister Laura's marriage to Paul (XI).

As in the case of Kirumbi, there are a few lineage "strangers" in the sub-village population. Jacob (III) is the son of a man who came to take up land and who married a clan sister of Mark's (II) and Peter's (I) mother, Irene. Carl (XIX) and Jack (XXII) are also sons of immigrants, while Conrad (XX) and Ian (XXVIII) are themselves immigrants. All, however, are related, however distantly, to other persons in the sub-village, either through clan ties with women or through the clan ties of their wives. Similarly, many of the wives have near or distant kinswomen in the sub-village. Hilda (XII) and Frances (XI) are full sisters who have married full brothers, while Edna and Dora (XV) are full sisters married to the same man—a case of orthodox sororal polygyny. The only persons not linked by kinship ties of some sort with every other member of the sub-village are Keith (XXX) and John (XXXI), a father and son. Both were born in Gasemba, Keith's father having been an immigrant, but so far as I was able to discover, they are completely isolated kinship-wise from their neighbours.

Kirumbi and Gasemba are stable communities. As I have suggested, stability in this context is a relative term, since none of the lineages in the two sub-villages has reached a depth of more than five generations of adults (six in the case of the *Baisensambaiza* of Gasemba if the children of Sam (VI) and Richard (IV), not shown on the chart, are counted as constituting a generation). But in Gasemba and Kirumbi one does find a structure which is the result of a natural process of lineage growth. One finds three to five generations of patrilineal continuity upon the land and a network of affinal ties between local lineages. The resulting communities can be described, quite accurately, as networks of kinship relations. Indeed, it is almost certain that I did not discover all the kinship relations among homesteads in Kirumbi and Gasemba and that really accurate genealogical diagrams of these communities would show an even greater density of kinship ties within them.

Bunyambale (Fig. 12) which seemed to me quite typical of Busambira sub-villages, is a community of a very different kind.

Of the fourteen homestead heads, only six can trace patrilineal kinship with one another. Two, Edwin (homestead IX) and William (X), belong to the *Baiseigaga* clan, which holds the rulership of Busambira and many of the headmanships of villages and sub-villages within it. Edwin and William, however, can hardly be said to constitute a lineage of any kind. Their patrilineal kinship, though traceable, is quite distant; their common ancestor is William's great-grandfather and Edwin's great-great-grandfather. Though the headman of Bunyambale is a member of the *Baiseigaga* clan, he does not live in the village and is not a close kinsman of either Edwin or William. He is a trader, living near Iganga township (see Map 8), and he is represented in Bunyambale by a *musigire* (steward), Harry (homestead I), who is an immigrant and has not a single kinsman in the sub-village. The other patrilineally-related group, members of the *Baisemagumba* clan, consists of John (V), Sam (VI), Mark (VII) and Tony (VIII). Of these, however, only Mark and Tony, who are brothers, are closely related.

Again, there are relatively few kinship ties of other kinds such as are present in Kirumbi and Gasemba. Sarah (III), Frank (IV), the late former husband of Pam (VII), and Kate (VIII) are distant clan-mates. Pam is a distant clan-mate of Edwin and William. These, however, exhaust the non-patrilineal kinship ties within the sub-village. The members of six homesteads (I, II, XI, XII, XIII and XIV) have no kinsmen whatever, near or distant, within the community. Only three persons, Mark, Edwin and Paul, out of an adult population of thirty-one, were born there.

This has been the impact of the sleeping sickness epidemics upon the network of kinship relations which I assume once existed in Busambira as it exists to-day in Gademba and Kirumbi. My assumption that it once did exist is based upon my belief that, allowed to operate over time in a relatively stable population, Soga kinship institutions inevitably produce this type of community structure. Soga land-holding, inheritance and residence rules, based as they are upon patrilineage membership, tend to produce local groups of lineage-mates, while the rules of exogamy and those associated with maternal and affinal relations tend to bind together the different lineages and to bind in immigrant strangers by in-law and mother's brother-sister's son ties. And conversely, as we shall see in a moment, the operation of Soga kinship institutions depends upon the presence of a relatively stable, kinship inter-related population. Where, as in such communities as Bunyambale, the network has been broken, kinship institutions operate with less consistency.

THE IMPACT UPON PEASANT KINSHIP INSTITUTIONS.

One index of the consequences for kinship institutions of the "broken network" type of situation is the statistical frequency in such situations of deviation from institutional norms. It is here that the differences, noted in Chapter IV but not discussed there, between the villages of Busambira and those of southern Bulamogi become relevant.

Before discussing these differences, however, let me take note of some of the shortcomings of these statistical data. In the first place, I shall argue that these differences in frequency of deviance are associated with, indeed result from, differences in population stability and kinship-inter-relatedness in different areas of Busoga. My samples, however, are in no real sense representative of the two areas which I should like to compare. They consist of five selected whole villages. Although I believe these villages to be reasonably representative of their respective areas, they were not selected according to rigorous statistical criteria. A really sound sample would consist either of a random selection of village populations or of a random selection of persons from the two total areas which I wish to compare: the area of south Busoga affected by sleeping sickness and that further north which was not so affected. A second deficiency pertains to the statistical data themselves. In many cases, the differences which I shall note are too small in terms of absolute numbers to make possible rigorous testing for significance.

Having stated these *caveats*, I feel that these statistical data are nevertheless worth presenting for three reasons. First, statistical treatment has seldom in the past been applied to structural features of non-Western social systems. The reasons are obvious: lack of basic demographic data of the census variety which so greatly simplifies sample selection; practical difficulties such as lack of efficient transport and the lack of trained local assistants and, most important, the very proper feeling on the part of social scientists that the gathering of qualitative data for such societies should have first priority because without it quantitative techniques are useless. To-day, however, these difficulties are being overcome. Statistical techniques are being applied in such societies and I feel that it is worth publishing attempts in this direction, however primitive, in the hope that statistically more sophisticated persons will be stimulated to take a hand in solving the special problems involved. My second reason for including these data is that, though many of the individual differences are not, by usual criteria, significant, they do in general point in the same direction. They are different ways of measuring what I believe to be essentially the same structural phenomenon. The differences do take on some added meaning by being consistent with one another. Finally, these statistics are worth consideration because they are concerned substantively with a widespread and important phenomenon. The sleeping sickness epidemic in Busoga is a unique event, but other events in other areas produce similar results. In other areas of Uganda, of Africa and of the non-Western world in general, modern economic and political developments often result in the shattering of the stable, kinship-inter-related local community and the re-grouping of persons into new communities which are, in kinship terms, quite atomistic. These data concerning some of the institutional consequences of such processes in one society may therefore be of comparative interest.

It is apparent that where, as in the villages of Busambira, the local unity and continuity of the patrilineage has been broken, individuals' day-to-day social relations will be less structured in lineage terms. Where few or none of a person's neighbours are lineage-mates, the lineage can hardly loom large as a context for social interaction. Individual persons may, of course, continue in some sense to believe in the institutional rules associated with lineage and may even attempt to maintain lineage relations at a distance. Indeed, certain modern developments in Busoga have, somewhat paradoxically, acted to make the maintenance of lineage relations under difficult conditions more, rather than less, possible. The mobility and rapid communication which good roads, bicycles, buses, and postal and telegraphic services have provided for the Soga peasant make it possible for him to maintain contact with lineage-mates over substantial distances. Many persons take advantage of these services and, particularly at weekends, there is a great amount of travelling about, much of it involving visits to distant kinsmen. Without these technological innovations, lineage structure would be even more effectively shattered in areas such as Busambira. Nevertheless, the peasant's daily social interaction is largely carried out with his neighbours and in Busambira few of the latter are lineage-mates or, indeed, kinsmen of any kind. It would seem likely that the persistence of an institutional norm as an effective part of an individual's social personality is, at least in part, a function of the frequency with which he has an opportunity to act in terms of it. If this is so, the motivation to follow lineage norms will tend to atrophy in the person who seldom sees his lineage-mates. Though it may be technically possible for him to maintain interaction with them, he will tend rather to be influenced by the easier and more frequent contacts which he has with his non-kin neighbours. Where the norms associated with lineage are not represented in his vicinity by living persons, he will tend to innovate—to "make other arrangements."

One aspect of the declining influence of the lineage in the villages of Busambira would appear to be a decline in the authority and respect granted older men. As I pointed out in Chapter VI, the elder has never had, in Soga society, the position of authority which he is granted in some African societies. Older men are, however, in a definite position of authority over their juniors in two important respects: in the succession lineage and in the territorial clan sections they normally hold the senior positions, while in the individual family a father retains his authority over his sons through his control of inheritance. (If in the past inheritance was exclusively from brother-to-brother, the concentration of authority in the hands of older men would have been even greater, since there would have been less likelihood of a young man's succeeding to a position of authority.) In accord with his position of authority, an older man ought, in terms of Soga values, to have a number of sons settled nearby and to maintain a large homestead of his own with many dependents. Though he very infrequently has married sons living in his homestead, he should, if possible, be polygynous and have a large homestead of wives and growing children. It is felt to be a particular misfortune—and a reflection upon his position—for an older man to live alone, either in his homestead or as the lone member of his lineage in the community.

In the three Busambira villages surveyed, men over forty-five years of age living alone are more than twice as common as in Budini and Buyodi. In Table IX, it may be seen that of the 106 men over forty-five who are heads of homesteads in the three Busambira villages, 12, or 11 per cent., are living alone. In Budini and Buyodi, only 5, or 5 per cent., of the homestead heads over forty-five are living alone. (This difference is significant at less than the 10 per cent. level.)

The isolation of older men may be, at least in part, a more or less direct result of the epidemics. Certainly, in many of the cases of which I have some knowledge, these men are the only surviving members of families whose other members died in the epidemics or were dispersed throughout Busoga. The epidemics, however, would not account for such persons being without wives and dependent children, since they took place more than forty years ago. The greater frequency in Busambira of elderly men living alone is rather, I believe, an aspect of the general decline in their prestige and authority which in turn is a result of the shattering of the kinship network type of community structure.

Another and related aspect of the decline in the position of older men in Busambira may be seen in the data concerning polygyny and divorce given in Tables XI and XII. In the more stable village of Buyodi (Budini may be neglected here because of the special influence of the mission there upon polygyny and divorce), men over forty-five have significantly more polygynous marriages (56 per cent.) than have men between sixteen and forty-five (37 per cent.) (difference significant at less than the 5 per cent. level). In the Busambira villages, there is no significant difference between the two age groups (56 as against 59 per cent.) in degree of polygyny. Furthermore, in Buyodi marriages tend to become more stable after men reach the age of forty-five. For men between sixteen and forty-five, 37 per cent. of all marriages contracted have ended in separation, while for men over forty-five this figure is only 28 per cent. (difference significant at less than the 10 per cent. level). In the Busambira villages, older men's marriages are not more stable. The percentage of all marriages broken stands at 46 for both age groups.

All these differences reflect, in different ways, the decline in the dominance of older men in communities where the lineages, which form the context for their authority, have been dispersed. Where the local lineage is intact, an elderly man has around him in the sub-village a group of sons and other lineage juniors who are dependent upon him for help in raising marriage payments, who in turn help him in cultivation, for whom he represents the sacred value of patrilineal continuity upon the land, and some of whom may hope to inherit from him land and other property when he dies. His wives, particularly the younger ones, may not enjoy being married to an old man, but they will stay with him because, just as his position among the men of the community is an elevated one, so theirs is high among the women. Furthermore, they are tied to their husband through their sons, who will tend to live nearby.

In Busambira, this sort of situation is much less common than in Budini and Buyodi. A man's sons are less likely to be able to settle near him because all available land will probably be taken up by persons who are not his lineage-mates. A strong local lineage can, as I have already said, exercise some control over the distribution of land, but the son of a lineage isolate must get land (through a process of semi-purchase to be described in Chapter VII) from the headman, if it is available, and his claim to land is no stronger than that of an immigrant. Often enough, he must leave the community in search of land. Mothers tend to follow their sons, thus increasing the separation rate among older men. The tendency of sons and wives to leave older men is, I suspect, increased by the decline in the religious value of land where patrilineal continuity of occupation has been broken. In Busambira, few men are tied to the land by the presence of many generations of ancestors' graves.

Just as the position of older men appears to decline where local lineages have been dispersed, so also does the position of men in general *vis-à-vis* women. In terms of Soga values, a woman is in many ways incapable of being an independent social person. Her position of formal subordination to men in the homestead has been described in Chapter IV. If she is married, a woman should reside with and should be under the authority of her husband. If she is unmarried, she should remain in her father's homestead and under his control. If she is widowed, she should either reside as a dependent of her son or else marry her husband's successor. In law she is in many ways incompetent to act on her own behalf. Though the position is changing to-day, particularly with regard to criminal offences such as theft, traditionally a woman was represented in court by her husband or her father. Adultery cases are still handled in the context of this set of values:

> I had noticed that in adultery cases, a not uncommon form of litigation in the Soga courts, the charge was always against the man, never against the woman. When I asked about this, ———, a Sub-County Chief, replied: "To us, it is like a case of theft. If a man stole your shoes, would you bring a case against the shoes? I know that Europeans think that women should have the same rights as men, but we still do not believe that.   One day we shall give women the right to vote.   When we do that, we shall also have to consider them equally responsible in matters such as adultery."

My informant's simile is slightly misleading.   Unlike stolen shoes, an adulterous wife is held responsible by her "owner" for having allowed herself to be "stolen," and he may beat her for it.   But the responsibility and the punishment are private matters, internal to the family; a wife is under the authority of and responsible to her husband much as a child is with respect to his parent.   Disputes between them cannot be aired in open court.   From the point of view of the public court, acting on behalf of society at large, the adulterous wife is indeed like stolen property—something to be litigated about, not a person to be litigated with.

In Soga values, a woman is thus properly a dependent of a patrilineal group of males—either that of her father and brothers or that of her husband and sons.   Where, as in the villages of Busambira, such patrilineal groups of males have been in large part dispersed, one finds greater frequencies of deviance from those institutional norms associated with women's dependent position.

Let us look first at the frequencies of separation shown in Table XII. It is first of all apparent, as I showed in Chapter IV, that Soga marriage is everywhere relatively fragile, even in areas such as Buyodi where population has been quite stable and where local lineages are intact. This represents an inconsistency in traditional Soga social structure. The Soga feel strongly that children should remain in their fathers' homesteads where they may grow up as members of and under the discipline of their own patrilineages. Frequent separation, however, means that many children grow up in the homesteads of step-fathers or maternal kinsmen. The latter is considered particularly unfortunate since a child's maternal kinsmen traditionally spoil him through lack of discipline, but it occurs whenever a woman leaves her husband without remarrying at once because an unmarried woman's proper place is that of a dependent in the home of her father or brother. Ultimately, children of divorced parents return to their fathers, since *pater* and *genitor* are always the same person in Busoga,[1] but during the formative early years of childhood they tend to remain with their mothers. A high divorce rate is thus one of the unresolved inconsistencies of traditional Soga society.

Table XII, however, shows that divorce is substantially more frequent in Busambira than in Buyodi. In Buyodi, of the 306 marriages contracted by men in both age groups, 99, or 32 per cent., have ended in separation. In the three Busambira villages, 333, or 46 per cent., of 719 marriages have failed. (Difference significant at less than the 5 per cent. level.) I attribute this difference to the differential prominence of local lineage groups in the two areas. Soga marriages are held together, I believe, less by the personal bond between husband and wife (though such a bond unquestionably develops in many cases) than by the wife's dependent attachment to her husband's lineage, which grows and is strengthened as she bears children who are members of that lineage. The marriage contract itself, involving the payment of bridewealth by the husband's people to the wife's people, is also a factor. The husband's kinsmen have paid for the wife and are interested in keeping her, while the wife's kinsmen would have to repay the bridewealth in case of a separation. Both thus have an interest in marital stability. These two sets of forces are in a sense two sides of the same coin. Internal to the family, the wife is bound to her husband through her emotional bond with her children, whose property rights and general legal status tie them in turn to their father and his lineage. External to the family are the father's and mother's lineages, each

---

[1] Pater and genitor are the same so long as the genitor is alive. Upon his death, his brother should become pater to his children.

with a corporate interest in the stability of the marriage. Both are lineage phenomena. Where the lineage is absent or weak, both the wife's tie with her husband through her children and the external pressures of the two lineage groups are likely to be lessened. This argument may at first seem inconsistent with that advanced in Chapter IV to the effect that lineage organisation is disruptive of Soga marriage. I contended there that lineage loyalties tend to divide husband from wife and thus to increase the rate of separation. These two notions are not, however, incompatible. When I suggest that patrilineages are disruptive of marriage, I have in mind a contrast with some other African patrilineal societies in which Gluckman feels that patrilineages act to stabilise marriage.[1] The societies which Gluckman describes have, I believe, features which counteract the disruptive effects of patriliny upon marriage. Soga society lacks these features; therefore patrilineages are disruptive of marriage and thus Busoga has a relatively high general divorce rate. Within this context of generally frequent divorce, however, those areas of Busoga where lineages have been dispersed have higher divorce rates than those where lineages are intact. Thus lineages produce a high general divorce rate in Soga society, as compared with some other societies, by dividing the corporate group loyalties of the spouses and thus militating against the development of a strong husband-wife bond. At the same time, patrilineal groups also have an interest in keeping divorce as low as possible and so, in a society where husband-wife solidarity is not strong, divorce becomes even more frequent in areas where lineages are weak or absent. This, however, is a rather complex problem which I do not wish to pursue further here since it is quite peripheral to the present study.[2] It is enough to say here that the shattering of the kinship network type of community structure tends to free women from their dependent subordination to the patrilineal groups of their husbands by loosening the bonds of marriage.

The greater frequency of divorce in Busambira has consequences for the kinship composition of homesteads there (see Table X). When a woman ceases to be married, she reverts to her former position as a dependent of her own patrilineal group and she takes back with her any young children she may have borne. With a greater frequency of divorce, Busambira homesteads therefore tend to contain more members of sisters' and daughters' families than do Buyodi homesteads. In the three Busambira villages, with a

---

[1] Gluckman, Max, "Kinship and Marriage among the Lozi of Northern Rhodesia and the Zulu of Natal," in *African Systems of Kinship and Marriage*, edited by A. R. Radcliffe-Brown and C. Daryll Forde, 1950, pp. 166–206.

[2] See Note 1, p. 85.

total homestead population of 840, 27 persons, or 3 per cent., are members of sisters' or daughters' families (that is, sisters' or daughters' children or, in a very few cases, their husbands). In Buyodi, only one such case occurs, representing much less than 1 per cent. of the homestead population. (Difference significant at less than the 5 per cent. level.)

The return of divorced women to their fathers' or brothers' homesteads is the institutionally approved solution to the problem of divorce. Though divorce is considered unfortunate, when it occurs it should be handled in this way. When this pattern is followed, divorce does not constitute a real emancipation of the woman from dependence upon a patrilineal group of males, since she simply transfers her dependence from one group of males to another. The greater frequency in Busambira homesteads of members of sisters' and daughters' families does not, therefore, represent the failure of patrilineal institutions to operate; rather it represents the action of such institutions in repairing, in so far as possible in accord with patrilineal norms, situations in which the patrilineal ideal of stable marriage has not been achieved. It may be noted, incidentally, that though Buyodi has a substantial divorce rate, nearly all these divorces must occur before the birth of children, since otherwise sisters' and daughters' children would be more common in Buyodi homesteads, though one would not, of course, expect them to be as common as in Busambira where the divorce rate is higher. Divorce before the birth of children is irrelevant to patrilineal institutions since it does not result in "misplaced" children.

Busambira homesteads do not, however, differ from Buyodi homesteads merely in containing greater numbers of returned daughters and sisters and their families. Busambira homesteads also contain a significant number of women who have been lost both to their husbands' and their own lineages. These women may be seen in Table IX, where homestead heads are classified by age and sex. In the Busambira villages, 13 out of 239 homesteads, or 5 per cent., represent women living either alone or as heads of homesteads. In Budini and Buyodi, only one such case occurs among 267 homesteads. (Difference significant at less than the 5 per cent. level.) These women homestead heads in Busambira represent the ultimate degree of deviance from the norms of Soga lineage institutions with regard to women. At least some of them own land in their own right and I know of one case in which a woman homestead head brought a court action for the headship of a sub-village on behalf of a young boy who was living as a dependent in her homestead. The boy, her brother's son, had no male lineage-mates in the area and so his father's sister took over the position of his guardian and acted on his behalf. This could not, I believe, happen in Buyodi or Budini. Finally, one finds in Busambira, but very rarely in Buyodi, homesteads being built up on the basis of affinal instead of patrilineal ties. In Table X it may be seen that in the Busambira villages a total of 25 members of homesteads, in a homestead population of 840, are kinsmen of homestead heads' wives or mothers. These constitute 3 per cent. of the homestead population, while the two such cases which occur in Buyodi constitute much less than 1 per cent. (Difference significant at less than the 5 per cent. level.) In these cases, the homestead tends to consist of the wife and her kinsmen, with the husband attached, instead of the other way round as the norms of patrilineal descent and patrilocal residence would imply.

These differences in frequencies of deviance from the norms associated with patrilineage are all indices of the decline in the importance of lineage as a context for behaviour where the spatial clustering of its members has been disrupted. It might be argued, of course, that these statistical differences in behaviour are not so much direct results of differential intactness or disruption of local lineages as general indices of acculturation. The latter term has been variously used, but here I mean by it the changes in persons' values and beliefs which result from contact with representatives of a different society. The differences which I have noted between frequencies of deviance in the two areas cannot, however, be explained in this way. Acculturation is of course a complex variable which could be measured only through further research. It does not seem unfair, however, to assume that literacy is as good a single index of acculturation as any in a situation such as that of Busoga over the past decades. Much of the contact between Soga and Europeans has taken place in a "teaching" context, in schools, churches or on the job in government. Literacy has been both a result of and a medium for cross-culture contact. In terms of literacy, however, Budini and Buyodi are more, rather than less, acculturated than the Busambira villages, as Table VII shows. The greater frequency in Busambira of deviance from lineage norms cannot, I believe, be a result of greater contact with European ideas and values.

There are other institutional consequences of the breaking up of the network type of community which are less easily expressed in statistical terms. I refer, not to deviance from traditional norms, which can be expressed in terms of frequencies, but rather to institutional features which are new in kind—which represent new developments under new conditions. Perhaps in the Busambira villages the most striking institutional adaptation to the disruption of local lineages has occurred in the area of inheritance and succession. Traditionally, the assembly of members of the succession lineage meets at a person's funeral to choose his heir and successor, but it is apparent from Fig. 8 that for a large number of men in the Busambira villages a group of lineage-mates sufficient to form a lineage council to decide upon such matters is not readily at hand. Lineage councils are not limited to lineage-mates living in the same village, or even to those living in a cluster of neighbouring villages. Members frequently journey some distance to attend. But there remain a substantial number of men who are effectively isolated from a group of patrilineal kinsmen. The problem is clearly an important one, since the rôle of the lineage councils in inheritance and succession is not only institutionalised in village society but is also recognised and sanctioned by the courts.

The answer to this problem has appeared in the legal fiction of a "clan" formed, not on the basis of patrilineal kinship, but by the association of men in the community without regard to kinship ties. The association has been given a name, formed after the pattern of clan names: *Baisekantu*. Translated literally, it means "they of the father Man" or "the clan of human beings." A local group is formed in each sub-village which elects a leader and collects dues from its members to defray the costs of members' funeral feasts. When a member dies, the group functions after the pattern of lineage councils. It buries the body, mourns for the usual period of two weeks, and then meets to choose a successor and an heir. In a case heard before the court of Sub-County Ssabawaali, Kigulu County, in 1950, it was held by the court that the "clan" of *Baisekantu* had the legal powers of a lineage council:

> Frederick was accused by James of wrongfully occupying a holding which formerly had been held by Albert. Both Frederick and James claimed to have inherited the holding from Albert. Frederick was able to bring as witnesses the chairman and another member of the assembly of *Baisekantu* which sat to consider the disposition of Albert's holding. Both testified that the assembly had been presented with a will naming Frederick as the heir and that the assembly had confirmed this will. James brought as witnesses four men who had been present when Albert died, as well as Albert's widow, who had subsequently married James. All testified that Albert, on his death-bed, had named James as his successor. The court held that the testimony of members of the assembly of *Baisekantu* took precedence over the testimony of James' witnesses concerning Albert's death-bed statement and the holding was awarded to Frederick.[1]

[1] Case Number 11/1950/Ssabawaali, Kigulu. This is a rather neat example of what Sir Henry Maine called "legal fiction" and it has developed in a context not unlike that of some of Maine's Roman examples. (See *Ancient Law*, 1861).

This fictional clan apparently exists only in southern Busoga. I was able to find no trace of it in Bulamogi.

Busambira also appears to be richer in associational groups of other types, such as introduced religious denominations and sects. Table XIV shows the religious affiliations of married men in the two areas. We may note, first, that in Budini and Buyodi, in spite of the presence of the large and long-established Roman Catholic and Anglican churches, and in spite of a higher general literacy rate, there remains a very substantial group of pagans, constituting more than one third of the total number of married males in the two villages. In Busambira villages, on the other hand, there is only a handful of pagans; nearly everyone is at least nominally Anglican, Roman Catholic or Mohammedan. Busambira also contains a few members of two of the sects which have thus far appeared in Busoga.

TABLE XIV

RELIGIOUS AFFILIATIONS OF MARRIED MALES

Religious affiliation	Budini and Buyodi	Bunyama, Wairama and Bukwaya
Anglican	73	115
Roman Catholic	89	11
Mohammedan	6	96
Malachite	—	3
Seventh Day Adventist ..	—	1
Pagan	94	7
Total	262	233

The Malachites are a syncretistic sect founded in Buganda in 1913 by a Ganda catechist of the Native Anglican Church (the orthodox Anglican organisation).[1] Although they have relatively few members to-day, they were at one time quite prominent in southern Uganda and the area around Busambira was one of their focal points in Busoga. The Seventh Day Adventists are a recently-developed group with very few members in Busoga. They have no church in Busambira; their single adherent there is affiliated with a church located a few miles to the east of Iganga.

Thus to-day traditional Soga kinship institutions operate with varying regularity in different parts of the country. In some areas, patrilineages remain intact and strong and village communities represent intricately woven networks of kinship ties; in other areas, many persons are without significant patrilineal ties and local communities tend to be atomistic with regard to kinship, though

---

[1] Thomas, H. B., and Scott, Robert, *Uganda*, 1935, pp. 337–338.

even here institutional substitution has acted to replace kinship institutions in some of their more strategic functions, i.e. the legitimation of inheritance and succession. What proportion of the total Soga population these two types of situation represent and to what extent there is a general trend toward the break-up of kinship institutions, I cannot say with any precision since my samples are so limited. Three points, however, are worth making in this connection. On the one hand, I have argued that in areas (like Busambira) where kinship atomisation has proceeded some distance, strong local lineages are unlikely to be re-established because of pressure on the land and lineages' inability in law to hold land in reserve. On the other hand, given a period of population stability, affinal and maternal, as well as some patrilineal, ties will develop; even communities which to-day are quite atomistic in kinship terms may well come to be networks of kinship ties, though without the patrilineal cores which are found in undisturbed areas. If this is so, one might hazard the prediction that in areas like Busambira kinship will continue to be prominent in village social relations but that it will be kinship of a more bilateral and less patrilineal sort. As we shall see in subsequent chapters, something of this sort also seems to be happening at the level of the modern political élite. Finally, there is no indication that, in undisturbed areas, patrilineal kinship is declining in importance. As the case of the fictional clan in Busambira would indicate, the functions of patrilineages in inheritance and succession are firmly-rooted in Soga peasant life. So long as the present system of land-holding remains intact, lineages are likely to remain strong.

Thus far in this study of Soga political structure I have discussed only those authority relations which are structured about kinship and these only in so far as they operate at the peasant level of society. Later chapters will be concerned with the wider political system of Busoga. In this wider system, kinship plays a part, but is not the whole story. Let us turn first to the structure of the traditional Soga state and its evolution over nearly a century of European contact and administration.

CHAPTER VI

A CENTURY OF POLITICAL EVOLUTION

THE POLITICAL STRUCTURE OF THE TRADITIONAL STATE.

In previous chapters, frequent reference has been made to earlier events and conditions in Busoga, but thus far no systematic account has been given of the traditional political system and the influences which have remoulded it to form the present-day African Local Government organisation. This chapter will provide such an account as a prelude to consideration, in Chapters VII, VIII and IX, of politics in contemporary Busoga.

The three institutional principles around which the states were organised were patrilineal kinship, ascribed rank and the patron-client relationship. In describing the interaction of these structural features, I shall follow the pattern established in previous chapters of taking as my primary examples the two areas of Busoga which I know best and supplementing the data from these areas, where it seems appropriate to do so, with briefer references to other areas. Although my knowledge of Busoga as a whole is too incomplete to allow me to say with assurance that these two areas illustrate all the important variations in political structure which occur in the country, they do, I think, illustrate two important contrasts. Bulamogi was one of the larger traditional states and one which was ruled over by a dynasty of the *Baisengobi* clan, who have traditional links with Bunyoro. Busambira was one of the small states of the south and its ruling clan, the *Baiseigaga*, are not linked with the legendary Nyoro immigrants. The striking thing which emerges from the comparison of the two states, however, is their structural similarity. Despite the differences in scale and in traditional history, the above three institutional principles appear to have operated in much the same way in both areas.

The first two of these principles—patrilineal kinship and ascribed rank—may conveniently be discussed together. I have described the general pattern of patrilineal kinship as it operates at the peasant level of society. Groups of lineage-mates are bound together by a corporate structure of authority—the lineage council with its senior members as leaders—and by corporate economic and religious interest in the land and the ancestors. In the structure of the state, the principle of ascribed rank set one patrilineal descent group— that of the ruler—above all others. Princes were, by birth, assigned higher status and an in-born fitness to rule. Like commoner lineages, the princes had a corporate authority structure and corporate economic and religious interests, but unlike commoner lineages, the royal group's unit of reference in authority, property and religion extended beyond its own members to the state as a whole. The authority of the ruler, as representative of the royal group, extended over members of all clans; the royal ancestors were in a sense "national" ancestors and the royal group, through the ruler, had interests in all the land of the state and its products. The royal group was thus more than a *primus inter pares* among patrilineal descent groups; it was the structural manifestation and the symbolic embodiment of the unity of the whole state and its internal structure was, in consequence, modified away from the general Soga pattern of patrilineal descent group structure.

The structural modification of the royal descent group was the result of the operation of the third of the institutions mentioned above—the patron-client relationship. Although the royal group as a whole shared in some measure in the ascribed rank of the ruler, it was not the instrument through which he governed the state. The ruler's administrative staff consisted rather of commoners of ability to whom he delegated authority over subdivisions of the state. The structural "need" for such persons was a consequence of the Soga type of descent system which has already been described at the peasant level of society. Soga descent rules were peculiarly ambiguous from the point of view of the persons involved. An individual—in this case the ruler—might choose his own heir, but his testament had to be reviewed—and might well be altered—by the council of his lineage. There was a bias in favour of the senior son, but this was not a fixed rule. In consequence, there was room for conflicting claims and ambitions among potential heirs.

In the case of the royal group this potentiality for conflict was increased by the fact that the inheritance in question consisted of the pinnacle of power and rank—the rulership of the state. All princes were of royal birth and hence potential rulers, but only one could in fact rule. From the ruler's point of view, therefore, the princes were ill-suited to subordinate administrative responsibility; they had always to be thought of as potential usurpers. Administrative authority was therefore delegated instead to able commoners who, being of non-royal birth, could not possibly aspire to rulership and who, owing their elevation to the grace of the ruler, were bound to him by ties of personal loyalty. Often these ties were further cemented by the marriage of the commoner to a princess or of the ruler to the commoner's sister or daughter. Such powerful commoners (*bakungu*), whom I shall call "client-chiefs," shared with the princes in corporate decisions which, in a peasant commoner lineage, would have been affairs involving lineage-mates only. Powerful client-chiefs shared in decisions involving the administration of the state and also in the choice of the ruler's successor. Not being themselves potential rulers, they could be used by the ruler to keep in check potential usurping princes. During interregnum periods, they exercised a disinterested restraining influence upon the competing ambitions of rival heirs. Thus, the client-chiefs acted to maintain the unity and stability of the state in the face of the devisive influence of the Soga type of patrilineal descent system.

Before proceeding to clothe these abstract statements of institutional form with descriptive data, it is perhaps well to note here that much the same sort of pattern is discernible in the structure of the villages described in Chapter V. Just as the unit of reference for the authority and the economic and religious interests of the royal clan was the whole state, so the unit of reference in these respects for the lineage of the village or sub-village headman is the village or sub-village as a whole. This is the significance of the oft-repeated statement, quoted in Chapter V, that the members of the headman's lineage are the "owners" of the village or sub-village. The headman's authority extends over the whole community and not just his own lineage-mates. The headman's lineage, through the headman, has certain corporate rights in all the land of the village (though in Chapter VII we shall see that these rights are not absolute but are limited by the rights of peasants and their lineages) and these rights are reinforced and legitimated by the presence of ancestor's graves. But again, as in the state, it was not simply a matter of the headman's lineage as a corporate group being superimposed upon corporate lineages of peasants. Ties of personal loyalty were established between the headman and leading members of peasant lineages and these ties were reinforced by ties of marriage. Thus, the headman, as head of the village or sub-village, like the ruler as head of the state, balanced his position within his own corporate lineage group with personal ties with important members of other corporate groups.

The village or sub-village is thus in a real sense a microcosm of the state—the lowest level in Soga society of state-type organisation. At each level in the society corporate unilineal descent groups were involved in the structuring of authority relations, but at no level, in constrast with the segmentary type of society, were they the sole political units. At each level, the unilineal kinship structuring of authority was combined with the patron-client institution to produce the composite type of political structure which may be seen in operation in the traditional states of Bulamogi and Busambira.

An account of the traditional Bulamogi state may appropriately begin with selections from the body of legend which surrounds the position of the Zibondo, the ruler of the state. What follows is taken from a history of Bulamogi prepared by the present Zibondo and an assembly of princes and clan heads during my visit to the area. It does not, of course, constitute "history" in the sense of modern historiographic scholarship; it is rather in the nature of a "mythical charter," in the Malinowskian sense, legitimating the ascribed rank and power of the ruler and the royal group. For the moment, therefore, its historical accuracy need not concern us since it is just this complex of legitimating belief, forming the basis for the ascription of rulership, which is of interest here. When we wish to trace out the "real" pattern of politics in the traditional state, we may draw upon other, less official, memories and traditions.

Appropriately, in a society in which unilineal descent is an important determinant of status, the legendary history begins with a genealogy:

> Lamogi I was the first ruler in this part.   He came with his brother, the ruler of Bunyoro, and they took their separate ways, the ruler of Bunyoro making his way to Bunyoro.[1]
> Lamogi made his way to the mountain Masaba (Mount Elgon, in Gishu country) and there came with him many of his people.   Then he began to distribute among his people parts of the land in this area and in this way he began to extend his rulership.   He remained for a long time as ruler of this area until finally he died.
> His son, Nadoi I, succeeded him and remained in the place of his father as Lamogi II.
> When Lamogi Nadoi died, his son, Wako, succeeded him and took his place on the stool of rulership of Lamogi.   He was Lamogi III.
> When Wako I, Lamogi III, died, his son, Mukunya I, succeeded him and he was Lamogi IV in the rulership of Lamogi.
> When Mukunya I Lamogi IV died, his son, Bwoye I, succeeded him and was Lamogi V in the rulership of Lamogi.
> When Bwoye, Lamogi V, died, his son, Isoba, succeeded him and he was Lamogi VI.
> When Isoba I, Lamogi VI died, his son, Namubongo I, succeeded him and he was the seventh ruler on the stool of Lamogi.
> When Namubongo I, Lamogi VII died, his son, Zibondo I, succeeded him and became Lamogi VIII on the stool of Lamogi.
> When Zibondo I, Lamogi VIII died, his son, Kiige I, succeeded him and he was Lamogi IX on the stool of Lamogi.
> When Kiige I, Lamogi IX died, his son, Musuuga I, succeeded him and he was Lamogi X on the hereditary stool of rulership of Lamogi.

[1] Lamogi is sometimes referred to as the brother of Mukama, the ruler of Bunyoro, sometimes as his son.

When Musuuga I, Lamogi X died, his son, Mukama I, succeeded him and became Lamogi XI.

That Lamogi XI, Mukama I, had a son and gave him the name of Zibondo Ngambani and when Mukama I died, his son, Zibondo II Ngambani, succeeded him and became Lamogi XII in the place of his father, Mukama I, Lamogi XI.

But all the people in the time of Zibondo II Ngambani, Lamogi XII, all who were in the whole area of the hereditary rulership of Lamogi, decided: "Now our ruler, Lamogi, will no longer be called Lamogi, but will be called Zibondo after our ruler of long ago.   But all of us, the people of our area, will be named after Lamogi and will be called 'Balamogi' and our country will be called 'Bulamogi'." From the time of Zibondo II Ngambani until to-day, we are all "Balamogi."

Zibondo Ngambani was the first with the title of Zibondo.   When Zibondo Ngambani died, his son, Namubongo II, succeeded him and he was Zibondo II on the stool which came down from Lamogi XI, Mukama I.

When Namubongo died, his son, Isoba II, succeeded him and he became Zibondo III in the hereditary rulership of Bulamogi.

When Isoba II, Zibondo III, died, his son, Bwoye II, succeeded him and became Zibondo IV in the hereditary rulership of Bulamogi.

When Bwoye died, his son, Mukunya II, succeeded him and was Zibondo V in the hereditary rulership of Bulamogi.

When Mukunya II, Zibondo V died, his son, Wako II, succeeded him and became Zibondo VI in the hereditary rulership of Bulamogi.

When Wako II, Zibondo VI died, his son, Namubongo Kisira, succeeded him and became Zibondo VII.

Zibondo Namubongo Kisira was the one who was there in Bulamogi as a great ruler when in 1873 Mutesa I, ruler of Buganda, called all the rulers who were near to him to tell them about the important matter of bringing the religion of God from England into Uganda. Our ruler, Namubongo Kisira, Zibondo VII, realised in his heart that the religion of God should come into Uganda.   Then he came back to his Bulamogi from Buganda, where he had been called by Mutesa I.

The religion of God came to Uganda in 1877 and at that time Namubongo Kisira was still hereditary ruler of Bulamogi.

Again, in 1889, the Government of Britain arrived in Uganda and the ruler of Buganda and his neighbouring rulers discussed the matter and asked them (the British) to come and guard Uganda and give it wisdom.   Again at that time our great ruler, Namubongo Kisira, Zibondo VII, was present at the discussion of those matters.

At the time of the mutiny of the Sudanese troops in Bunya in 1897–98, the rulers of the Soga states came to the assistance of the Government forces:

Then our ruler, Zibondo Kisira, was seized by an illness when he was at Bukaleba fighting the Sudanese.   All his people from Bulamogi who were with him, wanted to lift him and to bring him back to

Bulamogi while he was still alive, but he refused to be moved and died on 6th September, 1898. All the people of Bulamogi who were there lifted his body and carried it back to Bulamogi. It was buried in his palace in the village of Kaliro.

His son, Mukunya Wambuzi, succeeded him and became Zibondo VIII until he died in 1908.

His son, Ezekeri Tenywa Wako, succeeded him and became Zibondo IX on the hereditary stool of Bulamogi. And that ruler, E. T. Wako, Zibondo IX, began to be taught in the school at Jinja in the year 1905.

This rather skeletal account of Bulamogi's history from the founding of the state to the coming of British administration establishes, for those who hear it and repeat it, the hereditary right of the ruler and the royal group to paramount authority within the boundaries of the state. The account goes on to spell out the nature of this authority:

> From Lamogi I, the Lamogis and Zibondos had complete power to rule all the land of Bulamogi and all its people and all things of every kind which were created in all of Bulamogi. All trees and mountains and lakes in Bulamogi and all cattle, sheep and goats and wild animals and birds of the bush (were ruled over by him).
>
> Lamogi distributed land—gardens, villages and sub-villages—and chiefships of every kind. All were in his power and are still in the power of the present Zibondo.
>
> Disputes were first judged by the chiefs of the various areas, such as village headmen, sub-village headmen, and chiefs who were over a number of villages. They were the first to judge disputes and afterwards they might be taken to Zibondo.
>
> Since the creation of Bulamogi, there has been no man of Bulamogi who has rebelled against Lamogi. Zibondo was the one who had the final word in all disputes in his Bulamogi.
>
> All the people from all parts of Bulamogi brought to Lamogi gifts of every kind and it was their wish to do so.
>
> In Bulamogi, everyone was free to use the land if it was given him by Lamogi or by the chiefs of Lamogi. The chiefs had the power to distribute land in the parts which were given them by Lamogi or Zibondo.
>
> All the heirs of princes and great chiefs were announced before Zibondo when they succeeded their fathers.
>
> Zibondo was the one who gave power to the fishermen to build their homes along the lakes and to catch fish. The felling of trees was in his power and he was the one who gave orders to cut down trees to make boats for fishing on the lakes and for carrying people across the lakes.
>
> If it happened that there were enemies who attacked Bulamogi, all the great chiefs and princes and heads of smaller areas beat the war drum and all the people went to fight the enemies of Bulamogi.

When Zibondo went travelling to inspect his Bulamogi, he was conducted by his great chiefs and princes and by many other people and he was entertained by amusements of every kind.

From conversations with elderly men, one may learn something of the splendour which surrounded the ruler. The palace was a large establishment housing dozens of royal wives, children and servants. Physically, it consisted of a large enclosure of posts interwoven with elephant grass reeds, within which was the great conical thatched house of the ruler, the smaller huts of wives and servants, and kraals and sheds for the ruler's large herds of livestock. Each day the ruler held court in the courtyard in front of the royal house, where he might be visited by his chiefs and entertained by jugglers, musicians and story-tellers. Inside the house were the stools, spears, fetishes and drums, believed to have been handed down through generations of rulers, which were the symbols of rulership (see Plates II and III).

The paramountcy of the ruler and the semi-sacred character of his person is expressed in the ritual procedure which was followed upon his death:

It was different from an ordinary burial. At first they didn't tell the people that Zibondo was dead. They just prepared things to put in the grave. Then a *mwiwa* (child of a woman of the clan—see Fig. 1) beat the royal drum and the people were told: "The milk is spilled." Then the wives of the ruler and all of his people began to wail. Everyone tied plantain fibres to their heads and arms and waists as a sign of mourning. No one could work or cook food and if anyone was seen doing these things he might be beaten or killed.

The body of Zibondo was wrapped in many fine barkcloths and placed in a large grave with many things. Then a bull calf was brought. The heir stood there and was handed a spear by the *mwiwa*. First the heir speared the beast and then the *mwiwa*. Then the *mwiwa* threw the first earth into the grave and the grave was filled.

In the second generation after the death, in the time of the grandson of the deceased one, they went to take away the jaw-bone. They knew that by this time the jaw had separated from the skull. First they had to build a house. They cut poles and set them in the ground. Then they chose the house of an important clan-head and took the roof by force and put it on the poles. Then they thatched it quickly and plastered the walls with mud because they had to finish it in one day. The *baiwa* (plural of *mwiwa*) and the important chiefs and princes went secretly at night to get the jaw. They cleaned it and rubbed it with butter and decorated it with cowrie shells. They made it very beautiful. They then notified everyone not to sow millet and no one did so. The jaw and a milking cow were put into the hut with a wife of the deceased one to guard them. These things were left in the hut for two years. Then a bull, a male goat, a male sheep and a cock were prepared and a leg was taken from each. They might also catch a woman who was walking along the road. All these things were taken secretly at night to a forest at Nankodo in Gwere country. They left those things there and ran away. This was done because the first Lamogi, when he left Mukama, built his first palace in that place.

The installation of the new Zibondo demonstrated even more clearly his position as unifier of the whole state:

A great gathering of people assembled at the palace. Then the people who had special duties began to carry them out, one after another. The *mwiwa* of Zibondo who was also head of the *Baisekisige* clan placed upon the ground a barkcloth upon which the skins were to be spread. Upon this, the representative of the *Baisemususwa* clan placed a zebra skin. Next the royal stool, which was called *namulondo katitiizi*, was brought forward by a representative of the *Baisemuwanga* clan, who were the guardians of that stool. The representative of the *Baisenyanga* clan then brought Zibondo forward and seated him upon the stool. The *mwiwa* brought bowls of water and the representative of the *Baisekitandwe* clan pretended to shave Zibondo's head. Then the representative of the *Baisemususwa* clan brought forward the horns of the bushbuck, the totem of the royal clan, and placed them upon Zibondo's head, whereupon the sister of Zibondo waved an iron hoe above her head and shouted joyfully and everyone present followed suit. The representative of the *Baisekitandwe* then lifted up Zibondo and carried him to his palace, led by the royal drum *bamusuta* and followed by the representative of the *Baiseibolya* clan, waving a leopard skin. As the crowd moved toward the palace, someone shouted: "The rulership has fallen!" Others responded, speaking to the new Zibondo: "It will never fall if you support it!"

The assignment to representatives of each of several large and important clans of special ritual duties during the installation symbolised the ruler's position as central symbol of the state around which members of all clans were unified in a common loyalty. His special position *vis-à-vis* the royal ancestors also gave him a rôle akin to that of chief priest, for the royal ancestors were believed to influence greatly the well-being of the whole state, just as the ancestors of a peasant lineage were believed to influence the well-being of living lineage-mates. In time of war, the ruler could act on behalf of the nation, sacrificing to the ancestors to enlist their aid in the national cause. In time of famine, the ruler might lead the people in sacrificing to the spirits (*misambwa*) of the rivers, who were believed to control crops and the success of fishermen. Zibondo began the sacrifices by offering a cow to each of the major spirits.

His special relationship with the royal ancestors and nature spirits served both to support the ruler's position and to prevent his misuse of power, for these supernatural forces were believed to favour the general welfare and to punish rulers who became cruel or tyrannical.

As the above paragraphs indicate, royal power and rank centred particularly upon the ruler as an individual, but they were also shared to a substantial degree by the princes—other members of the royal clan. In particular was this true of sons of recent rulers. More distant patrilineal kinsmen of the current ruler were in daily life little different from members of commoner clans, though membership in the royal clan did confer a slightly aristocratic tone upon even its humblest member. But the sons of recent rulers had been reared in the atmosphere of the court and had once themselves been potential rulers. They shared in the royal blood and hence in the ascribed fitness to rule which was believed to be a quality of princes and rulers. Frequently they might exercise a kind of subordinate rulership over sub-divisions of the state. Although in theory the rulership of the whole state descended undiminished to a single heir, the revisionary powers which the assembly of princes and chiefs might exercise over the ruler's testament made succession uncertain. A ruler might, during his lifetime, give his favourite son control over an area of the state, but it might well happen that another son was ultimately chosen to succeed. In that case, the new ruler would find a "brother" prince entrenched in power in one area of the state over which he himself had, in theory, paramount authority.

In the time of Zibondo Kisira, the grandfather of the present Zibondo, there were in Bulamogi three such princely areas under the authority of descendants of former rulers. One, Muyodi, the grandson of Kisira's father, controlled an area of some twelve villages, while another, Namuyonjo, a brother of Kisira, controlled seven. A third cluster of villages was under the authority of Salamuka, a more distantly related prince. These princely areas were rather like states within a state. Though in theory Zibondo was their overlord, in fact his control was tenuous at best and depended in large part upon his personal administrative ability and force of character. Princes frequently refused to acknowledge the ruler's authority and might even attempt to overthrow him. In Kisira's time, Muyodi and Namuyonjo, together with a third prince, Salamuka, attempted to depose him and to seize power. They sought assistance from the ruler of Buganda, but, fortunately for Kisira, his own ties with Buganda were stronger and the rebels' request for aid was refused. Kisira succeeded in putting down the revolt and confining the rebels to their own areas. Rulers were not always so successful in asserting their authority. In the nearby state of Bugweri, where the ruling clan were the *Baisemenya*, there was a similar princely revolt in the time of Menya Nkutu, the great-great-grandfather of the present Menya. The dispute continued into the following generation when Nkutu's successor, Menya Kiuba, attempted unsuccessfully to reconquer the rebellious area. Menya's overlordship over the whole of the Bugweri state was only re-established years later, with the aid of the British Administration.

The ruler's administrative staff, through which he governed the area under his control and with which he protected himself against potential usurpers, consisted of commoner client-chiefs. Frequently such persons were chosen from among the many young boys who were sent to the palace to act as pages and household servants. Others were warriors of note, sometimes from other states, who offered their services to the ruler. In any case, they were always commoners with no hereditary claim to power. Having been raised by the ruler to positions of power and wealth, they were personally dependent upon him and thus were more reliable than princes. This conception of the commoner clients as protectors of the ruler against his brothers was and is quite explicit in the minds of Soga, being incorporated in songs, proverbs and stories. One tale of princely usurpation which was told to me ended with the statement: ". . . from then on, he (the ruler) ceased to trust the princes and relied instead upon the client-chiefs."

Frequently, the bond between royal patron and commoner client was further cemented by ties of affinal kinship. The client might be given a princess in marriage or the ruler might marry a woman of the client's lineage, thus adding to the patron-client bond the formalised respect relationship which obtained between in-laws. Such marriages had consequences in the following genera-tion. The commoner son of a princess became the ruler's sister's son with a special claim to royal favour. The son of the ruler and client's sister became the client's sister's son. This latter case assumed importance upon the death of the ruler, when a struggle over succession arose between his sons. Whereas a commoner's heir is chosen by his lineage council, the important commoner chiefs as well as the royal lineage had a voice in the selection of the new ruler. Indeed, the commoner chiefs often had the deciding voice because they held control of the state organisation. A son who could claim the support of a powerful chief on the basis of mother's brother-sister's son relationship was in a strong competitive position. Such political marriages also occurred at an inter-state level. An alliance between states would often be cemented by a marriage between the two royal houses. The mother of one of the present rulers was a princess from a nearby state and his chief wife is the daughter of a ruler in still another state. Such marriages were in part a matter of social class; a ruler required a wife with aristocratic up-bringing and the rules of exogamy excluded princesses from his own area. Partly also, however, it was explicitly a matter of political alliance.

Foremost among the ruler's client-chiefs was the *katikkiro*—the "prime minister"—who had charge of the palace and controlled access to the ruler. He managed the large staff of subordinate officials, pages, cooks, launderers, and entertainers who were required to maintain the palace in a fitting state of courtliness and interviewed those who came on official business. In particular, it was his duty to guard the ruler against his brothers and to prevent their entry into the palace.

Other commoner chiefs were posted in outlying parts of the kingdom in the villages held by the ruler. In the time of Zibondo Kisira, who died in 1898, there were in Bulamogi nine such territorial chiefs, placed at strategic points to guard against hostile invasions from neighbouring kingdoms and against uprisings by princes. From time to time, it is said, Zibondo Kisira made inspection tours of these outposts and maintained at each chief's headquarters a small palace where he could stay on such occasions.

Thus the ruler's staff of client-chiefs were in effective control of the machinery of government. They were subordinate only to the ruler himself. The power which they might exercise during inter-regnum periods, when there was always the potentiality for struggles between rival princes over succession to rulership, is revealed in an account of the arrangements which were made when a ruler was thought to be dying. It is taken from a published article written by one of the Soga rulers:

> When a big chief (i.e. ruler) was seriously ill, very few people were allowed near him. Perhaps his oldest wife, two or three chiefs, and a witch-doctor and his assistant were admitted. When he was seen to be dying, the headmen (i.e. client-chiefs) made enquiries as to where his property was kept, and they collected everything they could lay their hands on and hid it carefully away. His actual passing was kept secret at first, his attendants acting as if they were still nursing the sick man. This was continued until all wives, cattle, ivory, hoes, male and female slaves, etc., had been secured.
>
> But the very fact of the property being thus hidden led people to suspect a death and the deceased's brothers and sons hastened to search for any remaining property for themselves. Since . . . all went to the specially appointed heir—all others grabbed what they could. . . . When the corpse was in the grave . . . the princes,

including the one chosen as heir, were brought together. A large crowd of chiefs, relatives (i.e. *baiwa*—children of the women of the clan) and people, all armed with sticks, surrounded the heir. This was in case another prince should gather his own adherents to contest the inheritance and kill the heir-elect.[1]

Princes also maintained, on a smaller scale, staffs of client-chiefs to control the areas over which they had authority. Namuyonjo, one of the princes who rebelled against Zibondo Kisira, had his own prime minister, who was also his classificatory mother's brother, being the brother of Namuyonjo's father's mother. Other client-chiefs had authority over villages and sub-villages, thus making Bunyonjo, as Namuyonjo's area was called, a state in miniature.

Everywhere village and sub-village headmen constituted the base of the political pyramid. Some were minor princes, members of distant lineages within the royal clan. Others were clients of rulers or princes, while still others were commoners with what amounted to hereditary authority. While all commoner headmen were, in theory, clients of a ruler or a prince, it seems that in effect they quite often became hereditary. The patrilineal descent system made for a predisposition toward hereditary succession and while a hereditary chief at a higher level in the system would constitute a threat to the ruler's authority, the village or sub-village headman was simply the "little fellow at the bottom." So long as he co-operated with the ruler's client-chiefs, he could safely be allowed to pass on his position to his son or brother.

This hierarchy of ruler, princes, chiefs and headmen operated as a military, judicial, and tribute-gathering organisation. In case of war, each was responsible for providing for his superior a number of armed men. Each, together with his advisors, constituted a court of justice; a litigant dissatisfied with a decision could carry his appeal upward through the hierarchy to the ruler. For the support of the system, each was responsible for the collection of tribute in labour, foodstuffs, beer, barkcloth and iron hoes. These were collected in the first instance by the headmen, who kept a share for themselves and passed the remainder upward through the hierarchy. At each point in the system, subordination consisted in willingness to submit to one's superior in these respects. Refusal to pay tribute, to supply military aid, or to recognise the judicial decisions of one's superior was to deny his authority and to invite reprisal. On the other hand, if such acts of independence could be carried out successfully, for example by a prince, a permanent increase in authority might be obtained.

[1] Zibondo, Ezekeri, "Empisa Ezokuzika mu Busoga," *Uganda Journal*, Vol. II, No. 2, pp. 133–134.

In the smaller states of the south-west, the organisation was considerably less complex, though very similar in structure. In Busambira, for example, where the state consisted of only twelve villages, the ruler, whose title was "Kisambira," held a position not unlike that of Zibondo. He was an autonomous ruler whose authority was based upon patrilineal descent from Igaga, the legendary "first ancestor." Igaga, it is said, was created on Nhenda Hill, a large rocky outcrop in the village of Kabira, and there built his palace (see Map 8). Like Zibondo, Kisambira was said to be the ultimate owner of all the land of the state and the head of all its people and his position was a semi-sacred one. He held in his possession the ancestral stools, spears, drums and other symbolic paraphernalia of rulership and was looked upon as the chief link between the people and the royal ancestors and other supernatural forces.

Busambira also resembled Bulamogi in its structural arrangements for balancing the ascribed authority and rank of the princes with a staff of commoner clients directly responsible to the ruler. The Kisambira had his commoner prime minister who acted as an administrative assistant and protected him against the ambitions of rival princes. Other officials, subordinate to the prime minister, had charge of the palace household. Below this level, the concrete structure was different; since the state was very small, there were no large territorial sub-divisions under the authority of princes or client-chiefs. Within the state, the only territorial sub-divisions were villages and sub-villages. However, the same institutional principles which in Bulamogi governed authority relations in larger territorial units operated in Busambira at the village level. Because of the uncertainty of succession and the tendency of living rulers to give favourite sons positions of authority, many of the village headmanships were in the hands of princes who were the ruler's potential rivals. To counterbalance them, the ruler placed commoner clients in authority over his own villages and over sub-villages within villages held by princes. To facilitate comparison, the Busambira and Bulamogi systems are illustrated diagramatically in Fig. 13.

The structural importance of the commoner client in Busambira and the similarity of his position there to that of his counterpart in the larger state of Bulamogi is illustrated by an account of the career of Isumwa, prime minister of Kisambira Izizinga, who ruled during the latter part of the nineteenth century. The story was related by the son of Isumwa:

> Kisambira Izizinga asked Isumwa to come to this part from Bugweri, where he was a sub-village headman. He brought him

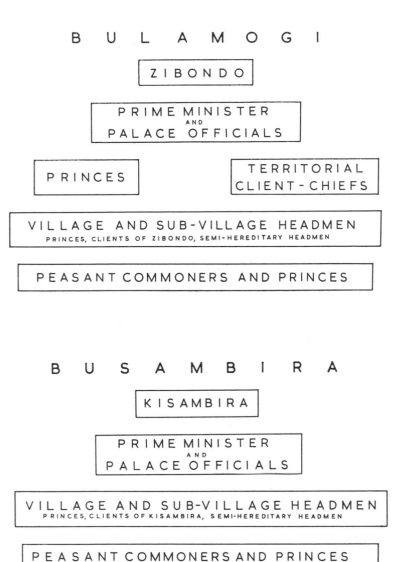

FIG. 13. The Traditional Political Structures of Bulamogi and Busambira.

because he was a brave warrior and gave him the sub-village of Namusenwa. He never lived in the sub-village because he was always away fighting. When Izizinga died, the heir was elected by the princes and the commoner clients. Isumwa supported Lukakamwa and when the latter was chosen to be Kisambira, Isumwa continued as his prime minister.

The case of Isumwa also illustrates the tendency of the commoner client-chief group to become unofficially hereditary. It was of the essence of the institution of patron-clientship that the position should not be officially hereditary since from the ruler's point of view one of the client's most important characteristics was his personal dependence upon the ruler. A client's brother or son, however, had an advantage over the sons of peasants in that he was frequently about the palace where he could learn about things governmental and where he might come to the ruler's notice. This is what happened in the case, first of Isumwa's brother, and afterwards of his son:

Isumwa died in the time of Kisambira Lukakamwa and Lukakamwa died soon after. Lukakamwa was succeeded by Kisamu. Biwawana, Isumwa's brother, had been a servant to Kisamu and when Kisamu became Kisambira Biwawana became his prime minister. When Kisamu died, Biwawana remained as prime minister under Kisambira Walinda. One time he was sent by Walinda on a journey to Kavirondo and died on the way. When Walinda heard that Biwawana was dead, he remembered that Isumwa's son, Waidha, had been a good servant. He appointed him prime minister and gave him a princess to be his wife.

Walinda's brother, Ntakambi, was his enemy and tried to chase him out of Busambira. Ntakambi received help from Ngobi (ruler of the state of Kigulu), so Waidha was sent to get help for Walinda from the ruler of Buganda. He went and introduced himself to the Ssekiboobo (chief of the neighbouring Ganda district of Kyaggwe), who sent him on to Mwanga, the ruler of Buganda. Mwanga arranged for Walinda to be restored to his rulership.

This story also illustrates the tenuousness of the independence of the smaller states of South Busoga, particularly toward the end of the last century when Ganda power was steadily increasing. Internal struggles for power within the smaller states provided opportunities for intervention by Buganda and the larger Soga states. Having been restored by Mwanga to rulership, Walinda became, in effect, his tributary dependent.

As this brief description of traditional Bulamogi and Busambira indicates, the Soga states were, on the whole, quite unstable, in part because of the peculiar combination of institutions on the basis of which the political structure was constituted. On the one hand, authority was for certain purposes vested in corporate patrilineal descent groups and this authority was reinforced by common reverence for and belief in the continuing influence of the ancestors. For commoner lineages, corporate interests focussed upon the peasant's holding, the guardianship of widows and orphans, and the headship of lineages, clans and sections of clans. For the royal clan, it centred upon succession to rulership. In no case, however, was the authority of the corporate unilineal kinship group complete. Authority was also, in part, distributed in terms of personal ties between patron and client. This meant, at the level of the central organisation of the state, that the ruler played two sets of rôles which were in part incompatible. On the one hand, he was a member of the royal descent group which shared royal rank as a corporate body. On the other hand, he was the head of the administrative organisation of the state which was made up of commoner clients and could have only one head. The sharing of royal rank—and hence potential rulership—by an extended kinship group, particularly in the absence of a fixed rule of succession, made for princely revolt and inter-regnum warfare. The clients of a ruler helped to suppress such fission within the royal group, but the clients of a rival prince—being his personal supporters—were a stimulus to it.

In a sense, the institution of corporate unilineal descent group membership and the institution of patron-clientship interfered with each other. The royal unilineal descent group could not act corporately as the head of the state because its members as individuals—the ruler and princes—had patron-client ties with non-members which were incompatible with such corporate action. At the same time, the stability of the hierarchy of patrons and clients was threatened by the corporate descent group membership of the ruler, which made it possible for rivals to threaten his position.

The mutual interference of these two institutions with each other was not confined to the central organisation of the state. As I have shown in Chapter V and will show again in Chapter VII, the headman of the village had a duality of rôles not unlike that of the ruler. He also was simultaneously a member of a corporate unilineal descent group and the head of a community of other persons with each of which he had personal ties. The patron-clientship institution also affected the structure of ordinary commoner peasant lineages. A member who had achieved high rank in the patron-client hierarchy of the state could exercise within his lineage an influence far beyond that to which his genealogical position entitled him. One example will suffice. The incident occurred during my visit to Busoga, but might equally well have occurred fifty or one hundred years ago:

> I attended the funeral of Henry, a village headman, with William, a County Chief. The council of Henry's succession lineage were meeting under a hastily-constructed sun-shade while large numbers of classificatory "mothers," "sisters," "in-laws" and other kinsmen were sitting about, chatting and eating food prepared for the funeral feast. Two of Henry's sons were hotly disputing the inheritance and the elders of the lineage council were having difficulty in reaching a decision. William, the County Chief, was a very distant classificatory "father" of the deceased and as such was taking no part in the proceedings of the council. Finally, one of the elders rose, came over to where William and I were sitting, and whispered a request that William come and try to settle the dispute. William, who attached some importance to proper procedure in clan matters, at first refused on the ground that he was a distant kinsman and had no right to interfere. Finally, however, he was persuaded, in the interests of harmony, to use his theoretically irrelevant authority as a County Chief and in a few minutes the dispute was amicably settled.

An important client-chief in pre-Administration times might have done the same. Considerations of status achieved outside the lineage system might also affect the choice of an heir by the lineage council. Conflict between such considerations and concern for lineage solidarity might arise:

> John was head of the clan in his area and so when he died his heir was chosen by a council of territorial clan heads under the chairmanship of the head of the whole clan. One faction within the council, led by the chairman, favoured Michael, an important chief, who was also known to have been his father's choice. The majority of the members, however, disagreed, arguing that Michael, being a rich and powerful person, would tend to keep aloof from his clan- and lineage-mates and would keep all his father's property for himself. In this case, lineage solidarity won out. The majority prevailed and a younger and much less prominent son was chosen.

It is situations of this sort which underlie the vagueness of the Soga when discussing the rules of succession and inheritance. A peasant's succession lineage may or may not prefer to choose the most promising son to succeed him; the headship of a lineage, clan, or clan section may or may not go to the most prominent among those eligible—frequently one who has achieved prominence outside lineage affairs; in lineage councils, great influence may or may not be exercised by persons of generally high achievement irrespective of precise genealogical position.

The instability of the traditional Soga state was not entirely due to structural strains. A further factor was the simplicity of its technological and economic base. The principal weapons, the spear and shield, were simple to manufacture and easily obtainable. This meant that one man was as good as the next in battle and that a ruler could not easily monopolise the means of force in defence of his position. Neither could the ruler monopolise to any substantial degree scarce goods of other kinds.[1] Although palace life represented a distinctly higher standard of living, it was different in kind from the life of the peasant's homestead only in its social aspects—courtly behaviour, constant entertaining, staffs of servants and the like. On the whole, the ruler simply consumed more of the same types of goods that the peasant consumed. His house, while much larger than the peasant's, was still of thatch; his dress, while more often new and more carefully manufactured, was of the same stuff as the peasant's skins and barkcloth; and while he ate more lavishly of meat and other delicacies, his diet contained little that was unknown to the peasant. The type of absolutism which has been possible in other, more technologically advanced, parts of the world was scarcely possible for the Soga ruler.

Although the state was unstable from the point of view of its concrete personnel, this very instability was, from the point of view of the system in the abstract, a kind of stabilising influence. The presence of potential rebel princes provided a ready source of leadership for revolt against serious misrule or breach of custom by the ruler. Many of the princely revolts which abound in Soga traditional history are described as arising, at least in part, from over-heavy demands for tribute and other tyrannical behaviour on the part of rulers. Thus traditional revolt frequently resulted in changes of personnel, but did not alter the system. In the changes which followed upon the advent of European administration, the system itself began to undergo gradual, but fundamental, alteration.

ADMINISTRATIVE BEGINNINGS: THE *Bwesengeze* SYSTEM.

At the time when the first Europeans arrived, two great states— Buganda and Bunyoro—were struggling for dominance in the area to the north of Lake Victoria. Warfare was more or less endemic along the border between the two states and spilled over into neighbouring territories in the form of competition for domination over the smaller states. Somewhat earlier, it appears, Bunyoro had exercised a vaguely-defined suzerainty over the northern Soga

---

[1] Toward the end of the nineteenth century, rulers began to have greater opportunities of this kind, trading ivory for guns, cloth and other goods.

states, but by the time Speke arrived, the tide had turned in favour of Buganda. The ruler of Buganda was receiving tribute from the rulers of Karagwe, in north-western Tanganyika, and Toro, in western Uganda, and from the rulers of several of the Soga states.[1] The arrival of Europeans served to hasten the spread of Ganda influence. As it happened, Mutesa, the then ruler of Buganda, and his successor, Mwanga, allied themselves with the missionaries and representatives of European Governments, while Kabarega, the ruler of Bunyoro, resisted them. As a result, the power of the Europeans was thrown into the local struggle on the side of Buganda, which was thereby enabled to expand further at the expense of Bunyoro. By 1894, when the British Protectorate was proclaimed, Busoga had become virtually a province of Buganda.[2]

The Ganda state had, at this time, reached a degree of stability and centralisation of political organisation which considerably surpassed that of the other Bantu states of the area. In form, the political system was similar to that which has been described for Busoga. The highest authority was vested in an hereditary ruler, the Kabaka, who in turn governed through a hierarchy of client-chiefs.[3] But it is significant that in Buganda the problem of princely revolt which so often threatened the stability of the Soga kingdoms was much less prominent. In Buganda, there was no royal clan. Although the commoner population was organised into patrilineal clans and lineages similar to those which existed in Busoga, the Kabaka was in a sense clanless. Only the "princes of the drum"—actual sons of Kabakas—were eligible for rulership. Often, it appears, princes other than the heir to the rulership were done away with. The interregnum struggle for succession remained, but the lack of a fully developed and ever-proliferating royal clan meant that, once established, the ruler was less likely to encounter resistance on the part of princes with hereditary claims to authority over subdivisions of the state. There were no large princely enclaves as in Busoga. All the major subdivisions of the state (*massaza*; singular: *ssaza*) were in the hands of commoner chiefs. Although there are suggestions that at an earlier time some of these chiefs may have been hereditary, during the latter part of the nineteenth century they were clients of the Kabaka.[4] The entire political organisation of the state was thus more completely in the hands of the personal administrative staff of the ruler than

---

[1] Speke, John Hanning, *Journal of the Discovery of the Source of the Nile*, 1863.

[2] Stanley, Sir H. M., *Through the Dark Continent*, 1878.

[3] Roscoe, John, *The Baganda*, 1911.

[4] Cox, A. H., "The Growth and Expansion of Buganda," *Uganda Journal*, Vol. XIV, No. 2, 1952, pp. 153–159.

was the case in many of the other Bantu states of the Lake Victoria area and Buganda was therefore more powerful and more effective in extending her power over neighbouring areas.

When the first British officer arrived to establish administration in Busoga, he found that the Soga rulers considered themselves tributary to the Kabaka and under the immediate authority of the Ssekiboobo, the chief of the neighbouring Ganda district of Kyaggwe. Present-day Soga, drawing an analogy with the British colonial system, say that the Ssekiboobo was the *gavana* ("governor") of Busoga.   For a number of years, at any rate, there was dual authority; the British officer in charge of the District attempted to set up a system of administration, while the Ssekiboobo continued to exercise authority and to collect tribute on behalf of the Kabaka.[1]

The Soga states were made more vulnerable to penetration by powerful foreigners by the endemic internal struggles discussed above.   Rulers and princes were constantly on the lookout for powerful allies and both the Ganda and the Europeans were ready to supply such aid in exchange for overall control.   Examples of Ganda intervention at the request of rival rulers have been noted above.   With the establishment of European administration, European officers found similar opportunities for intervention.   On his way from the coast to Buganda in 1890, Captain Lugard established relations of this kind with two Soga rulers and during the years immediately following, William Grant, the first administrative officer, spent much of his time settling intra-state struggles between princes.[2]   As present-day informants describe these early contacts between Europeans and Soga princes or rulers, it becomes clear that the Soga viewed the European much as they viewed the Kabaka of Buganda—as a powerful patron with whom they might ally themselves in the traditional manner.   They quite clearly did not see the relationship as a prelude to the fundamental alteration of the Soga political system which European administration ultimately brought about.

In 1900, under the terms of an agreement between Buganda and the British Government, the Kabaka relinquished all authority over Busoga and a separate District administration was established. This did not, however, mark the end of Ganda influence in Busoga. The British administrators had been greatly impressed by the Ganda political system.   The highly-centralised character of the Ganda state lent itself to the policy of indirect rule through indigenous authorities.   Furthermore, several years of missionary

[1] Uganda Government Archives, "Staff and Miscellaneous," 1893–1897.
[2] *Ibid.*

influence and contact with Europeans had resulted in the development in Buganda of a considerable body of chiefs who were literate
and well acquainted with European ways. Faced with administering a large territory with only a handful of European officers, the
Protectorate Government engaged numbers of Ganda chiefs to
remodel the political systems of neighbouring territories along
Ganda lines. For a number of years, the Bantu-speaking peoples
of the Eastern and Western Provinces, and even the Nilotic-
speaking peoples in the north of Uganda, were governed in this way
through Ganda chiefs. So it was that a uniform system of administration was developed throughout the whole of the Protectorate,
not only, as in Busoga, where a similar system had been indigenous,
but also in areas, such as the Nilotic north, where political organisation had previously been structured largely around lineage groups.

In Busoga, the "Ganda-isation" of the political system was
carried out by a Ganda chief named Semei Kakunguru, who from
1906 to 1914 acted as "paramount chief" of the District. A council
of Soga rulers was formed with Kakunguru at its head. Other
Ganda chiefs were brought in to serve as advisers to Soga rulers
and territorial units were redrawn and renamed in accordance with
the Ganda system. The larger states now became "Counties"
(Luganda: *ssaza*), while major chiefdoms within the kingdom came
to be known as "Sub-Counties" (Luganda: *ggombolola*). Below
the Sub-County level, a new unit was established which had no
counterpart in the traditional Soga system. Clusters of villages
were grouped together to form "Parishes" (Luganda: *muluka*).
Parishes within each Sub-County and Sub-Counties within each
County were, again in accordance with Ganda practice, ranked and
named in order of seniority. In descending order of seniority
these titles were: *Mumyuka, Ssabaddu, Ssabagabo, Ssabawaali,
Musaale*, and *Mutuba*. Thus an individual might be chief of the
Parish of Mumyuka of the Sub-County of Ssabaddu of the County
of Bulamogi. The villages and sub-villages remained, as they had
been in the traditional Soga system, the lowest levels of the political
hierarchy.

These changes in territorial units are summarised in Table XV.
The equivalences given in the table are not exact. In some cases,
notably in the south-western part of Busoga, the Counties represent
amalgamations of a number of small states. During Kakunguru's
time, there were three small Counties, Butembe, Bunyuli and Bunya,
in the south-western area, each representing amalgamations of
small states. After the sleeping sickness epidemics, which greatly
reduced the area's population, these were combined to form the
present County of Butembe-Bunya. Again, not all Sub-Counties

correspond strictly to the areas formerly controlled by princes or client-chiefs. In some cases, such as those mentioned earlier, Sub-Counties may correspond with small kingdoms in the traditional system. In other cases, areas formerly controlled by princes or chiefs have become Parishes. Bulamogi, for example, became a County, while Busambira was amalgamated with the state of Kigulu to form part of one Sub-County of Kigulu County. In general, however, the territorial units in the two systems correspond in the way shown in Table XV. This, at any rate, is how present-day Soga think and talk about the changes introduced by Kakunguru.

TABLE XV

CHANGES IN TERRITORIAL UNITS INTRODUCED UNDER KAKUNGURU

Traditional unit		New unit	
Lusoga term	English translation	Lusoga-Luganda term	English translation
— — —	— — —	— — —	District
nsi	State	ssaza	County
ttwale lya mulangira	Prince's area		
ttwale lya mukungu	Client's area	ggombolola	Sub-County
		muluka	Parish
— — —	— — —		
mutala	Village	mutala	Village
kisoko	Sub-village	kisoko	Sub-village

But more important than changes in political boundaries were the alterations in the actual operation of the political system which began in this period. The hierarchy of chiefs and rulers began to take on the form of a local government organisation within the framework of the British Colonial Administration. An ordinance passed by the Uganda Government in 1905 recognised the judicial authority of the chiefs and rulers and courts of record were established at the Sub-County, County and District levels.[1] A hut tax, later replaced by a poll tax, was collected by the chiefs for the support of the British Administration.

These operations required that transactions be carried out in writing. Early missionaries had developed an orthography for the Luganda language and during the administration of Kakunguru Luganda became the official language of Busoga. Every chief or ruler now either had to be literate himself or required the services of a literate clerk. The schools established in the eighteen-nineties and early nineteen-hundreds by the Anglican and Roman Catholic missions soon provided a supply of persons who could read, write

[1] Native Courts Ordinance, 1905.

and carry out simple calculations. As time went on, more and more of the chiefs themselves were mission-trained and within a few years, most of the chiefs and rulers had been converted to Catholic or Protestant Christianity.

Kakunguru also introduced changes in the economic aspects of the political system which tended to make his other innovations acceptable and even attractive to the Soga rulers and chiefs. Each County was divided into areas known as *butongole* ("official juris-diction") and *bwesengeze* ("personal estate"). With respect to the *butongole* Sub-Counties, the ruler was now simply an administrator carrying out the directives of Kakunguru and the British Administration. In his *bwesengeze* Sub-Counties, however, he could demand from the peasants personal tribute in produce and labour. In one

TABLE XVI

Division of Tribute from every Ten Peasants under the *Bwesengeze* System: 1922

	bwezengeze Sub-Counties	*butongole* Sub-Counties
County Chief (Ruler) ..	2 men	—
Sub-County Chief ..	1 man	3 men
Parish Chief	2 men	2 men
Village Headman ..	2 men	2 men
Sub-village Headman ..	3 men	3 men

sense this represented a whittling-down of the ruler's former pre-rogatives, since in the traditional system he received a share of the tribute from all areas of his kingdom. But in actual fact, he seems to have derived more profit from the new system than from the old because now his authority was backed by the power of the colonial government, whereas formerly his demands were restrained by his ultimate dependence upon the peasants for political support. The Native Authority Ordinance, 1919, gave chiefs the power to issue administrative orders and to punish under the ordinance persons who disobeyed such orders.

The introduction of cotton cultivation further increased the profit which the chief or ruler derived from the *bwesengeze* system. Cotton was a marketable commodity which made possible the conversion of the peasants' tribute obligations into money pay-ments. In 1922, tribute obligations were regularised in terms of a fixed division of the proceeds among rulers, chiefs and headmen. Each peasant was required to pay ten shillings or to do one month's free labour each year. Within each sub-village, the tribute owed by every ten adult males was divided as in Table XVI.

Thus the rulers, chiefs and headmen acquired money incomes made possible by the new cash-crop cotton cultivation. The labour of those who preferred to work for one month could be used to cultivate cotton on the chiefs' private lands. In addition to their income from tribute, the ruler and chiefs were given a rebate from the poll tax which they collected for the Protectorate Government. In 1924, it was estimated by an administrative officer that the ruler of Bugabula, the largest County, was receiving an annual income of more than £3,500 from all these sources.[1] These large money incomes enabled the rulers and chiefs to develop very rapidly a new chiefly style of life which included European-style houses, clothing and foodstuffs and to send their sons to mission schools. Thus there came to be an élite sub-culture in a sense in which that had not existed before. Whereas formerly persons of great power and high rank had lived a life which differed only in degree from that of the peasants, now they acquired goods and services and, through mission education, aspects of European non-material culture which were essentially alien to the peasant's world. To-day, chiefs who served during the period of the *bwesengeze* system speak of it with nostalgia. It was the golden age of chieftainship in Busoga when, from their point of view, all the advantages of the traditional and modern political systems were combined.

These developments occurred with remarkable smoothness and rapidity, no doubt largely because the rulers and chiefs found the new order of things so rewarding to themselves. By 1914, it was considered by the Administration that the services of Kakunguru could be dispensed with and by 1918 all Ganda chiefs had been removed. For a short time, the chairmanship of the District council rotated among the various rulers. Then, in 1919, one of the rulers, a young man who had spent a number of years in mission schools, was chosen by the council to be its permanent President and later was given the title "Isebantu Kyabazinga" ("The Father of the People Who Unites Them"). Shortly thereafter, a permanent headquarters, including an office building and a council chamber, was established at Bugembe, near Jinja. The organisation which was to become the Busoga African Local Government was beginning to take on its present-day form.

BUREAUCRACY AND POPULAR REPRESENTATION.

As yet, however, although the ranks of the rulers and chiefs now included many persons with European-style education, and although a number of innovations in the conduct of government had been

[1] Provincial Commissioner, Eastern Province, to Chief Secretary, Uganda Government Archives, 6025 I.

introduced, the bases of recruitment to office and the relationship between peasant and chief remained essentially what they had been in the traditional system. The peasant still owed personal tribute to his chief and to his ruler. The County chief was still an hereditary ruler and the Sub-County and parish chiefs were still princes or the personal clients of rulers. Gradually, however, and perhaps with no overall end clearly in view, the British administrators introduced changes which modified the system in accordance with their conceptions of just and efficient local government. More and more, the hierarchy of chiefs and rulers was remoulded after the pattern of a European civil service.

A decisive step in this direction was taken in 1926, when the Administration abolished the *bwesengeze* system. All Sub-Counties were now to be treated as *butongole*—areas in which the ruler's authority was that of an administrative official. The poll tax rebate was discontinued and tribute was reduced to four shillings or twelve days labour and made uniform for all areas. A "Native Administration" tax of six shillings was to be levied upon all adult males. From this source, rulers and chiefs were to be paid fixed salaries and pensions.

These new arrangements were, understandably, not accepted with enthusiasm by the rulers and chiefs, since their incomes were thereby substantially reduced. They also felt that the abolition of *bwesengeze* and the reduction of tribute constituted a threat to their power and prestige, since they were the economic expression of the personal tie which, in Soga values, existed between superior and subordinate. The scheme was accepted, however; at any rate none of the chiefs or rulers resigned or attempted to block its application. In his Annual Report for 1926, the Provincial Commissioner noted that:

> The announcement of the new Salary Scheme has been received on the whole by the chiefs . . . with complacency in view of the fact that they are considerable losers. The Busoga chiefs fear loss of power, but I think the pecuniary loss is felt far more.[1]

From the scheme introduced in 1926 to the complete abolition of tribute and the remuneration of chiefs entirely from salaries was but a short step. In 1936, the final shift was made, again apparently without significant opposition from the chiefs.

The readiness with which the chiefs and rulers accepted these fundamental changes in the definition of their rôles would seem to call for some explanation. To a great extent, it can be explained

---

[1] "Report of the Provincial Commissioner for the Year Ended 31st December, 1926," Central Offices, Jinja.

in terms of the very rewarding situation which the early years of administration had provided for them. Although the colonial situation had placed them under the authority of an alien power, this authority also buttressed their own position *vis-à-vis* the peasants and the *bwesengeze* system had given them increased wealth and prestige. In the meantime, many of the sons of chiefs and rulers had passed through mission boarding schools where, in more or less constant contact with European teachers and clergymen, they had come to accept the basic rightness of the aims of the British Administration. By 1930, more than half the rulers and substantial numbers of chiefs were men of this type. They were thus too far committed to the new order of things to oppose with much vigour the further innovations introduced by the Administration.

A further factor in the failure of the chiefs to make an issue of the change from tribute to salaries was their expectation that accretions to their wealth and prestige might be forthcoming from another source. In the early years of the Protectorate, a system of freehold estates was introduced in the neighbouring state of Buganda. As part of the agreement between the British Government and Buganda, somewhat more than half the area of the kingdom was allotted to the Kabaka and the chiefs in the form of freehold estates.[1] After the introduction of cotton, these estates proved a lucrative source of income for their holders, since money rents could now be collected from the peasants. A somewhat similar scheme, involving smaller areas of land, was also applied in the states of Ankole and Toro. The Soga chiefs hoped, and apparently had been led to believe, that the pattern would also be extended to Busoga. In 1930, the Protectorate Government offered to allot eighty-five square miles in freehold estates to leading families, but the offer was refused on the ground that this amount of land was inadequate.[2] The Government has since never indicated that a more attractive offer might be made, but the chiefs and rulers have continued to press their demands. Even to-day, chiefs express the hope that the Government might change its mind. Throughout this period the expectation that some day they might be rewarded by a grant of freehold estates has served to reconcile the chiefs to the acceptance of changes in other areas.

As we shall see in Chapter VII, these changes were not accepted by the village and sub-village headmen. When tribute was abolished

---

[1] Thomas, H. B., and Spencer, A. E., *A History of Uganda Land and Surveys* Government Printer, Entebbe, 1938, Chapter XIII.
[2] *Report of the Provincial Commissioner of the Year Ended 31st December,* 1930," Central Offices, Jinja.

and the salary scheme introduced, they refused to be absorbed into the official organisation. The reason for this difference in attitude may perhaps be found in the fact that the headmen had been to a much lesser degree involved in and committed to the colonial situation. It was the rulers and higher chiefs who had had personal contact with Europeans and who had been the main beneficiaries of the new situation in terms of income and education. A second important factor was the greater degree to which the headmen's position involved local personal ties. The village was and is a primary group community. Its members know each other as total persons and are related by ties of kinship and association which have extended over generations. The ruler or chief, on the other hand, even in the traditional system, operated at a level removed from that of local community. Although relationships between the ruler and his clients were personal, they were more confined to a political context. It is understandable, therefore, that the ruler or chief found it easier to accept redefinition of his rôle than did the headman.

The final transformation of the hierarchy of chiefs and rulers into a civil service now required alteration in the mode of recruitment to office. Although as early as 1906 a County chief had been appointed who was not an heir to rulership, it was still accepted in principle by the Administration that, subject to a co-operative attitude on the part of the incumbent, the County chieftainships would be treated as hereditary. As late as 1930, the heir to the rulership of the County of Bugabula was allowed to succeed his father. In 1938, however, the administration began to transfer County chiefs about and to post them in Counties other than those in which they had hereditary claims. This was shortly followed by an explicit change in the policy toward hereditary succession. Although hereditary County chiefs then in office might continue to serve, subject to transfer, no further appointments would be made on an hereditary basis. By 1952, all the hereditary rulers had been dismissed or retired and their places taken by persons appointed on the basis of personal qualifications.

Other innovations soon followed. The Administration considered that, having developed a bureaucratic civil service, it was now necessary to balance this with some provision for popular representation. In the traditional political system, chiefs and rulers had always been advised by informal councils known as *nkiiko*. The custom whereby the ruler "held court" each day at his palace provided a forum in which any person might state his views. The dependence of the ruler upon the support of his people ensured that no substantial body of opinion could be ignored. With the establishment of colonial administration, however, the rulers and chiefs had become less responsive to popular opinion. Since their positions were now guaranteed by the Administration, traditional checks upon their authority came to be less effective. Such councils as continued to be held at the headquarters of a chief or ruler tended to be made up more or less exclusively of members of the official hierarchy.

In 1938, a plan was introduced which provided for the establishment of formally-constituted councils at the Parish, Sub-County, County and District levels for the purpose of advising the chiefs and the European Administration. These councils were still dominated by the chiefs and headmen, but provision was made for the co-option of Soga clergymen, traders and other prominent persons. In 1949, the composition of the councils was altered so as to provide for an elected majority at each level. The lowest councils, those at the parish level, are elected by adult male suffrage. The councils at each successive level then choose from among themselves representatives to the next higher level. At each level, the chief serves as chairman and his subordinate chiefs are *ex officio* members. The Regulations governing the constitution of the councils are given in Appendix II. The District Council has authority to legislate within the framework of the laws of the Protectorate and is responsible for considering an annual Local Government budget.

Within recent years, the African Local Government organisation has continued to proliferate and to take on more and more of the functions commonly associated with "local government" in Western countries. In 1938, a Chief Treasurer was appointed to be responsible for African Local Government funds. To-day, he heads a staff of accountants and clerks who prepare the annual budget for consideration by the District Council. More recently the African Local Government has taken responsibility for the provision of other services, formerly provided by the Protectorate Government, with the result that the hierarchy of chiefs has been supplemented by a number of specialist officials. A Chief of Police now has charge of the police posted at each chief's headquarters and the prisons located in each county and at Bugembe. A Secretary for Agriculture and Forestry directs a staff of agriculture instructors who, in co-operation with the Protectorate Department of Agriculture, operate experimental farms and campaign on behalf of improved farming methods. A Supervisor of Public Works (at present a European who is assisted by a Soga Assistant Supervisor) is in charge of the building and maintenance of African Local Government roads and buildings. A number of other services not provided directly by the African Local Government are in part supported by funds voted by the District Council. African Local Government funds help support the schools operated by the Protestant and Catholic missions and the dispensaries operated by the Protectorate Medical Department.

In 1949, the office of Kyabazinga, which had since 1919 been occupied by one of the hereditary rulers, was made elective with a three-year term of office.[1] In the same year, the office of Secretary-General, also elective, was created. The latter is in charge of the clerical staff at the Bugembe African Local Government head-quarters and carries out liaison duties between the African Local Government and the District Administration.

The scope and complexity of the functions now carried out by the African Local Government organisation may be gathered from the abstracts of the Budget Estimates for 1952 given in Appendices V, VI and VII. In 1952, the African Local Government had 1,032 full-time employees and budgeted for more than £250,000. The sources of the African Local Government's revenue are given in Appendix VI. As more and more responsibilities have been given it, the Administration has increased the proportion of the poll tax collected for the African Local Government as against that collected for the Protectorate Government. In 1952, each able-bodied adult male was required to pay thirty-one shillings, of which six shillings went to the Protectorate Government and twenty-five to the African Local Government.

In this chapter I have summarised the traditional political structure of the Soga states and their development, over a period of less than a century, into a system of quite a different kind, resembling, in many of its features, what the Western world thinks of as "local government." We must now look more closely at the system as it operates to-day and examine the impact of these changes upon persons who play major rôles in it.

----

[1] The election is subject to confirmation by the Governor.

CHAPTER VII

POLITICS IN PRESENT-DAY BUSOGA: THE VILLAGE HEADMAN

LINKS WITH THE PAST.

To-day, as in the past, the lowest level of state-type political organisation in Busoga is represented by the village and sub-village headmen.

The changes which the past century has brought to Soga society have altered the headman's rôle, though not as profoundly as the rôles of persons at higher levels in the political system. At higher levels, there has been basic alteration in the mode of recruitment and hence a more or less thorough-going change in personnel. Positions once occupied by rulers and their personal clients are now occupied by civil servants. The headman, however, has not been bureaucratised. Though the context in which he plays his rôle has changed, any given headman is quite possibly the lineal descendant of the headman of the same area of fifty or seventy-five years ago. His link with the past is much more direct.

As I said in Chapter VI, there appear to have been three types of headman in the traditional state system. One was the client chief, who held a village as a sort of military and administrative centre from which he could govern the surrounding area in the name of the ruler. A second type was the junior prince, with claims to hereditary authority deriving from a grant from some previous ruler. Finally, there was the peasant-commoner headman—formerly perhaps the client of a ruler or prince—who had put down local roots and become, in effect, hereditary. Headmen were thus integrated with the structure of the traditional state. The terms upon which they held their positions depended upon their relationship with persons higher in the system. A powerful ruler might drive out existing headmen, either princes or commoners, and replace them with persons of his own choosing. Under a weak ruler, on the other hand, the autonomy of both princes and commoners tended to increase. The system was essentially a fluid one.

The establishment of the British Administration changed this situation fundamentally. Military considerations became irrelevant, since warfare was no longer possible. The rulers' and chiefs' positions were guaranteed by the Protectorate Government and hence defence against external invasion or internal princely revolt was no longer a problem. One of the consequences was that many (though by no means all) headmanships formerly held by clients of rulers and princes were taken over by the princes and rulers themselves. The client-chief or headman was less important because princes could no longer threaten one another. Another factor soon entered to stimulate this process. Although the tribute system gave the traditional state an economic aspect, the fundamental meaning of rulership, chieftainship or headmanship in earlier times had been the authority which it carried over persons. With the development of cash-cropping and a money economy, however, land itself came to have greater economic value. Persons in authority could now collect tribute in money or in labour which produced money. Furthermore, the Soga rulers and chiefs had grounds for the hope that the system of freehold tenure which had been introduced in Buganda might be extended to Busoga and that they might receive freehold rights over the land of villages and sub-villages held by them. Anyone, therefore, who could claim hereditary rights over a village or sub-village—and these tended in the main to be princes and rulers—hastened to do so.

These processes were further complicated by the activities of Kakunguru and other Ganda chiefs during the early years of administration when they were acting as agents of the Protectorate Government. The Ganda chiefs tended to reward faithful followers with grants of village and sub-village headmanships again, no doubt, with the model of the newly-established Ganda freehold system in mind.

Finally, as it became clearer that the freehold system was not to be extended to Busoga and as the upper levels of the system came more and more approximate to a civil service organisation, village and sub-village headmanship tended to be detached from the rest of the system. The rulers who had once governed the distribution of headmanships were no longer in authority. Gradually it came to be accepted that headmanship was hereditary to its current holder, whoever he might be. To-day, all headmen— princes and commoners alike—are uniformly hereditary on essentially the same terms.

This process of transformation has posed complex problems for Soga customary law. Disputes regarding headmanship which once were settled by the administrative action of rulers or by appeal to arms had now to be settled by the African Local Government courts in accord with some rule of law. However, claims of the most diverse kinds could be brought forward, some based upon inheritance, some upon grants by rulers or chiefs and still others upon grants by Kakunguru and his Ganda followers. The complexities with which the courts may be faced are illustrated by the following claim for headmanship of a sub-village put forward in 1949 by one whom we shall call Fred:

"This sub-village is mine for the following reason: It was given to our great-great-great-grandfather, George, by Ngobi Walulumba (the ruler). When George died, he was succeeded by his son, Henry. When Henry died, he was succeeded by his son, William. . . . William worked as headman in this sub-village until he died. In 1900 there came a famine and all the people in Busoga had to wander looking for food and therefore there was no son to take over this sub-village. When Kakunguru saw that there was no headman, he gave it to his man, Frank. At this time, my father went to Kakunguru to have our sub-village returned to us, but Kakunguru refused. In 1916 my father and I went to the County Chief and told him that since the Ganda were leaving we should be given our sub-village back, but again we were refused. . . . He said that Kakunguru was his great friend and that we must wait until his man, Frank, died. Then we might have our sub-village back. . . . Later, however, when Frank died, the princes took over the village and gave our sub-village to John. . . . That is why we are now claiming this sub-village."[1]

John, however, told the court quite a different story:

". . . the sub-village which I am claiming belonged to my ancestor, Albert. He was the owner of this sub-village during the time of Ngobi Walubbe (another ruler). When Albert died, he was succeeded by Adam, my father. When my father died, I succeeded him, but I was very young and the clan selected Steven to look after me. Steven introduced me to the village headman. . . . For some time I lived outside Busoga, but the village headman looked after the sub-village for me. Now I have been ruling the sub-village and this man, Fred, is trying to claim it as his. . . . He says that his ancestor was headman, but that is not true. His ancestor was a man of my ancestor who was merely given some land in the sub-village."[2]

---

[1] Case Number 121/1949/Musaale, Kigulu; Appeal Number 103/1949/ Kigulu County; Appeal Number 4/1950/Busoga District Native Court; Civil Revision 115/1950/High Court of Uganda.

In future references to cases, the following abbreviations will be used: CN = Case Number; AN = Appeal Number; CR = Civil Revision; BDNC = Busoga District Native Court; DC = District Commissioner's Court; HC = High Court of Uganda. All personal names, except those of historically prominent persons now deceased, are fictitious. I appreciate the objections against the use of English names in referring to Soga, but have followed this practice throughout this book, first because the use of unfamiliar names is confusing to the reader, and second because Soga names are often Soga-ised versions of English names. "Mark," for example, becomes "Mako," "John" becomes "Yokana," and so on.

[2] CN 121/1949/Musaale, Kigulu; AN 103/1949/Kigulu County; AN 4/1950/ BDNC; CR 115/1950/HC.

In such a case, the court can hardly base its judgment upon the merits of the claims put forward by the litigants, both because the events in question occurred so long ago that there can be no reliable evidence concerning them and because no rule of law can be made to cover events which at the time of their occurrence were subject, not to law, but to administrative action by chiefs and rulers. In this and in similar cases, therefore, the courts tend to rule in favour of the party who at the time is actually acting as headman, particularly if he has done so for a number of years without having his right disputed. In this case, since John had been acting as headman for some time before Fred entered his claim, John was confirmed as headman.

Another case, heard in 1950, illustrates even more clearly the tendency of the courts to recognise and legalise the *status quo* resulting from the operation of the traditional system, even though acts carried out under that system could no longer be legally carried out to-day:

> Jacob claimed that the sub-village in question was held by five generations of his patrilineal ancestors down to his grandfather, Michael. When Michael died in 1922, it happened that there were only two families living in the sub-village and so it was combined by the village headman with a neighbouring one. Jacob now claimed the sub-village on the ground that it was his by inheritance.
> Stanley, however, the headman of the sub-village with which Jacob claims his was combined, claimed that the entire area was taken away from Jacob's ancestor by Gabula Kagoda (the ruler) and given to his (Stanley's) ancestor.[1]

The court decided that the bulk of evidence showed that Stanley's story was correct and held that:

> ". . . it is true that the ancestor of Jacob was the owner of the sub-village but it was taken away and given to Stanley's ancestor by Gabula Kagoda. Therefore there is no evidence that the sub-village is his (Jacob's)."[2]

Ultimately, such cases will cease to arise since to-day the only recognised means of acquiring a village or sub-village headmanship is through inheritance. Furthermore, headmanship has, in recent years, become a matter of written record. The Poll Tax registers kept at Sub-County headquarters list taxpayers' names under the names of their village and sub-village headmen. Such cases as the two quoted above are products of the transition from the traditional system to the modern one.

[1] CN 128/1950/Mutuba II, Bugabula; AN 124/1950/Bugabula County.
[2] *Ibid.*

Thus the headmen of to-day everywhere occupy essentially the same position, though the origins of their claims to authority differ. Figs. 14 and 15, showing the genealogical relations among headmen in the two southern Bulamogi villages of Budini and Buyodi and in the three Busambira villages of Bunyama, Wairama and Bukwaya, illustrate this diversity of origin. The village headmanships of both Budini and Buyodi (Fig. 14) are held by princes (G and H), direct descendants of an earlier prince who was given the two villages by the ruler. The present ruler (J) holds no headmanships in this area, though he holds several elsewhere, but he is included in the diagram in order to show the genealogical positions of other persons with respect to him. Among sub-village headmen, six (B, C, D, E, F and I) are descended from the same common ancestor as the ruler and the two village headmen. Another, L, is also a prince, but is one more generation removed in relation to the others. Finally, there are five commoner sub-village headmen. A, K, M and N are all descendants of commoner headmen of the last century. Following a common pattern, one of these, K, has married a princess, thus relating himself affinally to the royal headmen of the area. The other commoner, O, illustrates a more modern phenomenon. He is the headman of the sub-village in which the Roman Catholic mission is located. Alone among the headmen of Budini and Buyodi, he has no hereditary claim to office but is simply appointed by the priests of the mission.

The three Busambira villages (Fig. 15) are even more heavily dominated by princes. All three village headmanships and all but two sub-village headmanships are held by members of the *Baiseigaga* clan. Traditionally, the ruler did not actually act as headman of villages and sub-villages held by him, but rather had commoner clients posted there. To-day, however, the ruler (J), who no longer has a recognised position in the wider political system, acts as headman of two villages (Wairama and Bukwaya) and four sub-villages. Bunyama village and thirteen of the remaining sub-villages are held by descendants of the ruler's father's brothers (A, B, C, D, E, F, G, K and L). One sub-village is held by the grandson of the ruler's brother (H). Finally, two sub-villages are held by commoners (I and M), both descendants of commoner clients of earlier rulers.

Despite these differences in origin, headmen to-day are sufficiently similar in the position they occupy for me to speak of them as a homogeneous group and describe the rôle of *the* village headman. The headman's rôle has two major aspects, corresponding with the two major groups with which he has political relations: On the one hand, he holds an authority position of a particular kind *vis-à-vis*

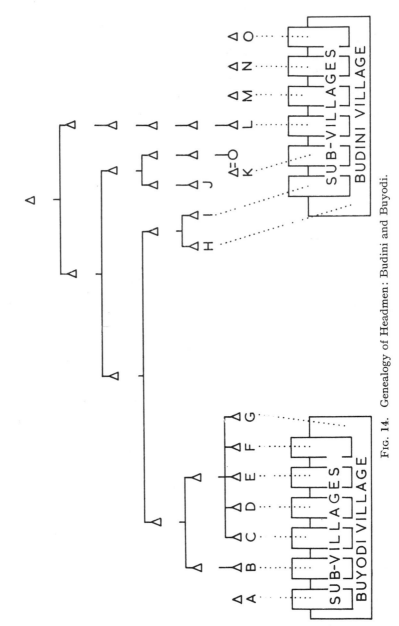

Fig. 14. Genealogy of Headmen: Budini and Buyodi.

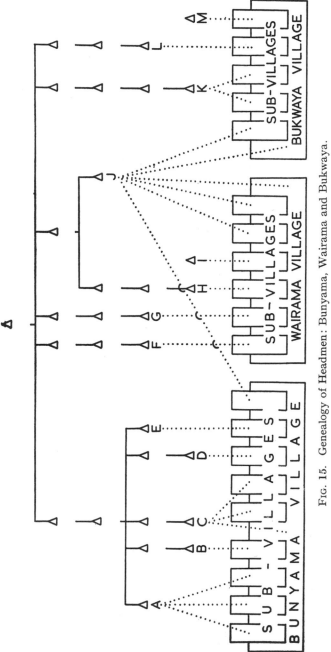

Fig. 15. Genealogy of Headmen: Bunyama, Wairama and Bukwaya.

the people of his village or sub-village. On the other hand, he is the link between his people and the wider political system and thus occupies a position in that system. We may examine each of these aspects in turn.

THE HEADMAN AND HIS PEOPLE.

Chapter V showed that villages and sub-villages in Busoga do not constitute localised lineage communities and it follows from this that the headman is not as such primarily a leader of a patrilineal descent group. This does not mean, however, that the headman has no kinship ties with his people. On the contrary, where population has been relatively stable, the community of which he is head is intricately interlaced with consanguineal and affinal relationships. In the genealogical diagrams of the sub-villages of Kirumbi (Fig. 10) and Gasemba (Fig. 11), the headman's involvement in the kinship network is apparent. In Kirumbi, the headman, Fred (homestead IV), is the head of the *Baisengobi* within the sub-village and he is related affinally with the other substantial local lineage, the *Baisemukubembe*, through the marriages of Tony (IX), Alfred (X) and Frank (XIII) to *Baisengobi* women. He is similarly related to Will (XIV), while Joseph (V), the remaining homestead head, is his maternal cross-cousin. Fred thus has significant kinship ties with every member of the community. The same is essentially true of George (XV), the headman of the sub-village of Gasemba. All but two homestead heads, Keith (XXX) and John (XXXI), are related to him through patrilineal, affinal or maternal ties. The headmen of villages and sub-villages in the Busambira area, whose structures were seriously disturbed by sleeping sickness epidemics, have far fewer kinship ties. In Bunyambale (Fig. 12), the headman, a member of the *Baiseigaga* clan who is not a resident of the sub-village, has only two distant patrilineal kinsmen, Edwin (IX) and William (X), and one affine, Mark (VII), in the community. His steward, Harry (I), has no kinsmen at all. But wherever, as in Kirumbi and Gasemba, there has been continuous and undisturbed settlement, the headman tends to be the centre of a complex kinship network.

Intra-village kinship ties involve the headman in a dilemma not unlike that of the ruler in the traditional state. Like the ruler, he is both a member of a solidary lineage group and the head of a territorial unit inhabited in large part by persons who are not his lineage-mates. The headman's affinal and maternal ties with many of these latter are analogous to the ruler's similar ties with many of his client-chiefs. Like the traditional rulers, headmen feel that they must emphasise these ties in order to counter-balance the claims of lineage-mates and to this end they often try to encourage settlement in their areas by persons outside the lineage. This practice is resented by members of the headman's lineage, who are apt to take more seriously the notion that the lineage as a whole "owns" the village or sub-village.

It is also significant that in each of these three sub-villages the homestead of the headman tends to contain more persons than do those of other members of the community. All three headmen are polygynous and two of them have married sons living with them— a situation which is unusual for Soga homesteads in general. Table XVII shows the mean number of wives and other dependents in the homesteads of village and sub-village headmen in the five survey villages as compared with the means for the homesteads of other

TABLE XVII

MEAN NUMBER OF WIVES AND OTHER DEPENDENTS IN THE HOMESTEADS
OF HEADMEN AND OTHERS IN THE FIVE SURVEY VILLAGES

	Village and sub-village Headmen	Other Homestead Heads
Mean number of wives	2·3	1·1
Mean number of other dependents ..	4·3	2·2
Mean total number of dependents ..	6·6	3·3

persons. Headmen have, on the average, more than twice as many wives and almost twice as many other dependents as have other homestead heads.

The larger homestead and the larger number of wives are both a symbol and a manifestation of the headman's position in his community. His homestead is the social centre of his domain. It is the scene of daily gatherings of men of the community for gossip and the discussion of community affairs. On such occasions, food and beer must be provided for all from the headman's plantain grove which consequently must be larger than that of the ordinary peasant. His wives are kept busy supplying this hospitality and maintaining the homestead in constant readiness to receive guests. The concern which most often draws visitors to the headman's homestead and forms the topic of the endless discussions which take place there is land. More than anything else, it is the headman's rights in all the land of his village or sub-village which form the basis of his prestige and authority.

The headman's position in the land-holding system can best be described in terms of the distribution of rights which the customary law makes among the several parties who have an interest in any piece of land.

My data on Soga land law are drawn almost exclusively from actual cases tried in the African Local Government courts. As I noted in the Preface, the records kept by the courts are relatively full. These records, supplemented by data gained through the questioning of litigants, judges and witnesses involved in particular cases provide, I believe, the surest basis for the analysis of customary law. I found that the attempt to elicit legal rules from informants by posing hypothetical cases usually failed because the informants, quite sensibly, refused to give an opinion without being in possession of all of the facts. Questioned about a hypothetical case, they invariably protested: "But how can I know? I must hear the evidence and know the circumstances." Given a concrete case, informants would sometimes comment upon what the law might have been had the circumstances been different in certain particulars, but it was essential to have the concrete case as a point of departure.

The case method does not provide a complete outline of the law. Through its use, one cannot discover what the law would be in circumstances which have not arisen or of which one cannot find an example. Such prediction is, however, impossible, strictly speaking, in any legal system. Law cannot really be said to exist outside the judgments of courts. I do not mean to imply, of course, that I have considered all cases which have arisen in Busoga; that would obviously be impossible. I have, however, examined all cases appearing before selected courts (one Sub-County and two County Courts) during selected periods (one year for each court). Though by this means some types of cases have undoubtedly been overlooked, most of the commoner situations which take people to court over land are probably included in my data.

The peasant who wishes to take up a new *kibanja* (a holding, usually consisting of a plantain garden plus land for annual crops), should engage someone to act as his *mukwenda* (representative) in his dealings with the headman. The *mukwenda* should be a person well-known to the headman who can vouch for the good character and future loyalty of the new tenant. He is paid for his services by the prospective tenant and is his legal representative in the transaction. In the event of future litigation, he may be required to testify in court concerning the terms of the contract.

> George was accused by Amos of not appearing to testify in a case brought by Amos, although the latter had paid George ten shillings to act as his *mukwenda*. The court held that, by not appearing, George had caused Amos to lose the case and thus to lose property

to the value of one hundred shillings and one goat.   George was ordered to compensate Amos by this amount.[1]

If the headman has a holding available, he and the peasant's representative agree upon the allotment fee to be paid and the time of payment.   The allotment fee, *nsibuzi* or *nkoko*, (literally "a hen") was traditionally, it is said, merely a symbolic payment of a hen or a barkcloth made in recognition of the headman's authority. To-day it is clearly of economic significance.   The sum paid may range from as little as twenty-five to as much as five hundred shillings, depending upon the size and quality of the holding, and the demand for land in the area.   It may be handed over in its entirety by the peasant's representative when the peasant assumes occupation or it may be paid in instalments, depending upon the terms of the contract.   It should be divided between the headmen of the village and sub-village in which the holding is situated. Often the village headman is also the headman of at least one of the sub-villages in his village and carries out land transactions there himself.   Such is the case in Bunyama, Wairama and Bukwaya. The headmen of Budini and Buyodi do not also act as sub-village headmen since both of them happen to be employed elsewhere, one as an African Local Government chief and the other as a medical assistant in a Protectorate Government prison.   Each is represented in his village by a steward (*musigire*) who carries out his duties as village leader and looks after his interests in the land.

Having settled the terms of the contract with the peasant's representative, the sub-village chief sends his own representative (*mubaka*) to establish the boundaries of the holding and to mark them with fast-growing barkcloth trees.   The marking out of the boundary should be done in the presence of a number of elders of the community who, because of their long and intimate knowledge of the area, are known as *bataka*, "men of the land."   All these persons, the representatives of the headman and the peasant and the "men of the land," are formal witnesses to the contract who may be called upon to give evidence in the event of a dispute.   With the spread of literacy, increasing use is made of written contracts, but even where this is done, it is the testimony of the living witnesses which is considered the most reliable evidence in the eyes of the courts.

If the tenant fails to pay the agreed allotment fee within the time specified in the contract, the headman may evict him.

John, a tenant, died before paying in full the allotment fee which he had contracted to pay to Henry, the headman.   John's heir,

[1] CN 31/1951/Ssabawaali, Kigulu.

William, assumed possession of the holding, but failed to fulfil the payments stipulated in the contract, whereupon Henry evicted him. William then sued Henry, but the court decided in Henry's favour on the ground that William, as John's heir, had assumed all of John's obligations under his contract with Henry. Having not fulfilled these obligations, he had forfeited his right to the holding.[1]

Once the allotment fee has been paid, the tenant and his heirs have perpetual, rent-free use rights in the land. Under the traditional political system the tenant could be called upon to pay tribute in produce to the headman and it is said that failure to make such payments was cause for eviction. In 1904, at the instigation of the Protectorate Government, the council of Soga chiefs agreed that so long as a tenant cultivated his holding and paid his poll tax, he could not be evicted. He was, however, required to pay a fixed sum in money tribute to the headman and chiefs in commutation of his former tribute obligations.[2] Later the tribute payment was abolished in favour of a Native Administration Tax (now called "African Local Government Tax"), evasion of which is cause for criminal prosecution but not forfeiture of land. To-day, therefore, the headman is entitled to no payment other than the initial allotment fee. Headmen may still request sand, timber and other building materials from peasants' land, but these are given only if the peasant himself has no use for them. The headman cannot claim in court the right to such materials.

Once paid, the allotment fee is not recoverable. If the tenant on his own initiative relinquishes his holding, he may sell the materials from any building he may have erected and also any standing crops, but he may not reclaim the allotment fee. The fee is forfeited and the holding reverts to the headman for allotment to another tenant. In reference to this principle, Soga quote a proverb: "Land is like a cow which never ceases to give milk." The headman never loses his residual rights in the land; he receives a non-recoverable fee from each new tenant. (An heir of a previous tenant is not a new tenant in this sense; he inherits without obligation to the headman.) However, the headman may not terminate the contract against the tenant's will merely by refunding the allotment fee. In the case reproduced in Appendix IV, the point at issue between headman and tenant was whether or not the allotment fee had in fact been refunded. The tenant, George, was willing to vacate the holding provided his fee was refunded. In commenting upon this case,

---

[1] CN 14/1951/Ssabawaali, Kigulu.

[2] Carter, Morris, *Report of the Committee Appointed to Consider the Question of Native Settlement in Ankole, Bunyoro, Busoga and Toro*, Government Printer, Entebbe, 1914.

the Sub-County chief remarked: "If George had not agreed to leave, Henry (the headman) would not have been able to force him to do so."

Although payment of the allotment fee assures usufructory rights in the holding to the tenant and his heirs, the tenant must fulfil certain conditions in order to maintain these rights; otherwise the headman may assert his reversionary right to the holding. The tenant must either live on his holding or cultivate it or, if he desires to rest it, must state his intention to do so to the headman in the presence of witnesses. If these conditions are not fulfilled, the headman may reclaim the land.[1] Furthermore, the tenant must not commit any act which might diminish the headman's reversionary right. If a tenant sells his holding to another tenant without the headman's consent, the headman may evict both purchaser and seller.

Frank sold his holding to Stanley and moved to another sub-village. Later, upon discovering that his new holding was not a good one, he returned and tried to claim his former holding on the ground that the sale was not agreed to by the headman and was therefore not valid. The court, however, held that by making an illegal sale Frank forfeited his right to the holding. The Sub-County chief commented that the headman could also evict the purchaser, Stanley, if he wished to do so.[2]

A tenant may allow another peasant to use part of his holding, but unless he is able to establish that the loan was for a delimited period, he will tend to lose his rights in the loaned portion and the borrower will become a primary tenant of the headman.

Frederick claimed that in 1947 he lent part of his holding to Mark, his brother-in-law. Mark, however, claimed that he was given the holding permanently. Frederick was unable to bring witnesses to establish that the land was only loaned, while Mark brought witnesses who testified that it was given. The land was therefore awarded to Mark as a regular tenant under the headman.[3]

The courts have also held that a headman may restrain a tenant from allowing a third party to build a permanent brick building on his holding, since this would tend to give a permanent interest in the land to a person with whom the headman has no contract.

Albert alleged that Michael, now deceased, allowed him to build a permanent shop on his (Michael's) holding. Theodore, Michael's

[1] Comment by Sub-County chief on CN 69/1951/Ssabawaali, Kigulu.
[2] CN 43/1951/Ssabawaali, Kigulu.
[3] CN 121/1949/Musaale, Bulamogi; AN 52/1949/Bulamogi County; AN 1/1950/BDNC; CR 39/1950/DC; CR 4/1951/HC. A similar judgment was given in CN 92/1950/Ssabagabo, Bulamogi; AC 60/1950/Bulamogi County.

son, together with the headman, protested when Albert began to construct a shop of bricks and asked the court to restrain him. The Sub-County court granted Theodore's request. The County court, on appeal, reversed the decision, but the District court again found for Theodore and this decision was upheld by the District Commissioner.[1]

Thus the customary law tends not to recognise sub-tenure. Land can be held only under the headman and as a result of an original contract with him. An attempt by a tenant to alienate any part of his own rights in the holding, other than by inheritance, would tend to diminish the headman's residual rights in the land and is therefore held by the courts to be illegal.

These are the respective rights of the headman and the original tenant. Upon the death of the original tenant, the rights of a third party—the lineage council, whose authority over inheritance was described in Chapter IV—come into force. The heir chosen by the council may take possession of the holding without payment of an additional fee and he acquires all the rights and obligations of his predecessor. If the heir is a minor, the council may appoint the deceased's kinship successor, who in any case is the minor heir's guardian, to be his trustee. However, as I have said in Chapter V, the council may not simply hold the land in reserve for the future use of some undesignated member of the lineage. If a peasant dies and no heir is named, the land reverts to the headman for re-allotment.

For purposes of inheritance, the headmanship of a village or sub-village is treated in the same way as a peasant's holding. Upon the death of a headman, his lineage-mates meet in council to choose an heir from among his sons.

It is said that in the past the lineage could restrain one of its members from willing his holding to a non-lineage-mate or from alienating any part of it during his lifetime, even with the consent of the headman, to a non-lineage-mate. I have been told that to-day there is a movement toward testamentary freedom and that cases occur in which persons successfully will land to non-kinsmen, though I have been unable to find a record of such a case. I did, however, find a case in which the court upheld the transfer of land to a non-kinsman during the lifetime of the holder.

William alleged that he was given a piece of land by Donald, now deceased. Gerald, the head of Donald's succession lineage, however, asserted the right of the lineage to choose an heir and when he observed William gathering plantains from the land in question, he

[1] CN 26/1949/Mumyuka, Butembe-Bunya; AC 61/1949/Butembe-Bunya County; AC 6/1950/BDNC; CR 6/1950/DC.

accused him of theft. The headman, however, testified that Donald had transferred the land to William with his (the headman's) consent. The Court decided in favour of William and acquitted him of theft.[1]

It is significant that this case occurred in Busambira, where the authority of the lineage has been weakened and where the fictional "clan" of *Baisekantu* has grown up. I very much doubt that in more stable areas, where lineage authority is still intact, such a case could have occurred.

Land litigation appears to arise most commonly from disputes between tenants who claim to hold by inheritance and headmen who claim reversionary rights on the ground that the rights of the line of heirs have been extinguished by failure to remain in effective occupation. The general principle governing this sort of situation is quite clear: a tenant or his heir or his trustee must establish a residence on the holding (this may be done in the case of an adult heir by setting up a subsidiary residence, with a wife) or, if he lives nearby, must cultivate it or establish his intention to rest it. Otherwise the headman may reclaim it. It should be pointed out that this reversionary right of the headman, by which he may reallot unused land, is not looked upon in present-day Busoga, as it apparently is in some African societies, as a trusteeship for the community, but rather as a personal prerogative of the headman. The tenant must remain in effective occupation, not because justice demands that unused land should be re-allotted, but in order to "indicate his willingness to be ruled by that headman." Although the rule is quite clear, in practice the likelihood of a claimant by hereditary right successfully asserting his right to a holding which has been re-allotted by the headman depends upon the weight of evidence which he is able to bring before the court. This, of course, is true of all courts of law everywhere. But where the events in question are often remote in time and where contracts are still largely verbal and depend for their validity upon the testimony of living witnesses, the question of evidence would appear to cover a particularly wide sector of law.

In general, the strongest type of evidence which a litigant who claims hereditary rights in land can present is the presence in the disputed land of the graves of his ancestors. This is readily understandable in view of the patrilineal nature of Soga society and the deep traditional reverence of the Soga toward everything pertaining to the ancestors. Against such evidence, however, the courts give considerable weight to evidence of undisturbed occupation. A tenant who has peaceably occupied and cultivated his holding for a

---

[1] CN 89/1951/Ssabawaali, Kigulu.

substantial period should not be dispossessed even in favour of one with hereditary rights. I have discovered no firm rule indicating how long a period of undisturbed occupation is required to outweigh firm evidence of hereditary right, but from the examination of cases of this type, of which very many occur in Soga courts, something of the type of reasoning which the courts apply to this common, and often intractable, type of case may be seen.

The longer a claimant waits after the critical events to bring his case, the less likely he is to be successful. If the headman attempts to repossess or to alter the boundary of a holding for which there is already an occupant by hereditary right in favour of a new tenant, the existing tenant has a ready remedy. If he can establish his hereditary right and if he quickly brings his case to court, the headman may be restrained. In two cases heard in 1950, attempts by headmen to revise boundaries in 1940 and 1949 respectively were successfully contested by tenants who could establish hereditary claims.[1] On the other hand, in another case heard in the same year, hereditary right was denied to a claimant on the ground that since he ceased to occupy the holding it had been successfully allotted by the headman to three tenants, the last of whom had occupied it for sixteen years.[2] The courts' reasoning in these matters may be seen in the following case:

> James asserted in 1949 that he had inherited a certain holding from his father, Allan. However, Amos, who now occupies the holding, was able to bring evidence to convince the court that he had been given the land in 1934 and had occupied it undisturbed since that time. He was further able to show that he was the fifth occupant of the holding since Allan and that when he (Amos) was allotted it, Allan was still living. The Court held that James no longer had a claim to the land. Since Allan did not bring the case to court before he died, the Court reasoned, he must have known that he did not have a valid claim.[3]

And in still another case:

> Mark alleged in 1951 that he had inherited a holding from his father but that while he was still a small boy the headman had allotted it to John. John, however, pointed out that this occurred long ago (twenty-eight years) and that Mark had long since come of age. The court agreed, awarding the holding to John, and added that Mark should at least have presented his claim to the lineage council of the headman, who had recently died. Since he did

---

[1] CN 70/1949/Mutuba I, Kigulu; AC 88/1949/Kigulu County; AC 3/1950/ BDNC; CR 29/1950/DC; CR 11/1951/HC. Also CN 71/1950/Mutuba III, Bugabula; AC 132/1950/Bugabula County.
[2] CN 230/1950/Ssabawaali, Bulamogi; AC 59/1950/Bulamogi County.
[3] CN 106/1949/Ssabawaali, Kigulu.

neither of these things, it had to be assumed that Mark knew his claim was not substantial.[1]

The court thus operates with two balancing principles. On the one hand, inheritance and the presence of ancestors' graves establishes land as the *butaka* (ancestral land) of the occupant. On the other hand, successful exercise by the headman of his powers of allotment over unused land establishes the land as *kitongole* (land over which the headman has authority). Ultimately, if the land is again inherited, it becomes the *butaka* of the heirs of the new tenant.

This is the complex of rights and obligations through which the headman is bound to his people in the land-holding system. He is, however, more than a landlord. To most of his people he is usually a kinsman of one sort or another and to all he is a patriarchal custodian of traditional values and community well-being. It is significant that this patriarchal rôle in some respects imposes upon the headman legally sanctioned duties quite apart from land matters. In one case, a headman was charged before a Sub-County court for failing to answer an alarm (*nduulu*) in his village.[2] A stylised alarm cry is raised whenever there is violence or disaster and it is the headman's duty to rush to the scene and take charge. In another case, a headman was fined for allowing one tenant to take plantains from another's garden, implying that the headman is in some ways responsible for the acts of his tenants.[3]

AN ARM OF THE STATE.

The headman is not, however, simply a local leader. Just as in the traditional political system he was the link between the state and the people, so to-day he mediates between the village and the African Local Government organisation.

The transfer of authority from the traditional state system to the African Local Government organisation as it affects the status of the headman requires some comment. Traditionally, the headman was, as I have explained, either a prince or a commoner dependent of a ruler or prince. With the increasing bureaucratisation of the upper levels of the political system, the traditional state has either disappeared or become ineffective and the headman has consequently become detached from it. The process has, however, been different in different areas.

To-day, the ruler of the small state of Busambira, for example, is himself in effect simply a village and sub-village headman and the head of the Busambira section of the *Baiseigaga* clan, of which

---

[1] CN 71/1951/Ssabawaali, Kigulu.
[2] AC 50/1950/Bulamogi County.
[3] CN 36/1951/Ssabawaali, Kigulu.

there are other sections elsewhere in Busoga. During the early years of administration, Busambira was a Sub-County and the ruler (the predecessor of the present ruler) was Sub-County chief. However, with the increasing bureaucratisation of the system, the hereditary status of the Kisambira ceased to be recognised and Busambira was amalgamated with three neighbouring villages to form the present Sub-County of Ssabawaali of Kigulu county. The ruler to-day holds a position of some influence in the area, but this influence is largely limited to the clan and to the villages and sub-villages of which he is actually headman. "Busambira" remains a social unit of identification and a focus of nostalgic memory, but is no longer an effective political unit.

The position in Bulamogi is somewhat different since the boundaries and name of the traditional state survive in the modern Bulamogi County. Furthermore, the present ruler served for many years as a County chief and as Kyabazinga of Busoga under the new system. In Bulamogi, therefore, and in others of the larger northern states which survive as Counties in the present system, attachment to the traditional state system has died more slowly. With the final withdrawal of recognition from the hereditary rulers, some of them have attempted to preserve their traditional positions by setting up hierarchies of chiefs parallel to the official hierarchy of the African Local Government. In at least one case, the ruler appoints "Sub-County and Parish chiefs" of his own—some princes and some commoners—who are supposed to try cases and to be in authority over the village and sub-village headmen.

The striking characteristic of this "shadow state," however, is its failure to provide an effective alternative to the official African Local Government system. One reason is that in fact it is little different from the official hierarchy. Most of its personnel, including the ruler himself, have themselves served in the official system and their notions of administration are taken rather more from that experience than from the really traditional state organisation, which none of them are old enough to remember clearly. Since all are Christian or Mohammedan and most are mission-educated, the system has none of the religious sanction which helped to support the traditional state. The chiefs appointed by the ruler keep written case records and try cases as they were taught to do by early administrative officers. A related source of weakness derives from the fact that these traditional leaders were for most of their lives identified in the minds of the people with the official, Government-sponsored hierarchy and many of them in fact owe their positions to this connection with Government. During the early years of administration, disputes over succession to rulership which traditionally would have been settled by force were settled by administrative officers. Chosen heirs were supported and trained by mission and Government and became the nucleus around which the early "Native Administration" system was built. One of the consequences has been that rival claimants to rulership, who traditionally might have been eliminated by war, have persisted. In nearly every one of the traditional states there are rival claimants to rulership and this weakens the rulers' claims to traditional sanction. Finally, the official African Local Government organisation has the support of Government. It in fact has the funds with which to pay its personnel and support social services and the ultimate power to enforce the decisions of its courts. Thus, though there is great loyalty to the ruler as a person and, occasionally, as a rallying point for discontent with unpopular Government measures, still, effective authority is in the hands of the African Local Government and the overwhelming majority of the people, whether out of a genuine satisfaction with its work or simply out of grim realism, accept it.[1]

The headmen, therefore, as links between their people and the wider political system, deal largely with the African Local Government. They are not formally members of the African Local Government organisation, however, because they have refused to accept the conditions to which formal incorporation would subject them. For many years after British administration was established in Busoga, the changes introduced made relatively little impression upon the position of the headmen. Although the traditional dues and services by which the officials of the old kingdom-states were supported were commuted to money payments, the income which they received was still in the nature of personal tribute. The headmen collected the tribute from the peasants and were permitted to keep for themselves a *per capita* share, the remainder being passed on to the chiefs and rulers. In 1936, however, the Administration introduced an innovation which changed the entire economic basis of the political system. Henceforth tribute was to be abolished in favour of a tax to be paid to the African Local Government treasury. The rulers, chiefs and headmen were to be paid fixed salaries. The rulers and chiefs accepted the new scheme and it became one of the major steps in their development into a bureaucratic civil service. The headmen, however, steadfastly

---

[1] The traditional rulers have not, it should be noted, been entirely excluded from the official African Local Government system. Though they are no longer hereditary heads of areas, they are *ex-officio* members of the District Council (see Appendix II). They are officially referred to as "clan heads."

refused to accept salaries, reasoning, with quite profound insight, that to do so would make them subject to transfer and to bureaucratic discipline, which in fact is what happened to the chiefs and rulers. In 1937, a delegation of village headmen told an administrative officer that "they would sooner be allowed to collect one shilling a year from each peasant as personal tribute than be paid a salary equivalent to twice that amount."[1] The headmen's concerted opposition is quite remarkable when it is remembered that there were more than 1,200 of them (counting only the village headmen) spread over an area which only forty years earlier had been split up among a number of mutually hostile states. One village headman, in explaining to me the stand taken in 1936 by him and his fellows, said: "If you pay me to wash my table it will then become your table." He saw his authority as locally-based, deriving in large part from his long and intimate association with his people and from the fact that his father had had a similar association with their fathers. To attempt to transfer his authority to another village or to subject it to bureaucratic control, would be to destroy it.

The headmen have therefore remained outside the formal organisation of the African Local Government. In fact, however, they behave and are treated as if they were an integral part of it and are indispensable to its day-to-day functioning. The African Local Government is even more dependent upon them than were the chiefs and rulers of the traditional states, because the new civil-servant chiefs are frequently transferred about from post to post and thus have little opportunity to acquire intimate acquaintance with the areas for which they are responsible. In the traditional system, the headman was the local magistrate. As the patriarch of the village or sub-village, disputes were brought to him for arbitration as a matter of course. To-day, the lowest court of record is at the Sub-County level and is presided over by the Sub-County chief, an African Local Government civil servant. The civil-servant chiefs recognise, however, that the volume of litigation in the courts can be greatly reduced if disputes are first taken to the sub-village and village headmen whose knowledge of the situation makes it possible for them to smooth over ruffled tempers and to arrive at an agreeable solution. Many civil-servant chiefs therefore refuse to allow a case to be entered for formal trial until the headman has attempted to arbitrate the dispute.

Civil-servant chiefs delegate numerous other duties to the village and sub-village headmen. The collection of taxes, the apprehension

---

[1] "Report of the Provincial Commissioner of the Year Ended 31st December, 1937," Central Offices, Jinja.

of minor criminals, the enforcement of public health regulations and the spreading of propaganda in favour of improved agricultural technique, all of which are formally the responsibility of the civil-servant chiefs, are in fact largely carried out by headmen. The latter are in practice so completely integrated into the life of the African Local Government that if for any reason a Parish chief is absent from duty a headman may temporarily take over his duties and be paid by the African Local Government for the period during which he serves.

THE HEADMAN'S DILEMMA.

From the headman's point of view, however, the rewards which his rôle provides are insufficient. The rewards cannot be sufficient because his rôle contains internal contradictions. He expects of himself and others expect of him patterns of behaviour which, given the situation, are mutually incompatible. On the one hand, he is the hereditary leader of his village or sub-village and the upholder of its traditional values. This part of his rôle is accepted by his people and is greatly valued by him. On the other hand, he is also in practice the local agent of the African Local Government organisation. It is his duty to help the civil-servant chiefs in numerous ways in the day-to-day governing of Busoga. This part of his rôle is also expected of him both by his people and by the chiefs because the African Local Government itself has come to be accepted as a Soga institution. The justice which its courts dispense and the social services which it provides have brought it the respect of the public. The headman himself accepts his rôle in the African Local Government because it allows him to participate in the dominant power system and because it is in keeping with his traditional position as mediator between his people and higher powers.

The headman's dilemma arises from the fact that in order to play these two rôles he has had to give up his traditional source of income without receiving a new one. The tribute which he received under the earlier system was important to him, not only as a symbol of his personal authority over his people, but also as a source of support for the hospitality pattern which he must maintain in order to retain his people's respect. Without some source of income beyond the produce of his own gardens, he cannot maintain this pattern. In some respects, his situation compares poorly with that of the ordinary peasant since he has duties which prevent him from giving his full attention to agriculture. On the other hand, he cannot accept the conditions of full membership in the African Local Government, which would provide a salary, because to do so would be in basic contradiction to his rôle as an hereditary, locally-rooted patriarch.

This is the situation in which the headman finds himself. The social system has, so to speak, changed beneath his feet in such a way that the two aspects of his rôle—his position as local leader and his position as lowest rung on the larger ladder of authority—tend to pull against each other. This is true of all headmen. Different individual personalities, however, handle, or rather try to handle the situation in different ways. No attempt will be made here to deal with these personality differences as such, but it is possible, short of this, to examine some of the different ways in which the headman's conflict of rôle emerges into social behaviour.

Three patterns occur with great enough frequency to be of sociological significance. The first type is the conformist, the headman who accepts the changed situation and attempts to fulfil both aspects of his rôle. He diligently carries out the duties delegated to him by the civil-servant chiefs and at the same time strives to maintain his position in his village or sub-village. It is this type of person who gains the approval of the chiefs and the European administrators. In the yearly competitions which are held by the African Local Government to choose the five most "progressive" villages in Busoga, headmen of this type take an energetic part.[1] There is a tendency, however, for such persons to be drawn off into the African Local Government organisation proper. They may be appointed to African Local Government civil service posts, often as Parish chiefs, whereupon they leave their villages or sub-villages in the hands of stewards or kinsmen.

A second type is the rebel, who feels deprived by the new situation and strikes back by engaging in activities which are considered by others to be illegal or anti-social. He attributes responsibility for his predicament to the Protectorate Government and to the African Local Government, which he identifies with the Protectorate Government, and is therefore hostile in his attitudes towards them. In interviews with headmen of this type, I was frequently reminded of the abolition of tribute and the deprivation which it had caused. I was also frequently told that "the Government is trying to take our land." In terms of the actual policies and practices of the Government, this seems an ill-founded charge, since very little land in Busoga has been alienated to non-Soga and, within recent years, almost none except for such public purposes as road-building and the extension of the boundaries of Jinja town.

[1] Cox, T. R. F., "Village Competitions in the Eastern Province of Uganda," *Journal of African Administration*, Vol. IV, No. 1, 1952, pp. 27–29.

The headmen are aware, however, that the Government is not sympathetic to their position in the land-holding system. Most administrative officers feel that the headmen are simply trustees for the peasants and that they should exercise their reversionary rights merely in order to redistribute unused land, not for personal profit through the collection of allotment fees. This view involves a misunderstanding of Soga customary law, but it has been the basis for Government actions which have tended to reinforce the headmen's view that the Government is hostile to them. Recently, for example, when the boundaries of Jinja town were being extended, the Government compensated the peasants whose land was condemned, but refused to compensate the headmen for loss of their rights in the same land on the ground that no economic loss was sustained by them. This particular case involved only a small area of land, but to many headmen all over Busoga, several of whom mentioned the case to the writer, it formed the basis of a belief that "the Government was trying to steal their land."

Such persons, therefore, though they generally carry out the duties delegated to them by the chiefs, do so grudgingly and at the same time bitterly criticise the Government and the African Local Government. They also engage in manipulations in land in an effort to replace the income from tribute which they feel was unjustly taken from them. The high allotment fees mentioned earlier are one manifestation of this. Another is the frequent attempt by headmen to increase the turnover of tenants and hence to increase their income from allotment fees by asserting their reversionary rights in circumstances where in fact the tenant is still in lawful occupation of his land. Although such attempts are notorious and are much talked about by the peasants, they quite frequently succeed because of the special position which the headman occupies with respect to land. Since he is traditionally the custodian of the land, the courts give special attention to his testimony in land cases. In cases in which he himself is an interested party, he can therefore influence the decision of the court to his own advantage. Headmen also attempt to increase their income from fees by letting land on short term to immigrants of other tribes who come to Busoga for one or two seasons to make a bit of money quickly by cultivating cotton on the rich soil. This, while not strictly illegal, is outside the customary law and is considered by Soga peasants to be an act of tribal disloyalty.

All these illegal or anti-social manipulations in land tend to undermine the customary law, which it is the headman's duty to uphold, and to increase the rate of land litigation. As Table XVIII shows, land cases are frequent and difficult to settle. Forming 7

per cent. of all cases at the Sub-County level, they increase to more
than half of all cases heard by the District court.

Such high rates of litigation over land increase insecurity of
tenure and thus discourage careful husbandry. The jealously with
which many headmen assert their residual rights in land also poses a
problem in connection with the future economic development of
Busoga. Within recent years it has become apparent that some
form of more definitely individual tenure approximating to freehold
will become desirable in order that persons anxious to do so may
apply more modern methods of agriculture. Some form of more
fully individual rights are required in order to increase security of
tenure and thus make greater capitalisation feasible and also in
order to make it possible for land to be sold or pledged. Under the

TABLE XVIII

LAND LITIGATION IN AFRICAN LOCAL GOVERNMENT COURTS, 1950

	Sub-County Courts	County Courts	District Court
Total cases	9,737	1,019	249
Land cases	635	307	139
Land cases as per cent. of total cases	7	30	56

customary land law, these things are not possible because rights in
land are distributed among tenants, headmen and corporate lineages.
No one can freely sell or pledge land. Most headmen, however,
would fiercely resist any attempt to change the law to allow individual tenure because this would involve their giving up the last
vestiges of their rights in land and their income therefrom—the
allotment fees.

A third type of reaction to the conflict situation is exhibited by
the headman who attempts to escape the dilemma by withdrawing
into passive inactivity. He neither co-operates with the civil-
servant chiefs nor pays much attention to his rights and responsibilities in connection with land and his position of authority within
his village or sub-village. He is apt to spend a large part of his
time at beer drinks and may even become a chronic alcoholic.
Passive withdrawal excites much less comment than do the aggressive activities of the rebel, since it less often brings an individual
into active conflict with others. However, the type is clearly
recognised by the peasants, who speak of such persons as "lazy

headmen who neglect their work of looking after the village and the land." Where the headman behaves in this way, it appeared to me that the customary land law again tends to break down, but in a different way. The headman is insufficiently motivated to assert his rights in the land with the result that a kind of *ad hoc*, but illegal, freehold pattern tends to grow up. The village or sub-village becomes essentially leaderless.

These are some of the ways in which village and sub-village headmen attempt to meet the situation in which change has placed them; undoubtedly there are others which did not come to the writer's attention.[1] It is clear, however, that, given the present state of the Soga social system, there is no satisfactory solution to the headman's dilemma. Attempts to resolve the dilemma tend either to bring him into conflict with institutional norms or to lead him to vacate his rôle, either by moving up into the African Local Government organisation or by retreating into inactivity. From the point of view of the system, however, it may well be that these patterns are a prelude to a restructuring of the situation so as to eliminate the dilemma. This question will be taken up in the last chapter, where an attempt will be made to treat the system as a whole as a field of social change.

[1] For an analysis of aggressive, passive and conformist reactions to a rather different sort of {conflict situation see: Merton, R. K., "Social Structure and Anomie," in *Social Theory and Social Structure*, 1949.

CHAPTER VIII.

POLITICS IN PRESENT-DAY BUSOGA:
THE CIVIL SERVANT CHIEF

Official Duties.

In Chapter VI, I described the transformation of the upper levels of the traditional state structure into a hierarchy of "civil servants." The end-product of the process of transformation—the Soga chief of to-day—must now be described in somewhat more detail.

Under the term "civil servant chief" may be included the Parish, Sub-County and County chiefs, persons who are salaried employees of the African Local Government and who are in charge of definite territorial units. As was pointed out in Chapter VI, the hierarchy of chiefs does not represent the whole of the African Local Government organisation. At the apex of the organisation are the elected President and Secretary-General and the specialist officers in charge of finance and special services. At each level, there are councils which serve the double rôle of advising the chiefs and interpreting and transmitting their directives to the people. And at the village and sub-village level, there are the headmen who, though not officially members of the hierarchy, carry out duties delegated to them by the chiefs. But it is the chiefs themselves who are responsible to their immediate superiors and to the British Administration for ordering all these elements in such a way as to make of the African Local Government an instrument of local government which is satisfying to the people and which meets the Administration's standards of justice and efficiency.

Within the hierarchy of chiefs, a further distinction should be made. It is the County and Sub-County chiefs who are both chiefs and civil servants in the fullest sense. County and Sub-County chiefs are pensionable officers, notices of whose appointments and transfers are published in the *Uganda Gazette*, the official Government publication. Under the Native Courts Ordinance, they are statutory magistrates and the Native Authorities Ordinance gives them the power to issue administrative orders having the force of law. The Parish chiefs, on the other hand, are non-pensionable and have no statutory judicial or administrative powers. As will be pointed out later in this chapter, the Parish chiefs' position is a rather anomalous one, since they have neither the locally-rooted authority of the headmen nor the statutory authority of the higher chiefs. For the moment, however, the focus of attention will be upon the County and Sub-County chiefs.

Physically, a chief's headquarters consists of a group of official buildings which are the property of the African Local Government. A Sub-County headquarters invariably includes an office building and a council room as well as official houses for the chief and his staff. As yet, most of these buildings are thatched and have mud and wattle walls, but under the new African Local Government building programme, a number of modern concrete and brick headquarters units have been built. The Sub-County staff normally consists of the chief, his *katikkiro* (really an assistant chief, though he bears the traditional title of a ruler's prime minister), a poll tax clerk, a judicial clerk and two or three policemen. Near each headquarters is an area of official land where members of the staff may cultivate plantains and other crops during their tenure of office.

A County headquarters is a more elaborate affair. Its offices are more spacious to accommodate the larger clerical staff and are equipped with typewriters and, in some cases, telephones. Nearby are the County prison, staffed by a detachment of African Local Government police, and the houses of the staff, including such specialist officers (agricultural and veterinary assistants, health inspectors and the like) as are posted in the County. All County headquarters are now equipped with permanent brick and concrete buildings. In order to carry out his duties, which require much travelling, the County chief must have a motor-car.

Much of the chief's time is occupied in judicial work. The Sub-County chief is president of the Sub-County court, which also includes two "official" members (two Parish chiefs serving in rotation) and two "non-official" members (two persons serving each month from a panel elected by the Sub-County council). After evidence has been heard, judgment is arrived at by voting, with the president exercising a casting vote. The County court is similarly constituted except that there the County chief presides over a bench of three "officials" (Sub-County chiefs) and three elected "non-officials." From the County court, appeal lies to the District court at Bugembe, where the Kyabazinga, or a County chief acting for him, presides over a bench of three Sub-County chiefs and three elected members. Beyond the District court, a litigant may take his case for revision to the District Commissioner and may appeal to the High Court of Uganda in Kampala. At each level, testimony and judgment are recorded by a judicial clerk. If an appeal is lodged, copies of these are forwarded to the court of appeal.

This is not the place to consider in detail the substance of the law administered by the African Local Government courts.   Section 11 of the Native Courts Ordinance, 1940, provides that:

Subject to the provisions of this ordinance, a native court shall administer and enforce only—

(a)   the native law and custom prevailing in the area of jurisdiction of the court, so far as it is applicable and is not repugnant to natural justice or morality or is not, in principle, in conflict with the provisions of any law in force in the Protectorate;

(b)   the provisions of all rules or orders made by a Provincial Commissioner, District Commissioner, or native authority under the Native Authority Ordinance and all Ordinances amending or replacing the same in force in the area in respect of which the court is constituted;

(c)   the provisions of any ordinance or other law which the court is authorised to administer or enforce by the terms of any ordinance; and

(d)   the provisions of any ordinance which the court may be authorised to administer or enforce under section 12 of this ordinance (providing that the Governor may confer jurisdiction under specified ordinances).[1]

The provision that the courts shall not administer such customary law as is "repugnant to natural justice or morality," of course, says little in itself.   In practice it means, as the writer of the *Handbook on Native Courts for the Guidance of Administrative Officers* has put it, that "there are some things which a British Government cannot permit, since they outrage our sense of what is right or just . . ."[2] The brief accounts of the customary law of marriage and land tenure given in an earlier chapter provide an indication of what this means. Subject to the limitations implied by Anglo-Saxon conceptions of personal freedom, customary law is allowed to take its course. It is said, for example, that prior to the establishment of British administration, a widow could be compelled to enter into leviratic marriage.   To-day, of course, such practices would be "repugnant," though the obligation of the widow's guardian to repay the bride-wealth in case the widow refuses to marry her husband's successor is not.   To-day, it is fair to say, the limits which "repugnancy" places upon the application of customary law have become accepted and could only with great difficulty be distinguished from the fabric of the customary law itself.   It is understood, both by administrative officers and by the Soga, that in certain spheres such as

[1] Native Courts Ordinance, 1940.
[2] *Handbook on Native Courts for the Guidance of Administrative Officers*, Government Printer, Entebbe, 1941, p. 9.

marriage, custody of children, land tenure and the like, customary law as administered by the African Local Government courts is the final authority. When such cases are brought to administrative officers for revision, they normally make no attempt to rule upon the substantive law involved, but limit their attention to matters of procedure and evidence.

Two other major "sources" of law are mentioned in the section of the Ordinance quoted above. These are Protectorate legislation, where African Local Government courts are given jurisdiction by the provisions of particular ordinances, and the authority given to chiefs and administrative officers under the Native Authority Ordinance to issue administrative orders having the force of law. An example of the first is legislation establishing the tax obligations of the Soga. Such legislation gives the African Local Government courts authority to try tax defaulters. Administrative orders include both "standing orders," such as the rule compelling peasants to uproot and burn cotton bushes at the end of the growing season in order to control cotton pests and particular orders which a chief or administrative officer may see fit to give in a particular situation, e.g. a chief may order an individual to help carry a sick or injured person to the hospital for treatment. Individuals who disregard such orders may be prosecuted for disobedience. Again, the limits within which such power may be exercised have become quite clearly defined and accepted. A chief may not, for example, exercise it merely for his own comfort or convenience.

Many Anglo-Saxon conceptions of procedure have also been applied and have come to be accepted in the practice of the African Local Government courts. Such principles as the speedy adminis-tration of justice, the finality of judgments subject to appeal to a higher court, the presumption of innocence in criminal proceedings, the distinction between criminal and civil actions, and the obligation to confront the accused with a clear charge have been accepted. The jurisdiction of the courts extends to all African residents of Busoga District. They are provided with the power to summon witnesses and may prosecute for contempt of court. By way of punishment, they may inflict fines, imprisonment or whipping. They may not try cases in which death is alleged to have occurred.[1]

It is perhaps worth noting two important respects in which the customary law as administered by the African Local Government courts differs procedurally from common law as it is known in Britain and America. First, the African Local Government courts lack any established system of precedent. Although the hierarchy of Sub-County, County and District courts constitute a ladder for

[1] Native Courts Ordinance, 1940, Section 10.

appeal, there is no regular means for bringing the judgments of higher courts to the notice of lower court judges. The assumption is that every member of the bench, having been reared under Soga custom, knows the customary law and is able to apply it. While such an assumption might have been justified at the time when British administration began in Busoga, it is hardly so to-day. Custom has changed and is changing in important respects. For example, contemporary Soga judges differ in their views concerning the competence of women to plead in court on their own behalf. All agree that women may themselves appear as defendants in such criminal cases as theft, but there is wide divergence of opinion concerning a woman's competence to appear as a principal in divorce proceedings. Most judges still hold that a woman should be represented in such a case by her father or guardian, but some are coming to believe that she ought to be allowed to act on her own behalf. Other instances might be cited from the sphere of land-holding. It would seem that without some system for assuring a degree of uniformity, change in custom must inevitably bring divergence in the customary law applied by different judges.

A second, and related, important difference between Anglo-Saxon common law and Soga customary law practice lies in the totally amateur character of the latter. Again on the assumption that every Soga knows the customary law, there are in Soga courts neither lawyers nor, in most cases, specialist judges. The assumption here is in large degree justified. Litigation is a prominent part of Soga culture and in general most persons are quite able to stand up in court and plead effectively. Chiefs and unofficial members of the bench acquire considerable expertise "on the job." But as both the judicial and other duties of chiefs become more complex and demanding, it has become apparent that judicial specialists are required. By 1952, three specialist Judicial Officers had been appointed in areas of particularly heavy court activity.

In most cases, however, the African Local Government courts remain the responsibility of the chiefs. An idea of the nature and weight of this responsibility may be derived from Appendix VIII, where the cases heard in one Sub-County court during 1950 are tabulated. These cases show, first, that litigation is an extremely common activity for the Soga. The population of the Sub-County in 1948 was 11,503, of whom 6,782 were adult.[1] If it is assumed that each of the 94 civil actions involved two principal litigants and that each of the 352 criminal actions, not counting the "state," involved one, then 540 persons, or one in every thirteen adults,

---

[1] *African Population of Uganda Protectorate*, East African Statistical Department, 1950, p. 20.

appeared in court as a principal litigant during the year. Secondly, it is of interest that of the criminal cases more than one-half represent offences against either particular orders given by the chief or standing orders which he is responsible for administering. For the most part, these concern local government rules and functions which are new to Soga society and which represent the attempt to make of the African Local Government a local government instrument adequate to the changing conditions of Soga life. Although these rules and functions are on the whole accepted by the Soga, action in accord with them has not yet become easy and automatic. Where Government is an innovator, the courts tend to be burdened with the enforcement of new patterns and habits of life. Finally, one may note in this tabulation of cases the tendency for court action to enter into the internal life of the African Local Government itself. The ten cases of "Failure to do Duty" represent prosecutions against African Local Government personnel for failure to carry out duties allocated to them. As for the Soga at large, the new rules and functions of local government are, for African Local Government servants, still rather tenuously established and must frequently be enforced by judicial sanction.

Tax collection is another responsibility which occupies much of the chief's energies. The actual collection of the poll tax is largely delegated to Parish chiefs and to village and sub-village headmen, but it is the Sub-County chief who is ultimately responsible for seeing to it that every eligible person pays. Every male who reaches the age of eighteen is required to report to the chief to have his name entered in the tax register. When an individual pays his tax for the year, a mark is entered in the register opposite his name and he is given a receipt. Since the peasant's main source of income is his crop of cotton and groundnuts, chiefs make an effort to collect as much of the tax as possible during the cotton and groundnut marketing seasons. Sub-County and Parish chiefs often post themselves at the buying stores and buttonhole the peasants before they have had an opportunity to spend their yearly earnings. Those who fail to pay are prosecuted in the Sub-County court.

The financial side of the chief's responsibilities include not only the collection of taxes, but also the payment of his staff and the handling of court fees and fines. Although he has a clerk to keep his financial records, he spends a great deal of time on these himself, since he is held personally responsible for any irregularity. European administrative officers regard a chief's handling of African Local Government funds as the source of his greatest temptation to deviate from the civil service norm of disinterestedness. Consequently, the best guarantee of favour in their eyes is a well-kept and accurate set of books.

The chief is also chairman of the council in his area of jurisdiction and an *ex-officio* member of the next higher council. It is his duty to represent the official view, i.e. the view of the African Local Government and the Administration, in council discussions. Appendix IX, which is a translation of the minute book of the Sub-County council of Ssabawaali, Bulamogi, for the years 1950 and 1951, illustrates the nature of the councils' activities. Some of these, such as the election of unofficial court members and the remission of poll tax for aged persons, are quite routine. In other cases, the councils are invited by the County chief to discuss matters under consideration by the District council and to send in their suggestions. Although only the District council has budgetary powers, proposals requiring the expenditure of funds may either be referred to lower councils or initiated by them and their suggestions may be taken into account by the Finance Committee of the District council when the annual budget is made up. Many of the discussions mentioned in Appendix IX are of this sort. In general, however, it cannot be said that the lower councils function as effective local government bodies. The matters over which they have actual authority are relatively few and many of the matters referred to them by the District council are so referred because of the District council's reluctance to risk unpopularity by taking action. Representative government is as yet rather poorly integrated into the Soga political system; political initiative still centres largely in the hierarchy of chiefs.

Appendix IX illustrates, however, another rôle played by the councils, the importance of which should not be underestimated. Although they are as yet rather ineffective instruments of responsible local government, in the Western sense, they do serve as forums for the public criticism of African Local Government and Protectorate Government policies. This safety valve rôle is illustrated by the discussions of 20th January, 1951, when a great diversity of complaints were aired.

In his Annual Report for 1950, the Provincial Commissioner complained that:

> The majority of the councils do not regard themselves as the advisors of the African Local Government. They feel, instead, that they should be concerned with the detailed administration of established policy, and they resent any interference with this conception of their duties. Unfortunately this confusion of ideas has been fostered to a large extent by the senior officials of the African Local Government, partly because they themselves have not understood the position

clearly, and partly because they are often reluctant to use their executive authority unless they first satisfy themselves that the action they propose will receive popular support.[1]

It would seem that at present the primary function of the councils *vis-à-vis* the African Local Government organisation is to provide a channel of communication and a forum for establishing consensus between the African Local Government and the people. This is, to some degree, the function of all deliberative bodies everywhere; it was certainly one of the functions of traditional Soga councils. But in Busoga to-day the potentialities for dissensus and lack of communication between the people and the "state" are particularly great, both because of the colonial situation, in which the African Local Government is liable to be charged with being a tool of the Administration, and because of the great gap in technical knowledge between the civil-servant chiefs and the people. The councils help to bridge this gap and to maintain consensus by putting the chiefs in the position of having to defend and explain.

These and many other duties keep the chief very busy indeed. At my request, one Sub-County chief kept a diary of his daily activities over a period of two months in 1951. It indicates more clearly than could any description which I might provide the scope and variety of the civil-servant chief's responsibilities. The diary is reproduced in Appendix III in the rather good English in which it was written. The only changes made are the deletion of names of persons and places and the translation into English of a few Luganda words which in Busoga are used in English conversation. The period represented by this diary was a particularly busy one for the chief. During the first part of the period, cotton was being marketed and so he was pressing the collection of taxes, court fees and fines. This involved frequent checking of his financial records and frequent trips to County headquarters to deliver tax money collected. He found time, however, to hear fifty-two cases in court and to deal with many complaints, most of which he attempted to settle by arbitration without formal legal proceedings. He also met a number of times with various specialist officers of the African Local Government and the Protectorate Government (Health Inspectors, Assistant Agriculture Instructors—all Soga), attended meetings of the County Team (meetings at which County and Sub-County chiefs and specialist officials of the African Local Government come together to plan and co-ordinate African Local Government activities in the area), and held numerous meetings at his own headquarters. During the period, he was visited only once, on 12th

[1] "Annual Report of the Provincial Commission for the Year Ended 31st December, 1950," Central Offices, Jinja.

and 13th March, by a European officer of the Protectorate Government. Except for the meeting at County headquarters on 28th March, when the District Commissioner was present, all his other official contacts were with Soga.

Many of the duties of the Parish chief have been noted incidentally to the description of the work of his superiors, the County and Sub-County chiefs. Unlike the latter, the Parish chief is not a gazetted official; he is not a statutory magistrate, has no subordinate staff, and is not pensionable. In general, however, he acts as an assistant to the Sub-County chief in such matters as tax collection and law enforcement and, within his Parish, resembles a Sub-County chief in miniature. Though his court is unofficial and has no power to enforce its decisions, it does accomplish a substantial amount of arbitration, thus reducing the volume of litigation in the Sub-County courts. The Parish court is often very informal in its constitution, though most Parish chiefs make an effort to secure the assistance of sub-village and village headmen and leading members of local lineage groups to form a bench on the model of the higher African Local Government courts. Often there is no official meeting place. Parish court and Parish council meet in the shade of a tree or in a plantain garden. One Parish chief whom I knew made it a practice to hold court each week at a nearby market, where he could meet the maximum number of people. There he arbitrated disputes, collected poll tax, issued the two-shilling beer-brewing permits which serve both as a source of African Local Government revenue and a discouragement to excessive brewing, and kept an eye open for violations of market rules.

In summarising the official position of the civil-servant chief, it may be said that in many ways his duties are similar to those of a Western civil servant. As a magistrate, he administers a rule of law which, though traditionally Soga in much of its content, is applied to all persons alike and is governed by procedures similar to those which prevail in Western courts. As a tax collector, he handles African Local Government funds as a Western civil servant would be expected to handle them, keeping accurate records and maintaining a strict separation between official funds and his own private resources. As co-ordinator of the work of African Local Government specialist officials and as representative of the official Administration in the councils, again, he operates in ways not unfamiliar to Western conceptions of government. Finally, not only his duties, but also his conditions of service have a fundamentally civil service character. He occupies official housing during his incumbency, is paid according to a fixed salary scale from a central treasury, is pensioned upon retirement, and is subject to transfer and bureaucratic discipline. We must now consider the ways in which chiefs are recruited into the service.

RECRUITMENT: THE PATHS TO POWER.

I have said a number of times in the course of this study that the African Local Government is an accepted institution in the sense that the Soga regard it as a legitimate heir to the authority of the traditional states. One of the aspects of this acceptance is the high prestige which is granted to the chiefs. A career in the African Local Government civil service is regarded as a desirable goal. To some degree, no doubt, this is because few other careers are open to Soga. Until recently, there have been few opportunities for jobs in industry and relatively few Soga have chosen business as a career. The major alternatives to employment in the African Local Government for persons of ability and education are limited to the Anglican and Catholic churches, both of which train African clergymen, teaching in the mission schools, and employment as functionaries of the Protectorate Government. The latter category includes nearly all professional positions, since persons who have qualified, for example, as medical doctors or as veterinary practitioners are nearly all employed by the Protectorate Government. Indeed one of the distinguishing features of present-day Soga society is the degree to which Government—the Protectorate Government and the African Local Government—dominates the power and status system. This point will be taken up again in another place, but for the moment the relevant point is the degree to which the African Local Government as a career appeals to the aspirations of young men. It is my impression, based upon many conversations with secondary schoolboys, that only the medical profession ranks higher than the African Local Government civil service in the esteem of ambitious Soga.

The high status of civil-servant chiefs—particularly County and Sub-County chiefs—may be seen in the deference which they are granted by ordinary people and in their position as part of a national élite for purposes of social life. On public occasions, such, for example, as the annual "Kyabazinga's Day" celebrations at the African Local Government headquarters at Bugembe, the order of precedence is clearly marked. At the church services, tea, feast and football match which go to make up the celebrations, County chiefs and senior headquarters officials are given the places of honour, followed by Sub-County chiefs, headmasters of schools, clergymen and priests and professional men. In the week-end visiting which forms such an important part of informal Soga social life, the County and Sub-County chiefs, together with educated persons in other professions, tend to form social cliques. Such persons share an élite style of life, based upon higher incomes, and in general speak each others' language—the language of high-level politics and of events beyond the ken of peasants.

There exists, then, the motivation to enter the African Local Government service. In theory, a civil service organisation should select from among a field of candidates those persons who are best qualified. One of the aims of the Administration in abolishing hereditary rulership was to make possible recruitment on this basis. However, probably no civil service has ever recruited its officials on the basis of completely free selection. Where entrance is by competitive examination, it may be possible to approximate free selection from among those qualified, but qualifications always include more than simply native ability. Normally, they include training, to which there usually is differential access. In addition, where means other than objective examinations are used as the basis for selection, factors of ascribed status may be involved. In Busoga, where little more than fifty years ago the dominant structural features in the political system were kinship, hereditary rulership and the patron-client relationship, it would be expected that such factors, inhibiting free selection, would be present in some degree. It would also be expected that where a civil service system is instituted in a society in which education is a relatively scarce commodity, access to education would be an important factor in determining who enters the service.

In order to find out the ways in which individuals are actually recruited into the African Local Government organisation, I collected genealogical and brief life history data from a number of County and Sub-County chiefs. The genealogical data for ten chiefs, four County chiefs and six Sub-County chiefs are summarised in Fig. 16. They illustrate some of the ways in which kinship appears to be a factor in recruitment into the African Local Government service. First, all chiefs shown in the diagram are in some way related to one another. They do not represent a random sample of all County and Sub-County chiefs, but on the other hand they were not specifically selected on the basis of their kinship inter-relatedness. They were simply the chiefs with whom I became best acquainted during the fieldwork period. I was not aware of many of the links until I had begun to collate the genealogical data after leaving the field. It may therefore be supposed that had I become well acquainted with other chiefs, similar links would have come to light.

The second point of importance is that the links among these ten chiefs cluster about three royal lineage groups (I, II and III) from three of the traditional states. The most recent ruler in each of the three royal lineages is included in order to show the genealogical positions of the chiefs *vis-à-vis* the direct royal line. However, only one of the chiefs shown (B) is a direct lineal descendant of a ruler. A and L are descended from near collateral lines within the royal lineage. Each of the remaining chiefs is related to one or more of the three royal lineages through maternal or affinal ties. C's mother was the daughter of the ruler in royal lineage I and has himself married the brother's daughter of the ruler in royal lineage II. D is also the son of a princess of royal lineage II. E, F and G are all sons of one man—one of the early commoner County chiefs

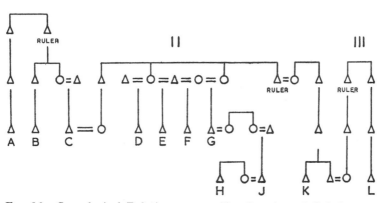

FIG. 16. Genealogical Relations among Ten County and Sub-County Chiefs.

appointed by the Administration—who married two princesses of royal lineage II. K is the grandson of a commoner client-chief in the traditional system who served under the ruler in royal lineage II, who married his sister. All these individuals relate in some recognisable way to the traditional political system. J, although he is related affinally to G, who in turn is descended from a princess, illustrates a more recent phenomenon. He was taken in by Catholic missionaries when a small boy and given an excellent education, ultimately attending Makerere College in Kampala for a number of years. Thus far, he would appear to be an example of a person occupying an important position in the African Local Government without having politically significant kinship ties. However, he has now married the sister of H, a former County chief who has recently become a senior African Local Government headquarters official. H is also a product of the Catholic mission schools and an individual without important kinship connections in the traditional system. But with this marriage of J to H's sister, a new network of politically significant kinship ties begins to arise.

In this group of chiefs it is striking that more of what appear to be the politically significant kinship links are affinal or maternal than are patrilineal. It was pointed out in Chapter IV that in the traditional political system affinal ties, which in the succeeding generation give rise to mother's brother-sister's son relationships, were important in cementing the bonds of personal loyalty between a ruler and his client-chiefs. Patrilineal, affinal and maternal kinship were each important in different ways in ordering relations within the kingdom-state organisation. Under modern conditions, patrilineal kinship in the sense of direct patrilineal succession can no longer operate as a mechanism of recruitment, since the Administration has insisted upon recruitment at least in part on the basis of merit. Maternal and affinal kinship, on the other hand, may more easily continue to be significant where recruitment is partially open. The marriage contract itself involves an area of free choice, so that marriages of convenience may take place and be of political significance even where political rôles are filled in large part on the basis of merit, just as happened in the traditional system in the case of the ruler-client relationship. Polygyny, of course, increases the possibilities here. For the same reasons, any extended kinship ties (as opposed to direct descent) are more suited to a more open system because relationships with particular persons out of a wide range of kin may be selected for emphasis. It may be added that it is probably easier under modern conditions to utilise maternal and affinal kinship links for political purposes because the Administration seems less aware of such ties. While administrative officers keep a sharp lookout for nepotism, most of them appear to think that only patrilineal kinship is important. They think of the traditional system largely in terms of direct patrilineal succession and so tend not to notice kinship ties of other kinds.

It appears, then, that kinship is in some way important in recruitment into the African Local Government civil service. Thus far, however, no account has been given of the formal system of appointment to office. In general, there are two ways of arriving at pensionable rank (Sub-County or County chief rank) in the service. One may either rise by promotion within the service, starting as a clerk or Parish chief, or one may be appointed directly to a Sub-County chieftainship. The formal procedure in either case is that a committee of the District council suggests to the District Commissioner names of persons to be appointed or promoted. The

District Commissioner also consults with the County chiefs, after which he is free to accept or reject the recommendations he has received. In fact, however, a number of factors combine to limit his range of choice. Appointment to lower positions in the service, i.e., Parish chieftainships and clerkships, are made by the County councils and the County chiefs. At the lower levels, then, there is opportunity for kinship to operate relatively freely. This is not to say that the councils do not take account of personal merit. They do, but they also take account of kinship connections. At one County headquarters which I visited, three of the four clerks were members of the royal clan. In the same County, eleven of the twenty-eight Parish chiefs were either members of the royal clan or "sisters' sons" of prominent royal clansmen. Since kinship connections are thus able to operate at the lower levels in the service, this means that when Parish chiefs come up for promotion to Sub-County rank, the field within which the District Commissioner may select has already been narrowed.

The District Commissioner's actual freedom of choice also varies considerably with his own familiarity with Busoga. Administrative officers are frequently transferred from one District to another and so are often not intimately acquainted with many of the chiefs. When a District Commissioner has little personal knowledge of the persons among whom he must select in making appointments and promotions, he becomes greatly dependent upon the County chiefs as sources of information. In fact, in discussing with chiefs their careers in the service, I was struck by the fact that in most cases they attributed their success in getting promotions to the influence of County chiefs who were their friends or kinsmen.

Where individuals are appointed directly to pensionable rank, the District Commissioner's freedom of choice is much greater. Such individuals are usually persons who have become prominent in other fields of endeavour. The proportion of persons appointed directly to pensionable rank may be seen in Table XIX . It may be seen that of the fifty-seven chiefs for whom data were available, fifteen had not previously served in the African Local Government. Comparison of the two groups shows first of all that those directly appointed to pensionable rank have on the whole had more education than those who have been promoted from the lower ranks. Ten of the 15 direct appointees reached Standard VII, while only 16 of the 42 who have risen from the ranks have reached that standard. All four of the chiefs who had attended Makerere College were direct appointees. Partly, no doubt, as a consequence of this higher educational standard, the direct appointees are much more likely to have held jobs in the Protectorate Government prior to their appointment to the African Local Government service. Ten of the 15 direct appointees have held such jobs, while only 12 of the 42 who were promoted from the lower ranks have done so. In a Protectorate Government job, particularly in such jobs as clerk or interpreter, an individual of ability may come to the notice of an administrative officer and be offered a post in the African Local

TABLE XIX

SOCIAL CHARACTERISTICS OF COUNTY AND SUB-COUNTY CHIEFS: 1952*

	Directly appointed to pensionable rank	Promoted from lower African Local Government positions
Clan membership:		
Royal	5	16
Other..	10	26
Age:		
31–35..	2	1
36–40..	—	12
41–45..	4	12
46–50..	3	13
51–55..	3	2
Above 56	1	—
Unknown	2	2
Education:		
Standard I–III	—	5
Standard IV–VI	5	19
Standard VII–IX	5	9
Standard XI–XII	1	7
Makerere College	4	—
Unknown	—	2
Previous Employment:		
African Local Government	—	42
Protectorate Government ..	10	12
Teaching	5	3

* Of the sixty County and Sub-County chiefs in service in 1952, data were available for fifty-seven. These data were made available by the District Commissioner, Busoga.

Government. Similarly, 5 of the 15 direct appointees have been teachers in the mission schools, while only 3 of the 42 others have been teachers. Having served as a teacher in a mission school, an individual may have the support of European missionaries in getting a post in the African Local Government service.

It is clear that education and employment in close proximity to Europeans confers a differential ability to secure direct appointment to the higher grades of the African Local Government civil service. It should not be thought, however, that persons who rise in this way do so entirely independently of social status and kinship ties. On the contrary, the child or the sister's son of a chief has more opportunity to acquire education and thus to find employment in the Protectorate Government or the mission schools. A considerable number of scholarships are now available, but most persons still must pay for education. And since the greatest source of wealth in Busoga has been service in the political system, this means that children or relatives of chiefs are more likely to be educated. In interviews with chiefs who had been appointed directly to pensionable rank, I was frequently told that educational expenses had been met by an individual's father or other relative who was an African Local Government chief. Further evidence pointing to the same conclusion may be found in Table XIX, where the clan affiliation of chiefs is given. Of all the 57 chiefs, 21, or 37 per cent. are members of royal clans. Since the royal clans do not represent anything like 37 per cent. of the Soga as a whole, it is clear that royal clansmen are somewhat more likely to become chiefs than are commoners. But the significant point here is that the proportion of royals to commoners among the direct appointees is not significantly different from that among those who have risen from the lower ranks (5 in 15 as against 16 in 42). It is clear that even where direct appointments to pensionable rank are made by the Administration, factors of kinship and social status continue to play a part in recruitment.

The tendency to appoint more highly qualified persons directly to the higher ranks of the African Local Government will probably increase as education becomes more available and as the duties of the civil-servant chiefs become more complex. Such a tendency would have certain consequences for the African Local Government as a local government organisation and as a career service. On the one hand, although the individual with higher education and with experience in other employment is more able to cope with those aspects of the chief's duties which require knowledge of finance and an ability to understand and co-ordinate the activities of the African Local Government specialist officials, such an individual labours under certain disadvantages in his dealings with the peasants. He is less familiar with peasant life and with customary law than is the person who has previously served as a Parish chief. Of one Sub-County chief who spent most of his life in mission schools and then served as a teacher for a number of years, it is said that he is quite unable to cope with his judicial duties. He is not adept at avoiding litigation by arbitration and in the courtroom has to depend heavily upon his Parish chiefs for advice concerning the application of customary law.

The practice of direct appointment to pensionable rank also tends to lower the morale of Parish chiefs, since the more appointments are made in this way the fewer are their opportunities for promotion. It was noted earlier in this chapter that the position of the Parish chief is in any case a rather difficult one. He is often transferred from one post to the next (of all Parish chiefs in five counties in May, 1952, 47 per cent. had occupied their posts for no more than two and a half years) and so does not have the local prestige and authority of the village headmen. On the other hand, he lacks the statutory judicial and administrative authority of the Sub-County and County chiefs. I noted a tendency in some areas for the chain of authority to by-pass the Parish chief. The Sub-County chief, feeling that the Parish chief had little authority, worked directly with the village headmen. In addition, Parish chiefs' salaries are, of course, lower than those of County and Sub-County chiefs. In 1952, County chiefs' salaries varied from £270 to £600 per year, those of Sub-County chiefs from £90 to £213 per year, and those of Parish chiefs from £28 16s. to £87 12s. per year.[1] If the Parish chief could have a reasonable expectation of promotion, these disabilities could be accepted as part of the civil service pattern requiring persons to start at the bottom and work up. But where a significant portion of the higher posts are filled by direct appointment, chances for promotion become fewer. I often heard Parish chiefs complain along these lines. One of the results is that many young men of education and ability are unwilling to accept Parish chieftainships. Although the salaries of County and Sub-County chiefs are high enough to attract them, Parish chiefs' salaries are not. Fresh out of school, they can earn more as clerks or as Protectorate Government functionaries and can expect to have an opportunity to enter the African Local Government at a higher level later on. Thus Parish chieftainship tends to become a career in itself for persons of lesser ability and education.

CONFLICTING DEMANDS.

The preceding pages have described the official position of the civil-servant chief in the African Local Government organisation and the mechanisms through which chiefs are recruited. We may now look at the position of the chief in the total Soga social system. For the chief is not simply a civil servant; he also occupies rôles in

---

[1] "Busoga African Local Government Estimates, 1952," Office of the District Commissioner, Jinja.

other institutions which have certain definite consequences for his civil servant rôle.

First of all, it may be noted that while the various specific duties of the chief have a clearly civil service character, his total rôle as a chief is unlike anything found in Western civil service systems, at any rate in modern times. Combined in one individual within a single hierarchy of authority are functions which are more usually spread over a number of individuals in co-ordinate authority hierarchies. The chief is a magistrate, an administrator of special services, a tax collector, and a leader of deliberative bodies. He is furthermore endowed with authority to issue, within "reasonable" limits, administrative orders which have the force of law. All these powers and responsibilities inhere in the idea of chieftainship as a single rôle. This is another way of saying that the Soga power system is to a great extent monolithic. There is essentially only one centre of authority: the hierarchy of civil-servant chiefs and, extending beyond it, the similarly monolithic authority system of the Protectorate Government. Furthermore, the dominance of the African Local Government in the political sphere is not balanced by co-ordinate systems of status and power in other spheres. Few Soga have made a success of business and relatively few have acquired wealth and prestige working as employees of private firms. Professional specialists by and large work for the Protectorate Government. This means that the chief is not only the most powerful person in his area but also the wealthiest person and the person with the highest social prestige.

This monolithic pattern might be seen from one point of view as a direct continuation of the structure of the state. The traditional chief was a judge, an administrator and a military leader. The ruler was all of these and in addition the chief priest. Economic life was relatively little developed and there were few specialists of other kinds. The tendency of the traditional chief or ruler to gather about him superiority in all spheres of life finds many parallels in the position of the modern civil-servant chief. Evidence for a direct continuity between the old pattern and the new may be found in the tendency of present-day Soga to think and speak of the African Local Government as the direct descendant of the traditional state. Though the system has changed, they think of it in terms of direct continuity through time. For example, when speaking of the client-chiefs in the traditional system, they often say: "so and so was *waggombolola* (Sub-County chief)" of a certain area, using the modern term for a civil-servant chief. Similarly, one often hears people say: "in the old days *bamasaza* (County chiefs) were hereditary," again using the terminology of the modern African Local Government.

Another bit of evidence is provided by the tendency of those persons who have achieved status in other occupations to model their behaviour upon the chiefly pattern. Soga clergymen, for example, often show this tendency.

On one occasion, I was present in the home of a clergyman when a little girl and her father arrived to ask the clergyman for a new certificate of baptism. The girl had lost her certificate and needed a new one in order to qualify for confirmation the following Sunday. The clergyman and the father treated the situation exactly as if the clergyman had been a chief and the father had been a litigant pleading his case. The clergyman sat in dignified silence while the father told the circumstances under which the certificate had been lost and the reasons why a new one was required. When the father had finished, the clergyman looked very grave and, after the manner of a chief delivering judgment, informed the father that his request had been granted, whereupon the father fell to his knees and profusely thanked the clergyman, moving his clasped hands up and down in the traditional gesture of gratitude for chiefly favour.

Similar patterns may be observed in all spheres of life. The pattern of courtly behaviour is carried over into interpersonal relations of all kinds. A subordinate in any situation may address his superior as *mukama wange*, "my lord," following the mode of address used by subordinates in the political system when addressing superiors.

The carrying over into present-day life of features of the traditional society is not surprising, of course, when it is remembered that those changes which have taken place have occurred within the life-span of living individuals. But the dominance of the chiefly ideal and the monolithic structure of Soga society need not be accounted for solely in terms of survival from earlier times. The colonial situation has in many ways tended to perpetuate and reinforce the traditional pattern. Until quite recent times, when the "responsible local government" notion has become dominant, the main aim of the Administration *vis-à-vis* the Soga political system was to make of it an instrument for the maintenance of law and order. The traditional monolithic authority system was ideally suited to this purpose and the Administration strengthened it by giving it statutory recognition. As a matter of fact, the Protectorate Government itself is in many ways similar in structure. Although there is a somewhat greater differentiation of function than in the African Local Government, the administrative officer (as distinguished from the specialist departmental officer) also has extremely wide powers and responsibilities. He is a magistrate, has wide fiscal responsibilities, may issue administrative orders which have the force of law, and is responsible for co-ordinating the activities of the special departments of the Protectorate Government in his area. It seems possible that the Protectorate Administration itself formed a model for the development of the African Local Government.

Soga society, therefore, tends to be dominated by the African Local Government organisation. Power, wealth and prestige all cluster about the civil-servant chief. This very fact places upon him great pressure to deviate from the civil service norm of disinterestedness. Lord Acton's statement that "power corrupts" was meant to express a general truth, but in a society in which extended kinship ties are of great structural importance, the pressure upon the holder of power to exert it in a less than disinterested way is particularly great. The chief is continually pressed to use his position to the advantage of his kinsmen. This pressure is manifested in a number of ways. He is, for example, expected to help as many of his kinsmen as possible to get an education. Since chiefs' families are usually polygynous, he normally has many children of his own to educate, but he is also expected to help the children of his brothers and sisters and even more extended relatives. If his headquarters are near a mission school, he always has a number of young kinsmen living in his household. These obligations are a great drain upon his financial resources and are one of the reasons for the not infrequent cases of embezzlement of African Local Government funds by chiefs.

Demands by kinsmen are sometimes more directly incompatible with the civil service norm of disinterestedness. Such is the case, for example, when a senior chief is pressed to use his influence to secure for a kinsman an appointment in the African Local Government service. As was indicated earlier in this chapter, the chief has opportunities to use his influence in this way and often does so. Chiefs may also be expected to favour kinsmen when deciding court cases. Since the extended kinship system makes it possible to trace significant kinship with a wide range of relatives, it not infrequently happens that litigants who appear in the African Local Government courts have some claim to kinship with the chief.

On one occasion, I was present when an old woman came into a Sub-County chief's office. She wanted to bring a case against her neighbour for possession of a plantain garden. Since she was a classificatory "mother" to the chief, she felt that she could bring the case directly to his court without first taking it to the headman and the parish chief for arbitration. The chief explained to her that this was impossible; she would have to go through the proper channels. When she had left, angry with her "son" for refusing to grant what she saw as a legitimate request, the chief turned to me and shook his head. "These people," he said, "just don't understand." He added that he knew that if she failed to receive satisfaction from the headman and the Parish chief she would be back and would expect her case to receive special consideration.

Chiefs often ask to be transferred in order to escape from kinship obligations. Busoga is a small country, however, and kinship obligations have a way of following one about. Most chiefs have kinsmen of some description in almost every part of the District. And if the chief takes a wife in the new area, he finds himself entangled in a further network of kinship ties.

Another consequence of the monolithic structure of Soga society is to bring politics into the African Local Government civil service. Aside from the civil service, there are few other spheres in which personal ambition for wealth and power may be satisfied. Opportunities in the economic sphere are scarce and the councils as yet have neither the power nor the prestige to be attractive to the ambitious individual. Where, as in most Western countries, the civil service is merely the administrative arm of an elected legislature and executive, its officials may be relatively insulated from the struggle for power. In Busoga, however, significant opportunities for exercising power may be found only within the civil service itself. A senior chief who has the confidence of the Administration can, by influencing recruitment into the service, build up for himself a considerable following of personal dependents in a manner not unlike that of the traditional ruler with his staff of client-chiefs. He can also effectively keep them in line through his influence with the Administration.

The ability of senior chiefs to use the Administration as a political weapon is increased, not only by the frequent ignorance of the administrative officer of conditions in the District and his consequent dependence upon the information which he receives from the senior chiefs, but also by the generally low level of communication which prevails between Soga and Europeans. Uganda does not have a single official language. A number of Bantu and Nilotic languages are used as official media in different parts of the Protectorate and consequently few administrative officers speak any of them well. This means that most administrative officers do not communicate easily with non-English-speaking Soga. Therefore, it is quite easy for a senior chief, who usually speaks good English, to reward his friends and punish his enemies among subordinate chiefs through the reports concerning their work which he gives to the Administration. Those whom he wishes to punish, he can prevent from receiving promotions and can even bring about their dismissal from the service. It is well known among Soga that more than once a senior chief has been able to fabricate a charge of embezzlement of African Local Government funds against another chief whom he wished to punish.

In 1949 and 1952, when elections for the offices of President and Secretary-General were held, the personal "political machines" of several of the senior chiefs were mobilised in support of one or another of the candidates. The campaign crystallised around two candidates, each of whom was an heir to rulership in one of the traditional kingdom-states. The African Local Government civil service divided itself into two factions, each chief using his influence to support the candidate to whom he was most closely tied by bonds of kinship. Strictly speaking, the President and Secretary-General are not really elected. The Governor of the Protectorate may or may not accept the result of the voting. But in most elections which have been held thus far, the Governor has accepted the result and has appointed the winning candidate. In both elections, the same factions have formed and have created incipient political parties within the African Local Government organisation.

However, in spite of all these pressures toward deviation from the civil service norm of disinterestedness, the norm is not simply something imposed from the outside by the Administration. It is a norm which is widely accepted by the chiefs and by the Soga. Partly, as was pointed out in Chapter VI, the norm is accepted because it has been introduced by stages and at each stage those who were in office at the time had committed themselves so completely to the Administration that they had no alternative but to accept further innovations. Partly, also, the norm has come to be accepted because many (to-day it would be proper to say nearly all) of the chiefs have been educated in mission schools where they have internalised it as an aspect of Christian ethics. But also the civil service system itself tends to produce in its members and in the Soga at large an acceptance of the norm. The chiefs' position as the core of a national élite tends to produce in them a group feeling— an *esprit de corps*—which supports the rules of the system in which they play rôles. Individual chiefs of ability wish to have their abilities rewarded by promotion for merit, even though they themselves may occasionally engage in nepotism. And the peasants have come to expect equality of treatment, even though they themselves may from time to time expect a kinsman who is a chief to give them special consideration.

It is of the essence of the present-day position of the Soga chief that he has placed upon him conflicting demands. He and those with whom he inter-acts accept the civil service norm of disinterest-edness. But also, both he and others accept the traditional obliga-tions between kinsmen. Both norms are institutionalised; both are accepted by the same individuals. A peasant demands special consideration from his kinsman who is a chief, but complains when special consideration is given to others. A chief may think it legitimate to utilise his kinship connections to secure promotion, but he feels outraged if another chief does the same thing. Each individual wishes to apply in a given situation the norm which is to his own advantage.

In order to continue to hold his position, the chief must somehow try to reconcile these conflicting demands. He cannot completely fulfil both sets of expectations, but must try to compromise a little with each. If he is too rigid in his disinterestedness, he alienates his kinsmen, and if his kinsmen include a senior chief who has influence with the Administration, this may bring about his dis-missal. Likewise, if he considers only his kinship obligations, he may bring down upon himself charges of nepotism and favouritism. Brought to the attention of the administration, these accusations may also bring about his dismissal. It is not surprising, therefore, that dismissals from the service are quite frequent. During the ten-year period from 1st January, 1941 to 1st January, 1951, seven County or Sub-County chiefs were dismissed.[1] The number who were in effect dismissed is actually probably somewhat greater than this. Often, a chief whom the Administration wishes to be rid of is allowed to retire so that he may not lose his pension. It is therefore likely that a portion of the twenty-four chiefs who retired during that same period were also persons who were not skilful enough in reconciling the conflicting demands. They are the perhaps unavoidable human wastage of a rapidly changing social system.

The conflicting demands may be in some measure reconciled or balanced by skilfully avoiding situations in which one must fully commit oneself in one way or the other. A chief may accomplish this in some measure by getting himself transferred into an area in which he has few kinship ties. It may also be partially accomplished by a careful selection of occasions for satisfying one set of expecta-tions or the other. The most successful (those who have been able to serve for long periods without making many enemies) appear to be those who are able to judge most shrewdly which kinsmen must be satisfied and which may safely be treated disinterestedly. All kinsmen are not of equal influence. A kinsman who is an influential

---

[1] *Uganda Gazette*, 1941–51.

senior chief must at all costs be propitiated, while an ordinary peasant perhaps need not be. Because of the degree to which the chiefs tend to be interrelated, however, even the most skilful sometimes find themselves in the position of having to choose between obligations to two persons, both of great influence. It is not sufficient merely to "butter up" the Administration while playing kinship politics behind the scenes. Administrative officers tend to be suspicious of the "good boy"; in any case, senior chiefs have a real measure of control over the Administration's sources of information.

In the present state of Soga society, there is no satisfactory solution to the situation of rôle conflict in which the civil-servant chief finds himself, just as there is no satisfactory solution to the rather different dilemma which confronts the village headman. Resolution of the conflict can only come through further change in the system.

Chapter IX

POLITICS IN PRESENT-DAY BUSOGA: THE PROTECTORATE GOVERNMENT

The Rôle of the Administrative Officer.

Thus far in this book, the British Protectorate Government has not been studied directly. It has been referred to as a source of influences impinging upon Soga society—often with very great effect—but such influences have so far been treated as "given" in the situation, factors impinging from outside the field of social life under analysis. No attempt has been made to examine the European Administration as a social field in itself or as part of a larger social field also embracing the Soga.

Such has been the most common practice among writers of anthropological monographs concerning peoples under administration and there are obvious arguments for following it. It is the anthropologist's task, one might argue, to analyse precisely those social phenomena which are, to Westerners, unfamiliar and hence in need of elucidation. It is his cross-cultural perspective which gives his work value; concerning persons or institutions of his own or similar societies, he is less able to be objective. Furthermore, it is sometimes argued, administrators may be offended at being treated as objects for study.

While recognising that there are difficulties, I nonetheless feel, for several reasons, that the attempt should be made to examine the European Administration as an integral part of the total political system in Busoga. On the one hand European administrative officers and Soga chiefs and headmen to-day really are members of a single political system. In what sense they are members of a single "society" will be discussed in Chapter X, but for the moment it is enough to observe that together they form a single hierarchy of authority. The rôle of the administrative officer is as much a part of the system as is the rôle of the chief or headman and an understanding of the total system therefore requires an understanding of his rôle.

In addition, in so far as studies such as this one are relevant to policy considerations, neglect of the administrative officer's rôle is in a sense unfair to him. An important aspect of an anthropologist's work in analysing social situations consists in his putting himself in the place of persons whose social positions he studies.

Part of what emerges, therefore, is an exposition of the average point of view or "outlook" of persons occupying the rôles in question. Thus, in Chapters VII and VIII, I have tried to look at the Soga political system from the point of view of the headman and the civil-servant chief respectively. (This exposition of the point of view of one playing a social rôle is, of course, only one part of the anthropologist's task; he must also concern himself with the structure and functioning of the system as a whole—the resultant of all the different social rôles which are contained in it.) If, therefore, one examines only some of the important rôles in the system, and not others, the result is, in a sense, a biased view. Particularly is this true where the system is in the process of radical change and therefore not well integrated. In such situations, any particular social rôle, as I have shown in the case of the headman and the civil-servant chief, is likely to involve for its occupant conflicting institutional pressures—"problems," "difficulties," "dilemmas." This is as true for the administrative officer as for other persons in the system. Thus, far from insulting him, a careful and dispassionate analysis of his rôle, such as I have tried to provide for chiefs and headmen, is necessary to an appreciation of the difficulties of his task and hence to an understanding of the problems of the system as a whole.

Thus the effort is, I believe, worth making, though difficulties remain. For one thing, it is less easy in the case of administrative officers than in the case of headmen and chiefs to generalise—to get away from individual idiosyncracy and to see the general rôle or structural position—simply because administrative officers are so few as compared with chiefs or headmen. Sociological analysis deals with the general, the typical. But only some eight administrative officers were posted in Busoga during my visit, never more than six at one time. While I have become acquainted with a handful of others posted in other Districts, still the number is unsatisfactorily small. I am in danger of presenting as aspects of the general rôle of administrative officer features which, in fact, pertain only to the personalities of particular persons whom I happen to have known.

One further *caveat* must be stated. Having implied that I am taking as my field for analysis, not just the social system of the Soga, but the social system of Busoga District, I shall be inconsistent and not really fulfil this programme. I have not and do not intend to deal as such with the substantial Asian community in Busoga, though in fact they are most important participants in the total social system of the District. Again, among Europeans, I shall concern myself almost exclusively with administrative officers, neglecting Protectorate Government officials of other types as well as Europeans engaged in private business, missions and other occupations.   As regards the Asian community, my excuse is that analysis of their place in the social system would require a working knowledge of the East African variants of Indian and Arab cultures —in itself a substantial research task.[1]   I justify the restriction of attention to administrative officers within the European community on the ground that the focus of this study is the political system of Busoga.   Among Europeans in Busoga, it is the administrative officers whose rôles are most directly concerned with politics. My delineation of the field for analysis, as is perhaps always the case in sociological studies, is thus a compromise.   I can only hope that the nature of and justification for this particular compromise have been made sufficiently explicit.

I must first describe briefly the organisation of the Protectorate Government within which the administrative officer works.   The chief executive of Uganda is the Governor, who is responsible for the administration of the Protectorate to the Secretary of State for the Colonies at the Colonial Office in London and thus, ultimately, to Parliament.   The seat of government is Entebbe, some twenty miles to the south-west of Kampala, in Buganda, where the central Secretariat and the headquarters of the main Government departments are located.   The Governor is advised by an Executive Council and legislative measures are debated by a Legislative Council of which he is President.   To these deliberative bodies we may return later in this chapter; for the moment our principal concern is with the executive organisation of Government.   Outside the headquarters organisation at Entebbe, the Protectorate is divided into Provinces and, within each Province, into Districts; here Government comes to life in the sense that policies decided upon at higher levels are put into effect.   It is at the Provincial and District levels that we may see the place of the administrative officer in the total complex of Government.

The administrative officer—the Provincial Commissioner at the provincial level and the District Commissioner and Assistant District Commissioners at the District level—is the principal executive officer within his area and is personally responsible to his superior (the Provincial Commissioner in the case of the District Commissioner, the Governor in the case of the Provincial Commissioner) for its order and well being.   Though specialist departmental officers (Agriculture, Education, Police and the like) stationed in the Districts and Provinces are under the authority of their

[1] Such a study is now being carried out by my colleague at the East African Institute of Social Research, Stephen Morris.

department heads at Entebbe, responsibility for co-ordinating their activities within the administrative unit lies with the administrative officer. In particular, he is responsible for co-ordinating all Government activity relating to Africans. In Uganda where, as we have seen, settled communities of other kinds are relatively small, this tends to cover nearly the whole range of Government activity at District and Provincial levels.

Busoga is an administrative District within the Eastern Province. The town of Jinja, however, contains three administrative headquarters. Both the District and Provincial headquarters are located there and in 1952 there was a separate organisation for Jinja Township, which had its own District Commissioner and thus constituted a separate administrative "District."[1] Jinja is thus not a typical District headquarters; the official European community is larger and more varied than is the case in most Uganda District stations. Table XX lists the European officials of the various departments who were stationed in Jinja during 1952. Of the total of 78 officials, only 6 were administrative officers and of these only 4, the District Commissioner, Busoga, and 3 Assistant District Commissioners, were posted to Busoga District, the other two being the Provincial Commissioner, Eastern Province, and the District Commissioner, Jinja. All the other officials posted in Jinja were members of specialist departments.

Thus the administrative officer is a non-specialised official with the general responsibility of co-ordinating the work of specialists of many kinds. This rôle has many counterparts elsewhere in the bureaucratic structures which are such a prominent feature of modern Western society. The "line" officer in military organisations and the executive in large business firms share a similar sort structural position *vis-à-vis* specialist officials. Indeed, the position of generalised executive co-ordinator is probably inherently necessary in the modern Western type of occupational organisation, emphasising as it does a high degree of division of labour, but at the same time rational planning. The rôle of the colonial administrative officer, like that of the military line officer or the business executive, involves, however, certain difficulties for its occupant. Although he is responsible for over-all planning and co-ordination, he often does not share the specialised training and experience of the persons whose activities he is charged with co-ordinating. In accord with the modern Western emphasis upon specialisation, specialist officials are apt to resent the superior authority of one who appears to them to have no special competence. Administrative officers

[1] The administrative organisation of Jinja Township is described in Sofer, Cyril, and Ross, Rhona, "Jinja Transformed," *East African Studies* (in press).

usually have had general university education, but few have special professional training.[1]   Indeed, the emphasis in conversations among administrative officers concerning the training desirable in their field is upon general education and leadership qualities. Put another way, administrative officers feel that they are specialists in decision-making and responsibility-taking, just as departmental

TABLE XX

EUROPEAN PROTECTORATE GOVERNMENT OFFICIALS
STATIONED IN JINJA DURING 1952*

Department	Number of Officials
Administration	6
Accountant General	2
Agriculture	2
Co-operative Development	1
Education..	2
Forests	1
Geological Survey	2
Judicial	1
Labour	2
Medical	14
Police	10
Prisons	1
Social Welfare	1
Public Works	23
Stenographic†	2
Survey, Lands and Mines	2
Township Authority	2
Veterinary	1
Miscellaneous Services	3
Total	78

* Source: *European Staff List*, 1952, Government Printer, Entebbe.
† Exclusive of temporary secretarial employees.

officials are specialists in the application of particular types of technical skill or knowledge.   This difference in point of view is sometimes productive of misunderstanding and ill-feeling within the Governmental organisation.   Departmental officials sometimes feel that "the Administration" stands in the way of progress in their particular fields, while administrative officials feel that the

[1] Of the 109 regular administrative officers in service in Uganda in 1952, 68 held university degrees.   Of these, 53 were graduates of Oxford or Cambridge.   (Source: *European Staff List*, 1952, Government Printer, Entebbe, 1952.)   The number of university graduates in 1952 was probably abnormally small, since acute staff shortages at the end of World War II were met by recruitment from other sources, such as the armed forces.   In normal times, one gathers, recruitment is to a greater degree concentrated upon university graduates.

specialists become so engrossed in their particular areas of concern as to lose sight of general problems and aims. It must be emphasised again, however, that this problem of friction between the specialist and the general executive is not peculiar to colonial government; it is a common feature of bureaucratic organisation everywhere in the modern world.[1]

Another feature of the administrative organisation which is shared by bureaucratic systems elsewhere is the frequent feeling of frustration by the man on the spot with what seems to him irrelevant or misguided directives from above. Administrative officers often feel that they, being directly involved in the problems of administration, are better able to decide what should be done than remote officials in Entebbe or London. Inevitably the broad outlines of policy are laid down at higher levels and inevitably these often fail to take account of all the different conditions obtaining in different areas. Often, too, policy decisions at the highest (i.e. Colonial Office) level are influenced by considerations of world politics as well as by local conditions, or so it frequently appears to the administrative officer. Again, this problem is not peculiar to colonies. The problem of reciprocal communication between policy-making and application levels is common to complex bureaucratic organisations everywhere. I take note of it here because, though not unique or even unusual, it is an important feature of the situation in which the administrative officer finds himself.

What is peculiar to the colonial situation, and in particular to the Uganda type of colonial situation, is the type of decisions and responsibilities which administrative officials are required to undertake. The long-term policy aim of Britain in Uganda is the transformation of the Protectorate into a modern, self-governing state.[2]

---

[1] This is a feature which, incidentally, may also be expected to become more prominent in the African Local Government organisation as it approximates more closely to the Western type of civil service bureaucracy.

[2] A statement by the Governor in connection with recent proposals for constitutional reform in Uganda reiterates this policy: "The Secretary of State for the Colonies on behalf of H.M. Government stated in the House of Commons on 23rd February, 1954, that 'the long-term aim of H.M. Government is to build the Protectorate into a self-governing state' and that 'when self-government is achieved the government of the country will be mainly in the hands of Africans.' He also stated that 'when the time for self-government eventually comes H.M. Government will wish to be satisfied that the rights of minority communities resident in Uganda are properly safeguarded in the constitution, but this will not detract from the primarily African character of the country . . . .' In accordance with this statement of policy, the ultimate aim of constitutional development in Uganda is a responsible Government answerable to an elected Legislature of the whole Protectorate, with proper safeguards for the rights of minority communities resident in Uganda." *Agreed Recommendations of the Namirembe Conference*, Government Printer, Entebbe, 1954, Appendix B, p. 15.

Toward this end, it is felt, the administrative officer has a double responsibility. On the one hand, he must encourage Africans to take responsibility and must help them to develop institutions adequate to self-determination. On the other hand, he must himself remain responsible, in the meantime, for seeing to it that his area is governed in accord with what are felt to be proper standards of "good government." He must slowly let go of his own authority while at the same time remaining responsible for the just and proper exercise of the authority which he is relinquishing. This double requirement of encouraging self-government while at the same time maintaining good government (meaning, roughly speaking, government according to modern Western standards of disinterested administration) places upon the administrative officer a heavy burden indeed. Someone has remarked that socialism would be an excellent system, but that a socialist society could only be properly governed by geniuses and archangels. Whatever the case with socialism, something very similar could with much truth be said of the colonial policy of "training for self-government." The carrying out of his responsibilities requires of the administrative officer very great devotion, intelligence and restraint.

I should perhaps repeat again the declaration of neutrality which I made in Chapter I. I most emphatically am not undertaking to pass judgment upon Uganda Government policy, just as I do not pass judgment upon any particular point of view represented among the Soga. Statements concerning the difficulties of the administrative officer's rôle I regard as statements concerning social fact about which, of course, I may be mistaken. My saying that the rôle is a difficult one does not in any sense imply that it should, in a moral sense, be otherwise. Commonly enough, difficult situations may be morally evaluated as "inevitable" or "the best possible under the circumstances."

It is for obvious reasons difficult to particularise concerning the problems facing the administrative officer in his task of training the Soga for self-determination; to cite particular examples would sometimes be to abuse personal confidence. Enough has been said in my account of the African Local Government, however, to indicate the sort of difficulty which arises. The administrative officer is charged with tutoring the African Local Government both toward greater responsibility and toward the discharge of this greater responsibility in what Westerners conceive to be a just and disinterested manner. The Western civil service norm of disinterestedness has achieved a substantial degree of acceptance within Soga society, but this acceptance is as yet not unqualified. It is qualified in that, though the norm itself is accepted as "good," other norms, such as personal loyalty between kinsmen and between patron and client, are also still institutionalised in the social system. The Soga, as individuals and as groups, are literally of two minds about how authority should be exercised. Hence the civil service norm is often violated and hence the administrative officer must restrain and sometimes punish. It is accepted, however, that the African Local Government can only develop greater responsibility and adherence to the civil service norm by being given greater opportunities to exercise responsibility. Greater responsibility, however, means greater opportunity to deviate from the norm of disinterestedness. The administrative officer is often held personally responsible for such deviation when it occurs. Thus in cases of misappropriation of African Local Government funds by chiefs or other African Local Government officials, the administrative officer may in certain circumstances be held personally responsible for making up the loss because he is broadly responsible for seeing to it that the District is well governed. He must thus oversee the work of the African Local Government with sufficient thoroughness to prevent serious maladministration but not so thoroughly as to stifle the development of initiative and responsibility. Needless to say, the middle way in these matters is most difficult to determine.

It is generally held among administrative officers that the difficult judgments which they are called upon to make are only possible for a person who is intimately acquainted with the people among whom he serves. The African societies which make up the Uganda Protectorate are recognised to be very diverse in their traditional culture and social organisation. It is further recognised that, in the nature of the contemporary situation, as I have outlined it for Busoga in previous chapters, politics in these societies is often of the "underground" or "back room" variety and hence difficult to penetrate and to understand. It is therefore believed that the administrative officer, in order to carry out his complex and delicate task of cautiously relinquishing authority, must have a good working knowledge of the society. He must acquire the confidence of the people and know their ways. For these reasons, high value is placed upon continuity of personnel within the District and upon frequent and extensive touring. Many administrative officers make great efforts to learn the local language and to develop personal association and friendship with chiefs and other African Local Government officials.

A number of factors, however, militate against close and continuous association between administrative officers and Soga. One such factor is a by-product of the very policy of indirect rule and devolution of responsibility which the administrative officer is charged with applying and which has, broadly speaking, governed policy in Uganda almost from the beginning. As more and more responsibility passes out of the hands of Europeans and into the hands of Soga, the points of contact between Europeans and the Soga as a whole become fewer. The application and teaching of Western ideas and techniques tend more and more to be carried out by Africans. This process occurs over a much broader field than the African Local Government itself. First steps have been taken toward the gradual Africanisation of the Protectorate Government service. During my visit in Busoga, the Protectorate Government post of Medical Officer of Health was held by a Soga and it has been announced that Africans will soon be appointed to administrative officer posts. The educational system, too, tends to be Africanised as more Soga teachers are trained. Not, of course, that there are fewer European officials and teachers in Busoga; on the contrary, there are more of both to-day than ever before. But the process of Westernisation operates over an increasingly wide area and affects more and more people. Of the total volume of Westernisation occurring in the country, a larger and larger proportion occurs in relations between one African and another instead of in relations between Europeans and Africans.

Among Soga chiefs, for example, the younger ones, who on the whole are better educated than their seniors, have nevertheless had less personal contact with Europeans. Nearly all of the older chiefs had intimate personal contact with early missionaries and teachers. Many were mission boys who were taken into missionaries' homes and educated by missionaries themselves. To-day most mission schools are completely or in large part staffed by African teachers and students passing through them have little personal association with Europeans.

Technological progress has also tended to decrease the intimacy of Soga-European contacts. Early administrative officers came to Uganda without their families. Touring was often done by foot *safari*, and relatively long periods were spent at chiefs' headquarters. Such informal sociability as officers enjoyed was perforce spent in the company of Soga. Later, however, improved health conditions permitted officers to bring their families and the self-contained European social life of the District station, with its European club and its round of reciprocal entertaining, developed. Motor cars and improved roads made it possible for officers to tour more quickly and thus to spend more leisure hours in Jinja.

All these developments are the inevitable by-products of "progress." They mean, however, that personal association between the Soga and Europeans, including administrative officers, is somewhat less intimate than before. This is often remarked upon by Soga chiefs, particularly older ones who remember earlier conditions.

A young Sub-County chief and an elderly County chief were having dinner with me. When food was served, the County chief quite naturally began eating in the European way. The younger man, however, hesitated and said to me with some embarrassment, pointing to the cutlery: "You must show me how to use these. I have never eaten with a European." He had had some secondary education, spoke excellent English, and had a very respectable knowledge of world affairs derived from extensive reading of newspapers and books. The older man laughed and remarked, in much less fluent English: "You young men do not know the Europeans." He then went on to tell us stories of his boyhood life in the home of an Anglican missionary.

There are, it should be noted, dangers for the administrative officer in too-intimate association with Soga chiefs and other officials under his authority. I have described elsewhere the pattern of patron-clientship which was so important a feature of traditional Soga political structure and which survives to-day in the African Local Government organisation. The desire for personal attachment to a powerful superior is very much alive to-day and administrative officers may easily become the object of such desires. In the circumstances of Soga society, casual friendliness may easily be interpreted as favouritism. I was struck, for example, by the frequency with which chiefs attributed their success in the service to personal relations with administrative officers. The patron-client pattern is, of course, alien to the norms governing the administrative officer's rôle just as it is alien to the official norms of the African Local Government. Officers must be wary of being "captured" by particular persons or groups within the African Local Government and thus becoming involved in its internal factional politics. Aloofness, however, also has its dangers. As I have noted, personal knowledge of the District and its people is felt to be a prerequisite to good administration. Furthermore, the official impersonality which in the Western world is accepted as part of the civil service pattern may in Busoga take on overtones of racial discrimination in the minds of Africans.

The bureaucratic nature of his position and the increasing complexity of his duties also militate against the administrative officer's maintaining close and continuous contact with the people under his administration. Though everyone deplores the fact, administrative officers are transferred from one district to another with great frequency and hence have insufficient opportunity to acquaint themselves with the Districts they administer and to learn the languages. In the twenty-year period from 1931 to 1950, for example, Busoga had fifteen different District Commissioners.[1] In part this high frequency of transfers was due to wartime conditions and efforts are now being made to achieve greater continuity. The structure of the Administrative Service itself, however, would appear to make relatively frequent transfers inevitable. Districts, and even Provinces would appear to be too small to form self-contained units for purposes of promotion. Promotion thus often involves transfer to another District or Province. The system of extended home leave in England following each tour of duty also tends to encourage transfers. It is felt that Districts cannot be left for long periods in charge of junior officers and so a senior officer tends to be brought in from another District and the officer on leave to be sent elsewhere upon his return.[2]

As government, both Protectorate Government and African Local Government, becomes more complex, so do the duties of the administrative officer. Added functions mean added paper work and this, he often feels, chains him to his desk in Jinja and prevents his touring the District with sufficient frequency to enable him to know it well. Again, the trend is deplored by all, but it would seem to be inevitable. An increasingly important part of the communication between administrative officers and the African Local Government is carried out, not through personal contact by officers on tour, but through written communication between the government Central Offices in Jinja and the African Local Government Headquarters at Bugembe.

GOVERNMENT BY MINUTE PAPER.

I have noted in Chapter VIII some of the consequences of the lack of easy communication and mutual understanding between administrative officers and Soga for the maintenance of the civil service norm of disinterestedness in the day-to-day governing of the District. Poor communication increases the possibility of undetected graft and corruption and, by making the administrative officer dependent upon information received from English-speaking

---

[1] *Uganda Gazette*, 1931–50.
[2] The Uganda Government has recently attempted to eliminate this source of frequent shifting of personnel by making leave periods shorter and more frequent. Thus, it is hoped, it may be unnecessary to replace officers on leave.

senior chiefs, increases the effectiveness of "framing" as a weapon in the internal factional politics of the African Local Government. Poor communication also affects the success of Protectorate Government programmes for economic and political development in the District. Often the Soga and the Administration start from different value premises in thinking about "progress" and in consequence the same proposal may have quite different meanings for them. Again, the Soga frequently do not understand proposals put forward by the Administration and therefore suspect officers' motives. For their part, administrative officers are often unaware of important features of Soga culture and social structure and are thus unable to understand "why the Soga are so suspicious."

These doubts, suspicions and misunderstandings are reflected in the written communications which pass between the Administration in Jinja and the African Local Government offices at Bugembe. Administration proposals are sent to the District Council and its major committees (e.g. the Standing and Finance committees) and are replied to in the letters and minutes of meetings which are returned to the District Commissioner. The fact that much of the communication takes place in writing increases the likelihood of misunderstanding, since the African Local Government officials at Bugembe and the interpreters who prepare translations are often marginally literate in English. Particularly in complex technical or legal matters, their command of the language is frequently inadequate. Whereas the more rapid and subtle give and take of verbal communication allows misunderstanding to be relatively quickly corrected, communication through writing in an imperfectly understood language results in malcommunication which is much less easily and less quickly resolved. Often extended exchanges of letters and minutes occur in which the communications of each side seem to the other to be irrelevant or worse.

Sometimes fundamental differences in values are at the root of the trouble. The following exchange between the District Commissioner and the District Council in 1946 illustrates this type of situation. The District Council minuted on 18th June:

". . . To apply for a special ward for chiefs and other prominent people to be provided in the Civil Hospital in Jinja. The above matter was discussed and unanimously decided by the Council to apply to the Government for a special ward for chiefs and prominent people which does not exist at present, to be provided in the Civil Hospital in Jinja. In favour: 80; Against: 0."[1]

[1] Access to the minutes of the District Council and its committees was kindly granted to me by the District Commissioner and the Secretary General of the Busoga African Local Government.

On 29th July, the District Commissioner replied:

". . . Chief's Wards, Jinja Hospital. This is a Government Hospital and there are more important requirements which have priority."

This, the Council felt, was not a satisfactory answer and on 29th October they again minuted the District Commissioner:

". . . Ward for chiefs and prominent people in Civil Hospital, Jinja. Subject No. 6 of the previous Council. After reading the District Commissioner, Busoga's reply . . . which said that 'This is a Government Hospital and there are more important requirements which have priority, the Council rediscussed this matter as follows:

(i) The Council failed to understand the District Commissioner's reply when he said that 'The Jinja Hospital was a Government Hospital and that there were more important requirements which have priority.'

(ii) Such a hospital is supposed to be there for the good and treatment of all people protected by the Government and chiefs and other people holding high offices are some of the people who should be considered to be given better treatment in the same way as it is done in other things.

(iii) The Council feels that all sick people should be given as better treatment as possible and that at the same time chiefs and prominent people in the tribe are treated according to their dignity. In favour: 60; Against: 0."

At this, the District Commissioner gave up and on 1st November replied:

". . . I shall be pleased to explain and amplify the letter you refer to."

Apparently the District Commissioner did amplify and explain—verbally—since no more is heard of the matter in the Council minutes. The cause of the difficulty here is obvious. The Council, in accord with traditional Soga values, felt that special treatment ought to be accorded important and powerful persons, while the District Commissioner, equally in accord with Western values, felt that a Government facility ought to be equally available to all according to need. These differing notions concerning equality and inequality are frequently productive of discord. On 28th January, 1950, the Standing Committee, apparently feeling that existing arrangements did not give sufficient recognition to the dignity of the Kyabazinga, minuted:

". . . Special Uniform for Kyabazinga's Orderly. This was agreed upon in principle but the matter as a whole was referred to the Finance Committee to deal with. The following points were also mentioned for their guidance when discussing:

(i) What would be the salary.

(ii) Rank..

(iii) Fez (headgear).

(iv) What uniform and how many uniforms per annum.

(v) Boots."

To this suggestion, the District Commissioner replied:

".. . Special Uniform. I see no necessity for such a post or uniform."

On 14th March, however, the Standing Committee again recommended the establishment of the post of Kyabazinga's Orderly and again proposed that expenditure for special uniforms be allowed.

Let me cite one final, and somewhat more serious, example of disagreement over the rights and obligations attaching to high rank. For some time, the Administration has pressed the Soga to adopt some form of graduated taxation in order to provide funds for further expansion of African Local Government activity. In 1945, one such proposal was referred by the District Council to the lower councils. After receiving the minutes of discussions in the lower councils, the District Council minuted, on 20th December:

".. . Graduated Tax. Minutes discussed by all councils on the graduated tax were read before the Council after which the matter regarding the introduction of the graduated tax was carefully discussed by the Council. After discussion, and voting, it was decided by the Council that the graduated taxation should not be introduced in Busoga at present time on account of the following grounds.

(a) The time is not ripe yet for the introduction of graduated taxation.

(b) In Busoga there exist no rich men who are known to possess large sums of money invested in banks on their own account.

(c) There are no traders in Busoga who are known that they are gaining much money from their various trades like other countries.

(d) Here in Busoga are no farmers who have got farms of various economic crops out of which they can derive wealth. As far as agriculture is concerned, people are still being taught by both Governments.

(e) In Busoga there are no Companies belonging to people themselves by which they can make money like the Companies that exist in other countries.

(f) Although cultivation of cotton in Busoga is under practice, yet most people are found in a poor state. The money they make through cultivation of cotton cannot bring them up to a position where they are considered to be rich men.

(g) The education in Busoga is still low and this is mainly due to the poverty of people that they are unable to take their children to secondary schools. . . .

In favour (not to be introduced now): 51;
Against (to be introduced now): 32."

To this minute, the District Commissioner replied, on 4th July, 1946:

". . . Graduated Tax. . . . It appears that the present Council consists largely of rich men who reject the theory that poor men should pay lower taxes than themselves."

The Council, of course, did contain a heavy concentration of the wealthier people of Busoga since it included the more highly-paid officers of the African Local Government. From their point of view, however, the crucial point was that, relative to other countries, such as European countries of which they had heard or read, Busoga was poor. Differences in wealth within Busoga were less important than their undoubtedly exaggerated impression that, for example, most Europeans were much wealthier than any one of themselves. From the District Commissioner's point of view, however, the Council's attitude was both selfish and unrealistic, particularly in view of its tendency to recommend increased African Local Government expenditure. Indeed, from the modern European point of view, differences in wealth within Busoga are substantial and hence ordinary justice, as well as fiscal prudence, would demand some form of graduated taxation. It might be pointed out, of course, that this is a recent point of view, even in European countries. It is one of the administrative officer's difficulties that he is called upon to apply a modern welfare state pattern of taxation and local government administration to a society whose views concerning equality and inequality are more similar to those of medieval or renaissance Europe than to those of the modern West.

An even more serious and, from the administrative officer's point of view, more frustrating source of friction is the common suspicion of the Soga concerning the Government's motives. Often such suspicion is a response to Government proposals which in turn involve misunderstanding of Soga society and culture. The most common and most important focus for misunderstandings of this sort is land. As I noted earlier, it has long been Government policy that no land in Busoga should be alienated to non-Soga and that no Soga should be removed from the land he occupies except for public purposes. The legal position is that all land is ultimately vested in the Crown. The policy, however, is that Soga shall continue to occupy and use land in accord with the customary system of tenure. The Administration, however, has never really accepted the customary system of tenure. Government actions regarding land are usually based upon the assumption that the village and sub-village headmen are simply trustees and distributors of land for the peasants and that they have no legitimate economic interest in the land. It is believed that this was the traditional pattern and that deviations from it represent perversions of custom. The allotment fees which headmen collect are felt to be in the nature of illegal extortion—"key money." It is undoubtedly true that the economic aspect of the allotment fee has substantially increased with the rise of cash-crop cultivation, though, as I pointed out earlier, this is in part in replacement of the headmen's former income from tribute. To-day, in any case, the headman's right to a substantial allotment fee from each new tenant is firmly established in the customary law as administered by African Local Government courts.

These differences in interpretation of customary land law have become a focus for friction in connection with the establishment and extension of townships. Although the Administration disapproves of the practice of headmen's demanding allotment fees, they make no real effort to stop it in rural areas. Within townships, however, where more rigid health and other rules are applied and where land may be required for public purposes or for shop sites, the question of compensation sometimes arises. According to the Administration's interpretation, only the peasant cultivator has an economic interest in the land and hence only he is entitled to compensation. The Soga view, however, is that headmen also have an economic interest in the land and that therefore they also ought to receive compensation when deprived of their rights. During November and December, 1950, the following exchange took place between the District Council and the District Commissioner:

". . . Kisoko and Mutala chiefs (village and sub-village headmen) and Compensation in Respect of their Land. The subject of compensation for Kisoko and Mutala chiefs when deprived of their Kisokos and Mutalas when forming Townships etc. was discussed upon by the Council and it was referred to the lower councils. In favour: 78; Against: 0."

The District Commissioner replied:

". . . No question of compensation arises except in the case of an individual who loses crops, buildings, etc. I do not therefore see that any useful purpose can be served by further discussion on this point."

The same question has arisen in connection with the resettlement of areas formerly depopulated by sleeping sickness. On 1st

December, 1954, the District Commissioner wrote to the Council in this regard:

> ". . . Sleeping Sickness Areas Reclaimed for Settlement. . . . While we do not wish prematurely to break down the kisoko and mutala system, we cannot allow mutala chiefs the last word in deciding where people shall live. . . . Obviously mutala chiefs are hoping to make a good thing for themselves out of 'presents' for redistribution of land. . . ."

Such views on the part of the Administration provoke anxiety in the minds of many Soga concerning Government's intentions with regard to the land and this anxiety is exacerbated by the complex of religious and economic sentiments which attach to land in Busoga. Further suspicion is aroused by the designation of land as "Crown land." The Soga do not understand the legal implications of the common Western practice of reserving ultimate rights in the land to the state in order to provide for future public needs. To the Soga, the application to their country of the term "Crown land" means that it is liable to alienation to non-Soga, though the Administration has repeatedly stated that this is not so. All such anxieties concerning land are further stimulated by the sharp awareness on the part of the Soga of the presence of a substantial European settler population in neighbouring Kenya Colony.

The administrative officer, in carrying forward the policy of economic development and devolution of political responsibility, is thus faced with what seems to him an exasperating complex of suspicion, misunderstanding and incomprehensible opposition. Many further examples could be added to the ones already cited, but the point, I think, is clear. In a society which is in a sense two rather different, but partially interpenetrating, societies, different value premises and different modes of perceiving and understanding are often brought to the same situation by different participants. To-day the Soga and the Administration partly share the same value and belief systems and yet partly operate with different value and belief systems. Development of greater mutual understanding and fuller sharing of value premises is inhibited by the conditions under which administrative officers and Soga come into social relations with one another: lack of a satisfactory common medium of communication and, because of the frequent transferring of administrative officers, relatively brief association. And finally, mutual adaptation is made more difficult by the fact that the situation is not a stable one. The administrative officer is charged with furthering, under these difficult conditions, a policy of planned change so that further innovation tends to outrun such mutual understanding as does develop.

Self Determination: Busoga or Uganda?

The ultimate aim of British policy in Uganda is the development of a self-governing modern state. It is toward this ultimate end that the policy of development and devolution is directed. It is felt, however, that the achievement of this end involves development and devolution not only at the level of the District or Province but also at the centre. Institutions for responsible government, it is felt, must be developed for Uganda as a whole. This conception is clearly set out in a recent Government statement:

> ". . . the future of Uganda must lie in a unitary form of central Government on parliamentary lines covering the whole country with the component parts of the country developing within it according to their special characteristics. . . . The Protectorate is too small to develop into a series of separate units of government, even if these are federated together. The different parts of the country have not the size, nor will they have the resources, to develop even in federation with each other the administrative and political organs which modern government requires. This can only be done by a central Government of the Protectorate as a whole with no part of the country dominating any other part but all working together for the good of the whole Protectorate and the progress of its people."[1]

It is envisaged that the existing central Government—the Protectorate Government—will gradually take on a more representative character and will become more independent of Colonial Office control. The African Local Governments, it is hoped, will form, within this more independent and more representative state, "local governments" in the Western sense, with responsibility for local legislation, finance and services. Development at the centre has moved ever more rapidly within recent years. Efforts are being made to bring more Africans into the Protectorate Government service. To-day, the central legislative body, the Legislative Council, consists, besides the Governor as president, of twenty-eight "representative members" (fourteen Africans, seven Asians and seven Europeans), seventeen *ex-officio* Government members (senior Colonial Service officials) and eleven Government-appointed "cross-bench" members who may speak and vote freely except on issues of confidence, of whom six are Africans. Thus, though there remains an official majority, twenty of the fifty-seven members of the Council are Africans and a total of twenty-eight are non-officials. African representative members are elected by District councils, while the European and Asian representative members are nomin-

[1] *Government Memorandum on the Report of Mr. C. A. W. Wallis of an Inquiry into African Local Government in the Uganda Protectorate*, Government Printer, Entebbe, 1953, p. 3.

ated by the Governor. The membership of the Executive Council, the Governor's "cabinet," has also been widened to include, in addition to senior Protectorate Government officials, six non-official members, two from each of the three major ethnic communities. As this is written, further proposals for extending popular representation in the institutions of central government are under discussion.

The development of more representative central government institutions has not, however, met with an entirely enthusiastic response from the Soga and other African peoples of Uganda. The very success of Government over the past half century in building up local government institutions on the basis of traditional tribal political organisation is to-day proving something of a stumbling-block in the way of the creation of a unitary state. In a number of the tribal areas (Buganda, Bunyoro, Toro and Ankole), formal agreements were entered into, during the first decade of this century, recognising the traditional state systems as subordinate Governments under the over-rule of the Protectorate Government. In Busoga, which was traditionally divided among a number of separate states, no formal agreement was concluded, but much the same result was achieved by building up Busoga-wide political institutions to form the present Busoga African Local Government. Similar processes have occurred in other Districts, with the result that Africans have been encouraged to think largely in terms of the tribe or, in ethnically less homogeneous areas, of the District, as the focus of their ambitions for greater self-determination. Central Government institutions tend to be thought of as alien to their interests, particularly so since they are dominated by Europeans. Africans in other districts tend rather to look upon the Buganda Kingdom, which holds a peculiar position of greater autonomy within the Protectorate, as their model for progress.

Mr. C. A. G. Wallis, who in 1952 carried out, at the request of the Government, an inquiry into local government in the Protectorate, noted the barrier of tribalism which further political development in Uganda tends to encounter:

". . . There are in Uganda two constitutional ideas about local government. The first is . . . that policy should be directed at building up an efficient and democratic . . . system of local government. The second is that of native states.

. . . All the Standing Committees made it plain that they are bent upon reaching the status of a native state. Their object is to achieve a constitution as like that of Buganda as possible, and they believe that they will eventually supplant the Protectorate Government as the Government of their areas in nearly all affairs. In short, they aim at Home Rule and think that this was the Protectorate Government's intention in handing over, as they say, the power to govern their areas.

Moreover, it seems to them that this is the logical development of past administrative policy. Clan barriers have been broken down, sections have been amalgamated, a tribal organisation has been created and a tribal loyalty has been developed. In their own estimation they have arrived and they cannot understand why the Protectorate Government, having granted them the name of Governments, still withholds the realities of power. . . ."[1]

This description fits precisely the attitude of most Soga. The District Council has steadfastly resisted Administration attempts to integrate them politically with their neighbours. In 1943, it was proposed by the Administration that an Eastern Province Provincial Council be formed with representatives to be elected from the councils of the constituent Districts. On 13th and 22nd September, the Busoga District Council discussed this proposal and rejected it in the following terms:

". . . the Council has further discussed the matter of selecting six members to go to Mbale to meet members of other districts. . . . The council has come to the conclusion that a letter should be written to the District Commissioner informing him that we would not like to send six members to Mbale . . . on the following grounds:

(a) That we the Basoga, our customs differ from the peoples of Teso, Bukedi, Bugishu and Karamoja.

(b) That our language is different from the various languages of those tribes. We cannot understand each other.

(c) That when Bugwe and Samia Counties were under Busoga, they were taken away from Busoga in 1917 and amalgamated with Bukedi District . . . on the ground that the Bagwe and Basamia were a different people from the Basoga in custom, languages, etc., that they were more or less like the peoples of Bukedi than Busoga and they were accordingly amalgamated with the peoples of Bukedi with whom they look alike in customs, language, etc.

(d) In Busoga we have a different system of land tenure. . . ."

The District Council has reacted similarly to the representation of Busoga in the Legislative Council and has refused to elect a member. The present Soga member, like the members from Buganda and from Bukedi District, are consequently nominated by the Governor.

Although Administration efforts to integrate Busoga and other areas of Uganda into the official institutions of central government

[1] Wallis, C. A. G., *Report of an Inquiry into African Local Government in the Protectorate of Uganda*, Government Printer, Entebbe, 1953, p. 13–14.

have as yet met with limited success, recent years have seen the beginnings of a pan-Uganda African nationalism which in the future may result in a weakening of the present strong tendency toward tribal exclusiveness and solidarity. Over the past decade various attempts have been made, for the most part with little success, to form political parties on an inter-tribal basis. The most successful of these efforts thus far is represented by the Uganda National Congress, which was founded in 1952. Although having its centre in Buganda, the Congress is inter-tribal and African nationalist in its ideology and has succeeded in establishing active branches in a number of other areas, including Busoga. Whether the Congress and similar associations will prove able to develop and maintain themselves on a Uganda-wide basis and whether their activities will ultimately be directed toward the official institutions of central government so as to provide the foundations for a party system and thus contribute to parliamentary governmnet, it is at present too early to say. It may be noted, however, that other developing institutions also contribute to the strengthening of inter-tribal, Uganda-wide identification and sentiment. The mission churches are long-standing institutions of this sort. Christian ideology is, of course, fundamentally anti-particularistic in its orientation. Recent years have witnessed, in addition, the development within the Anglican Church of a fundamentalist revival which appears to be even more radically anti-tribal and universalist in its appeal.[1] The ever-widening educational system, and in particular institutions for higher education, have a similar influence. Makerere College, the University College of East Africa, brings together students not only from all areas of Uganda but also from the other East African territories. Like students elsewhere, they tend to develop within the university situation wider identifications and interests. Expanding trade and industry also play a part. The large urban centres, such as Kampala and Jinja, are tending more and more to become multi-tribal communities. At Jinja, where a dam and hydro-electric station on the Victoria Nile are nearing completion, it is hoped that substantial industry, including cotton-spinning, may develop. Though this is no place for detailed prediction, it may be safely assumed that these trends will continue and that over the long term the peoples of Uganda will move toward closer unity. Just as over the past half-century the separate Soga states have become a single social unit, so, perhaps during the next half-century, the Soga and their neighbours will become one people.

[1] A brief account of the revival in Uganda is given in Warren, Max, *Revival: An Enquiry*. London, S.C.M. Press, 1954.

Chapter X

REVIEW AND REFORMULATION

Problems: General and Particular.

As is so often the case with contemporary social anthropological studies, this one is a hybrid compounded in part of description of a particular society and in part of discussion of general problems of concept and theory.   This hybrid kind of product would seem to be inevitable, particularly for one writing about a society not already well described in the literature, for the social anthropologist has a double professional obligation.   On the one hand, he should contribute to the general fund of comparative data upon which social anthropologists must draw in developing new concepts and testing new hypotheses.   But, in the belief that description without theory is impossible, and in any case would be fruitless even if it were possible, he must present this descriptive data in terms of hypotheses and concepts.   Inevitably also, these two tasks to some degree interfere with each other.   Descriptive data presented in connection with a particular hypothesis or frame of reference is in the nature of the case highly selected and therefore never entirely satisfactory for use by other social anthropologists concerned with other hypotheses or frames of reference.   Equally, the concepts and hypotheses in terms of which one presents data from a given society invite application also to other societies exhibiting the relevant features, for social anthropology is a comparative discipline.   Though one may have hypotheses concerned only with a single society ("In society X, institution a has consequence b for institution c"), most social anthropologists feel that societies are in some degree commensurable and that the confirmation of such an hypothesis in one society is a first step to be followed by its testing in other societies (societies Y and Z which also exhibit institutions a and c).

Seen in the context of the total development of social anthropological thought, however, these difficulties are not as great as they seem.   While a given study may appear an uneasy compromise between description and theory, it is the indispensable building-block for the discipline as a whole.   Each of us begins from the fund of ethnographic data and ideas assembled by his predecessors and contemporaries and, if possible, restates or reformulates these ideas against a new body of descriptive data.   Such new, or at any rate reformulated, ideas as may emerge from this process may then be tested against the existing body of comparative data and finally passed on to colleagues for further testing or reformulation. It is with this wider process of growth in social anthropological thought in mind that I wish now to summarise and restate the concepts and hypotheses which have guided me in this study.

I began with the general problem of integration and conflict among a society's institutions and posed the question of their limits and dimensions. Stated in this broad, general way, these are hardly possible research questions, at any rate not in the context of a case study of a single society. The dimensions which one sees in integration and conflict in society are rather a matter of concept—of the frame of reference in terms of which one finds it possible to ask questions of research. The limits of conflict and integration, while perhaps ultimately discoverable, given a frame of reference, can be found only in the long term through the combined efforts of generations of social scientists. This study can therefore yield no firm conclusions on this most general level, though it is useful, I think, to keep such general problems in mind when dealing with more particular ones, if only because his wider frame of reference and his views concerning long-term problems inevitably and quite properly influence the social anthropologist's work in more restricted fields. Thus, while restricting this study to the analysis of particular types and degrees of conflict and integration among political institutions which have characterised traditional and modern Soga society, it is useful to see this limited task against the backdrop of more general problems.

In summarising and restating the results of this analysis, I should therefore like to proceed in terms of the two dimensions of institutional conflict and integration which I referred to briefly in Chapter I. These are, on the one hand, the dimension of conflict and integration among particular institutions and, on the other, the consequences of the operation of such institutions for persistence and change in the society as a whole. I have two cases to deal with, since I have tried to analyse Soga political institutions at two points in time. This chapter, therefore, will proceed as follows. First I shall briefly restate my conclusions concerning conflict and integration among Soga political institutions during each of these time periods. Since the particular institutions involved (corporate lineage, state, bureaucracy) are of types which occur elsewhere, I shall also briefly review these conclusions in the light of comparative data from other societies. Then, again using the Soga material as data, I shall consider some of the consequences of the operation of Soga political institutions at these two points in time for stability and change in the society as a whole.

LINEAGE AND STATE.

In Chapter I, I ventured the hypothesis that the simultaneous structuring of authority within a society in terms of both corporate lineages and the state was productive of strain and instability. I want to review traditional Soga political institutions in terms of this hypothesis, but first I should define more clearly what I mean by "strain" and "instability." As I said in Chapter I, I do not assume that two institutions in the same society necessarily have substantial consequences for one another. Institutions which do not apply to the same persons or situations may be neutral with regard to each other. Where, however, institutions do come together they may have either positive or negative consequences for each other. To the degree that institutions positively contribute to what Parsons has called "complementarity of expectations"[1] among the society's members, they may be said to be integrated. Where they interfere with this complementarity, they may be said to be conflicting. Integration and conflict may be looked at from two points of view: from the point of view of the society's members as social persons, integration among institutions means that the expectations which others have of them are complementary; satisfaction of one set of expectations contributes to the satisfaction of the other. From the point of view of the institutions themselves, integration means that conformity to the norms of one contributes to conformity with the norms of the other.[2] In the case under consideration, integration between lineage and state would mean that persons satisfying the demands placed upon them by lineage norms would at the same time be satisfying the demands placed upon them by the state and that, consequently, conformity to state norms would contribute to conformity with lineage norms. "Strain" and "instability" I use to describe the situation in which these conditions are not fulfilled. "Strain" I take to mean the interpersonal and intra-personal conflict which ensues when institutions are not integrated; by "instability" I mean the failure of the institutions themselves to operate under these conditions. In

---

[1] Parsons, Talcott, and Shils, Edward A. (eds.), *Toward a General Theory of Action*, 1951, p. 15.

[2] This is of course Parsons' familiar "actor-situation" dichotomy. (See Parsons, Talcott, *The Social System*, 1951, p. 25 ff.) The distinction is an analytical one. Conflict within and between persons and failure of institutions to be conformed with are, on a more concrete level, the same things. The analytic distinction is, however, useful because it allows one to recognise that conformity with the same institutional norm may, in terms of individual personality system, be quite differently motivated. Similarly, the same institutional conflict may produce different conflicts and reactions in personalities, as in the case of the different types of reaction to the same conflict in village headmen which I discussed in Chapter VII.

order, therefore, to test my hypothesis, I must show that in Soga society lineage and state placed upon individuals demands which brought them into conflict within themselves and with each other and that, from the point of view of lineage and state as institutions, the social units defined by them were frequently unable to operate in terms of the norms of these institutions.

The essential characteristic of unilineal kin groups in Busoga was their corporateness and solidarity; in those spheres in which authority was structured in terms of lineage, it was the authority of the group which was emphasised and not that of particular members. Internally, relations between the members were more or less egalitarian. I have noted the high value which was placed upon lineage unity and the reflection of this tendency in kinship terminology.[1] Let me briefly review the patterning of authority in those concrete social units which were structured in terms of agnatic kinship.

The smallest and lowest-order agnatic group was that consisting of a man and his sons. Among siblings there was a conspicuous lack of differentiation in terms of authority. The essential equality of siblings was epitomised by the lack of any clear-cut rule for choosing from among them the one who was to be his father's heir.[2] The father, it is true, was a distant and authoritarian figure *vis-à-vis* his sons, but this pattern was tempered by a number of factors. In the first place, the father's authority over his sons declined with the latters' maturity and this tendency was both a result of and strengthened by the general absence of extended family homesteads in which aged patriarchs might dominate adult sons.[3] The father's dominance was further tempered by the corporate authority of the succession lineage with regard to inheritance. Though the father might choose his heir, this choice was subject to review by the lineage. Finally, if one accepts the view of most Soga that traditionally inheritance, like succession, passed from brother to brother, even this source of paternal dominance drops away in any consideration of traditional Soga society. The son would not be his father's potential heir and hence would presumably be less subject to his authority.[4]

In the succession lineage, the next highest-order agnatic group,

---

[1] See Table VIII and Figs. 1, 2, 3, 4 and 5.

[2] See p. 90. As I noted earlier (pp. 90–92), most Soga believe that in the past inheritance was from brother to brother. If this were true, then none of the sons would be his father's heir. Throughout this discussion of conflict and integration among traditional political institutions I use the past tense, though, as we have seen, many of these institutions continue to operate to-day.

[3] See pp. 71–73, 79–81.

[4] See pp. 90–92.

group solidarity and the lack of marked authority differences were even more prominent. Within each generation of classificatory siblings, each man was a future successor to his senior in the birth order and great stress was placed upon preventing fission and maintaining unity. The mode of selection of the heads of lineages and of the territorial clan sections which constituted the highest-order agnatic units further exemplified the stress upon group action. The head of a succession lineage or a clan section might (though he need not) be succeeded by his son, but only if he were chosen by the relevant higher council. Once in office, he was *primus inter pares*, acting more as a co-ordinator and chairman of council deliberations than as an independent executive. Though there seldom was formal voting in such bodies, the will of the majority prevailed, usually through the establishment, after prolonged discussion, of a "Quaker meeting" kind of unanimity. Headship of a clan or lineage council was, furthermore, a part-time position. The head directed no permanent organisation or staff, but functioned only when the council was called upon to meet.[1]

The authority of unilineal kin groups, exercised through councils and group heads, applied primarily to such intra-group matters as succession, inheritance, breaches of exogamy and the like. It has been suggested to me by informants, though such suggestions are so vague that I have not referred to them elsewhere in this book, that in earlier times unilineal kin-groups in Busoga also had judicial functions in other matters, handling intra-lineage disputes of a type which to-day are tried in African Local Government courts. It has also been suggested that heads of different unilineal kin groups might meet to arbitrate disputes between their respective members. The evidence on this point, however, is too vague and flimsy and I shall therefore assume that the authority of such groups concerned only such matters as they have had jurisdiction over in recent times.

Finally, the ancestor cult, uniting patrilineal kinsmen in a common reverence, served to emphasise and sanction the solidarity of the group. The ancestors were believed to favour group interests and intra-group harmony and to be able to punish persons who threatened these values.[2]

So much for Soga lineages. Let us turn to the traditional state system which, according to my hypothesis, was in conflict with the lineage principle. Up to a point, the lineage principle was incorporated in the state organisation. The royal clan, and in particular the lineage of the ruler, was sometimes spoken of as "owning" the state as a whole. All members of the royal group shared in some

[1] See pp. 86–95, 171–172.
[2] See pp. 92–93.

measure a common aristocratic status, though those genealogically more remote from the ruling line were little different from commoners in daily social interaction. In fact, however, authority in the state system was exercised by and emanated from, not the entire royal group, but the ruler as an individual. Perhaps it is a general sociological principle that complex, continuously-functioning administrative organisations tend to have a single head. In any case, Soga rulers commonly felt that paramount authority could not be shared with lineage-mates. The state organisation was consequently hierarchical in form—a ladder of authority culminating in the ruler as an individual and otherwise manned by the ruler's personal commoner clients. Within the state structure, the institutionalisation of differential authority was as prominent as was the lack of it in the lineage. In the state structure, a client was his patron's total personal dependent and servant. Furthermore, the state hierarchy was not a solidary group but rather consisted in chains of dyadic relationships of subordination and super-ordination. Rights and responsibilities related to superiors and subordinates as individuals.[1]

Thus the norms governing the exercise of authority in the two structures differed. In the lineage, authority was the property of a solidary company of near equals; in the state, it was a property of individuals arranged in hierarchy of superiors and subordinates.[2] For two institutions to be different, however, does not make them conflicting. The situations or persons to which they apply may be so segregated that no conflict arises. In order to demonstrate that the co-existence of these two institutions in Soga society was productive of strain and instability in the sense in which these were defined above, it must be shown that they applied to the same persons or situations in such a way as to make the fulfilment of both sets of norms impossible. It would appear that in fact both sets of norms often did apply to the same persons and situations— that the two sets of norms could not successfully be segregated. As I argued in Chapter I, the reasons for this would seem to derive from the fundamental nature of kinship-structured institutions. On the one hand, kinship institutions tend to apply to every member of the society. While every Soga did not have a rôle in the state hierarchy (unless, of course, one considers that every commoner

---

[1] See pp. 135–137.

[2] Agnatic groups were also "hierarchically" arranged, but in a different sense. If the successor and heir to a succession lineage head had to be chosen, a council of the territorial clan section might be called. There was thus a hierarchy of more and less inclusive agnatic groups, but within each group there was relatively little differentiation in authority. The state, however, was a hierarchy of subordinate and superordinate individuals.

held such a rôle as a subordinate), everyone was a member of one or more lineages and was thus bound by lineage norms. Lineage and state could therefore not be segregated in terms of the persons to whom they applied. On the other hand, it is difficult, because of the highly diffuse and solidary character of kinship relationships, to treat an individual as a kinsman in one situation and as a non-kinsman in another. State and lineage could therefore not be segregated in terms of the situations to which they applied. As I showed in Chapter I, in societies where kinship structuring of rôles is essentially limited to the nuclear family, kinship institutions may, in spite of these considerations, be segregated quite effectively from other institutions. In modern, urban, middle-class United States, for example, kinship may with some success be segregated from occupational structures (including the state) because each nuclear family tends to have only one member (the adult male) who also plays an occupational rôle. In Busoga, however, this was not possible because there kinship defined relatively large solidary groups (lineages) containing many adult males. State and lineage could not therefore be kept apart; the differing norms governing authority in the two institutions inevitably came into conflict.

In previous chapters I have described many of the situations in which the simultaneous applicability of these two sets of norms produced conflict. Let me briefly recapitulate the major structural points at which interpersonal conflict and instability of institutions arose. Of these, the conflict which centred upon the ruler had the most pervasive consequences because it involved authority over the state as a whole. The ruler himself was both the head of the state hierarchy and a member of the royal clan and lineage. His unique position at the head of the state was, however, in conflict with his membership in the royal company of equals. If he emphasised his link with his commoner clients, he violated lineage values. If he did not, he stood in danger of losing his paramount authority to his lineage-mates.[1] Similar conflicts to-day, and presumably also in the past, afflict the hereditary village headman. He also had to balance territorial headship against lineage membership and thus might become involved in conflict with his lineage-mates.[2] Finally, the recognition in the state system of achieved status tended to produce conflict within commoner lineages. Persons who had achieved power and wealth in the personal service of a superior might claim, on that ground, great influence within the lineage and this claim might be resisted as a threat to lineage solidarity.[3]

[1] See pp. 134–135.
[2] See pp. 162–163.
[3] See pp. 141–142.

Each of these points of contact and conflict between state and lineage norms may also be viewed in terms of institutional instability—the failure of institutions to operate in terms of their norms. The ruler could not uphold the norms of both state and royal lineage. To the degree that he emphasised his ties with clients in the state system, the conception that the royal lineage ruled the state was violated and the royal lineage failed to function as such; to the degree that he did not do this, the conception of the ruler as the personal head of a hierarchy of patrons and clients was violated and the state as a concrete unit might disintegrate into a series of principalities. Similarly the village headman could not act both as a *primus inter pares* head of a lineage community owning the land as a corporate group and as a personal superior *vis-à-vis* each villager without regard to kinship. Most villages appear to have represented compromises between these two ideal community structures, but both norms were felt to operate and to the degree that one was followed the other could not be. In commoner lineages, a member who had achieved high rank in the state system could not be treated both as an ordinary member of the corporate group and as a person of great authority. Conflicts concerning which way he should be treated might split the lineage.

If it be accepted that lineage and state were in conflict in traditional Soga society, what of the many other societies in which these two types of structuring of authority have co-existed? Such cases have clearly been very common. Ideally, comparative testing of my hypothesis concerning the functional incompatibility of these institutions should begin with the neighbouring Bantu states of the Lake Victoria region. It is a common and, I believe, sound notion in social anthropology that comparative analysis can most fruitfully be carried out within groups of societies known to be historically closely related. Eggan, in his comparative study of the Pueblo Indian societies of south-western United States, has noted some of the advantages of this procedure:

> "In order for the comparative study of correlated social phenomena in a series of tribes to be valid, it is necessary to make first comparisons between phenomena which belong to the same class or type or, alternatively, between phenomena derived from the same historical source. Only by exercising such controls can we be sure that the phenomena compared are comparable for scientific purposes."[1]

It is not argued, of course, that wider comparisons among societies more remote from one another in time or space are not

[1] Eggan, Frederick, *Social Organisation of the Western Pueblos*, 1950, p. 9.

valuable, but rather merely that within an area of similar culture and environment more of the unknown number of variables affecting social structure may be held constant and thus the influence of particular social structural variables may be more easily isolated. Such an area of broadly similar culture and environment is formed by the Bantu states lying to the north and west of Lake Victoria. Chapter I showed that these peoples speak languages which are very similar, often to the point of mutual intelligibility. They share common traditions of origin and a broad area of common culture. Although there are environmental variations within the area, all practise some mixture of agriculture and pastoralism.

Comparative analysis within this area will ultimately, it may reasonably be hoped, prove most enlightening and it is in part toward this end that the present study is presented. Studies of a similar kind have recently been carried out, or are in progress, in Buganda, Bunyoro, Toro, Buhaya, Buzinza and Ruanda. Little of the data resulting from these studies, however, has as yet been published. Although there has been much consultation and mutual stimulation among field workers in the area, detailed comparative analysis must wait upon further publication. I must therefore present this as a preliminary analysis and limit reference to existing published sources, many of which are quite inadequate by present-day standards.

It is quite clear that, at any rate in a number of the Inter-Lacustrine Bantu states, conflict between lineage and state structures did arise in connection with the rulership. Speke, whose accounts of the peoples through whose countries he passed show him to have been a social analyst of no mean ability, speaks of the conflict between royal brothers as an endemic cause of instability and disorder throughout the area.[1] This view is supported by later writers. Among the Nyoro, Ganda, and Nkole, interregnum war and princely usurpation were common. The structural sources of such conflicts appear to have been broadly similar to those operative in Busoga. Like Busoga, all these societies are patrilineal, and in all of them rulership was held in a royal patrilineal kin group. In Ankole, the Mugabe was chosen from a section of the *Bahinda* clan.[2] In Bunyoro, the Mukama held his position as a member of a lineage within the *Babiito* clan.[3] In Buganda, though there was, in the totemic sense, no royal clan, the Kabaka was chosen from among the *Balangira ab'engoma* ("Princes of the Drum"), the

---

[1] Speke, John Hanning, *Journal of the Discovery of the Source of the Nile,* 1863, p. 5.

[2] Roscoe, John, *The Banyankole*, 1923, p. 5.

[3] Roscoe, John, *The Bakitara*, 1923, p. 14.

patrilineal line descended from previous Kabakas.[1] As in Busoga, also, there was in none of these societies a firm rule of seniority among sons. All writers agree that the ambiguity resulting from the essential equality of princely siblings was productive of frequent strife. Oberg notes that in Ankole the Mugabe:

> ". . . must be the strongest of the last king's sons. . . . If one brother had fewer followers than the other, he generally got killed or fled to another country. . . . During the accession war which might last for several months, the country was in a state of chaos."[2]

A similar pattern is described by Roscoe for Bunyoro:

> "There was always at least a general understanding which prince the king wished to reign after his death, and that prince was ready to assume the place. . . . He had to prepare for trouble, for rarely did a prince ascend the throne without opposition from at least one brother, and he had to be prepared to meet any claimant in battle and prove his right to the throne as the stronger man, the victor in battle."[3]

The princely threat was sometimes not eliminated by the interregnum war. Surviving princes might attempt rebellion, sometimes successfully:

> "In the reign of Nyamatukura a prince . . . called Kaboyo, rebelled and fled from the country. He was taken into Buganda by a man Byakweyamba, who took him to Mutesa, then king of Buganda, and from there he returned and became a great chief. His son, Nyaika, continued to extend his power. . . ."[4]

Kaboyo's area became the autonomous state of Toro, which maintained a more or less separate identity until the arrival of the Europeans.

And in Buganda, Roscoe says:

> "Civil wars also broke out from time to time . . . between rival princes who laid claim to the throne. These latter wars were by far the most disastrous that could happen to the country; and during the few weeks that they lasted, untold damage was done and a great loss of life took place."[5]

The commoner client-chief as the ruler's administrative subordinate and his shield against princely revolt is also a feature common to all these societies. Like the Soga rulers, the Kabaka of Buganda had his *katikkiro* (prime minister) and territorial *bakungu*

---

[1] Roscoe, John, *The Baganda*, 1911, p. 187–188.
[2] Oberg, K., "The Kingdom of Ankole in Uganda," in Fortes, Meyer, and Evans-Pritchard, E. E. (eds.), *African Political Systems*, 1940, pp. 157–158.
[3] Roscoe, *The Bakitara*, p. 123.
[4] *Ibid.*, p. 88.
[5] Roscoe, *The Baganda*, p. 346.

(client chiefs), none of whom was ever a prince.[1] According to Roscoe, three of these commoner chiefs chose the new Kabaka and defended him against his brothers:

> "The choice of the prince who was to succeed his father as king was a matter for the *Katikiro*, the *Kasuju* and the *Kimbugwe* to decide. The reigning king generally made his wishes known to the *Katikiro* and the *Kasuju*, and his wishes were adhered to, if possible; but if these chiefs thought that there was another prince who would make a better sovereign, they did not hesitate to appoint the latter."[2]

A rival prince who tried to contest the decision could only hope to succeed if he had the support of other members of the hierarchy of commoner chiefs:

> "If there was any chief who was not satisfied with the choice made, he now came forward, carried off the prince whom he wished to have on the throne, and called upon his associates to fight . . . the *Katikiro* always appeared on the scene with a strong armed force in order to quell any disturbance that might arise."[3]

Similar functions are attributed by Oberg to the senior commoner chief of the Mugabe of Ankole:

> "The Enganzi has been variously called the 'prime minister,' the 'head chief,' the 'beloved one' and the 'favoured one,' but we shall here call him the 'favourite chief.' . . . The first act of the Enganzi after the accession war is the establishment of the new Mugabe. In this sense he is a king-maker. Although the Enganzi was a rich and powerful man, he was always selected from a clan other than the *abahinda* and, therefore, could not lay claim to the Mugabeship himself. . . . After the death of the Mugabe, the Enganzi would support the favourite son of the Mugabe in the struggle for the Mugabeship. In this struggle, his power would often turn the scales against the other sons. The Enganzi then often formed a link between the two reigns. . . ."[4]

The Bunyoro material is less clear. The implication in Roscoe's account, however, is that Bamuroga, who had functions similar to those of the *katikkiro* in Buganda and the *enganzi* in Ankole, was also a commoner client-chief, administrator and king-maker.[5]

Existing published accounts are not full enough on the relevant points to make possible comparison with my Soga data concerning

---

[1] A. H. Cox traces the traditional histories of the major chieftainships in "The Growth and Expansion of Buganda," *Uganda Journal*, Vol. XIV, No. 2, 1950, pp. 153–159. Sir Apollo Kagwa's *Basekabaka Be Buganda*, 1901, lists successive prime ministers and other chiefs and their clans.

[2] Roscoe, *The Baganda*, p. 189.

[3] *Ibid.*, p. 190.

[4] Oberg, *op. cit.*, pp. 138–139.

[5] Roscoe, *The Bakitara*, pp. 51–52, 118–135.

conflict between lineage and territorial headship at the local community level and conflict within commoner lineages resulting from members' achievement of status in the state system.[1] Detailed comparison in these matters must await the publication of the new material referred to above. It is also likely that these recent studies will reveal differences in detail among the Inter-Lacustrine Bantu states which will shed further light upon the interaction of lineage and state. Although the broad pattern would appear to be similar to that found in Busoga, there is evidence, as I said in Chapter VI, that in Buganda, for example, the state structure was somewhat more stable than in Busoga, in part at least as a result of the operation of mechanisms for restricting the royal patrilineal group to a single line of fathers and sons. There was thus no constantly proliferating royal lineage to threaten the ruler's position. In addition, there appears to have been an explicit policy of killing off the Kabaka's brothers in order to prevent princely revolt.[2] If the foregoing interpretation be correct, it of course supports my hypothesis. I have argued that conflict and instability are the result of the structuring of authority in terms of both lineage and hierarchical state. Greater stability in Buganda would appear to be associated with the fact that, at the level of the rulership, the lineage principle gives way to the state structure.

[1] Beattie describes the rights over village lands held by clients of the Mukama in Bunyoro and suggests that, prior to the disruption of local communities during the wars around the end of the last century, local clan communities also had corporate land rights. (See Beattie, J. H. M., "The Kibanja System of Land Tenure in Bunyoro, Uganda," *Journal of African Administration*, Vol. IV, No. 1, 1954, pp. 18–28; "A Further Note on the Kibanja System of Land Tenure in Bunyoro, Uganda," *Journal of African Administration*, Vol. VI, No. 4, 1954, pp. 178–185.)

This suggests a clash of state and lineage at the village level similar to that which I have described for Busoga. In the material thus far published, however, Beattie does not explicitly discuss such conflict.

[2] Roscoe, *The Baganda*, pp. 188–189. The situation with regard to the Ganda royal agnatic group is not very clear. It was not a clan in the totemic sense since the Kabaka assumed the totemic and exogamic avoidances of his mother's patriclan. At the same time, all those persons descended from Kabakas are spoken of as *Balangira* and *Bambejja*—"princes" and "princesses"—as a group. To-day, I am advised by Dr. A. I. Richards, the princes and princesses do operate in much the same way as other Ganda clans, being internally segmented and engaging in corporate activities. (Private communication.) Whether or not one considers them to have constituted in traditional times a clan in substance, if not in name, depends in large part upon the interpretation one places upon the various mechanisms said to have been used to restrict the group in effect to a single line of fathers and sons. Concerning the restriction of succession to the Kabaka-ship to "princes of the drum"—actual sons of Kabakas—there seems to be little doubt, but it is less clear how efficacious and how consistently applied was the practice of killing non-succeeding sons of Kabakas. I have been told by Ganda that those princes who were not killed tended to run away and become absorbed into other clans, often those of their mothers.

My hypothesis concerning the inevitability of conflict between lineage and state clearly invites testing in other areas as well. Extensive comparative analysis would be out of place in a study of political institutions in a single society, but some suggestions for future work in this direction may be noted.[1] Perhaps the most attractive area for comparison with the Inter-Lacustrine Bantu states is that of the Southern Bantu. Southern Bantu societies also have both strong agnatic groupings and centralized state systems. Although these two features also exist sporadically in the area between Lake Victoria and southern Africa, few of the societies in this intervening area are well documented, whereas for the Southern Bantu we have such excellent accounts as those of Schapera, Gluckman, Krige, Kuper, Ashton and others.[2] A preliminary review of this literature would indicate that the major difference between the Southern and Inter-Lacustrine Bantu situations is to be found in differing patterns of seniority and inheritance within lineages. Whereas Inter-Lacustrine Bantu lineages emphasised the equality of members within any generation, Southern Bantu lineages were highly stratified internally and ranked *vis-à-vis* each other. There was a clear-cut pattern of seniority among siblings and hence inheritance and succession to rulership were never problematical. Under these conditions it would appear that members of the royal lineage were much less a threat to the position of the ruler than was the case among the Inter-Lacustrine Bantu; being quite precisely ranked among themselves, princes were to a lesser degree competitors for rulership. In consequence, princes could be and were given positions of administrative authority in the state system. The state organisation was more in the hands of the royal lineage as a group. None the less, in spite of the system of ascriptive ranking within the lineage, princely usurpation and revolt did occur in these societies. It would appear to be difficult for a society so firmly to institutionalise ascriptive ranking among lineage collaterals as to eliminate the fundamental tendency towards sibling equivalence which brings lineage organisation into conflict with state hierarchies.[3]

[1] I hope in the near future to carry out a systematic comparative analysis of African societies having both patrilineal descent groups and centralised state structures.

[2] Schapera, I., *A Handbook of Tswana Law and Custom*, 1938; Gluckman, Max, "The Kingdom of the Zulu in South Africa," in Fortes, Meyer, and Evans-Pritchard, E. E., *African Political Systems*, 1940, pp. 25–55; Kuper, H., *An African Aristocracy*, 1947; Krige, J., *The Social System of the Zulus*, 1936; Ashton, Hugh, *The Basuto*, 1952.

[3] It would seem likely that the "equivalence of siblings," though of course subject to modification in degree in accord with social structural variation, is a general human tendency arising out of the circumstance that siblings

Continued on page 238

Let me emphasise again that these comparative suggestions are of the most tentative and preliminary sort—"hunches" to be tested in the future. Now let us return to Soga society and re-examine the tensions and conflicts which characterise its present-day political institutions.

BUREAUCRACY IN A PARTICULARISTIC SETTING.

In modern Busoga there is, superimposed upon the traditional tension between state and lineage, a new conflict arising out of structural incompatibility between both of these institutions and the European-introduced conception of civil service bureaucracy. As I have noted in earlier chapters, the conflict springs from differing norms concerning the exercise of authority—what Weber would have called differing bases for the legitimation of authority. In the two traditional authority structures—lineage and state—authority relations were defined in terms of relationships between particular persons or groups. A person was under the authority of the members of his own lineage or the person who was his own patron. Such criteria governing social relations I have called, following Parsons, "particularistic."[1] In the civil service bureaucracy, on the other hand, authority is situational. It is a property of an office, not a person, and its validity depends upon general rules governing the office, not upon the person who holds it. Thus, for example, whoever happens to hold the office of Sub-County chief holds authority of a particular kind over his area of jurisdiction. The particular person who holds the office is irrelevant to the exercise of authority within it. This type of definition of social relations, again following Parsons, I have called "universalistic."[2]

[1] Parsons, Talcott, *The Social System*, pp. 61–65.
[2] *Ibid.*, pp. 61–63. These are clearly polar types rather than mutually exclusive categories. Although in traditional Busoga a man had authority relations of a special kind with his lineage mates as against other persons, so that authority was from this point of view particularistic, still within the lineage his relations with all kinsmen of the same sex and generation were similar and thus, to this degree were universalistically defined. Similarly, although the African Local Government civil service to-day holds within Busoga a universalistically-defined kind of authority, still, as we have seen, the Soga are reluctant to take part in similar authority structures extending outside Busoga. To this degree, the African Local Government has particularistic elements. All concrete cases are no doubt mixed cases in terms of these categories and hence differences are differences of degree.

Continued from page 237
share a common socialisation situation including a common subordination to parents. (See Radcliffe-Brown, A. R., *Structure and Function in Primitive Society*, 1952, p. 64.)

It may be noted that it, as the Soga believe, rulership was in the past handed down through the line of collaterals in strict birth-order, then an ascriptive modification of the equivalence of siblings similar in its consequences to the Southern Bantu system of lineage ranking would result.

Again I am arguing not merely that there is here an opposition of abstract ideal types, but rather that where such opposing authority norms are institutionalised the opposition does and must result in concrete interpersonal conflict and in instability in institutions. Thus the Soga civil-servant chief's position is defined in such a way that both sets of norms may be brought to bear upon the same situation. As regards recruitment to office, conflict may arise between the claims of kinsmen or clients and the principle of recruitment according to ability. In the daily exercise of authority, again there may be conflict between particularistic loyalties and the norm of disinterested and impartial administration. Both sets of norms cannot be satisfied, but since both are institutionalised a decision in either direction may result in inter-personal conflict and in lack of conformity with some institutionalised norms.

The tension between the introduced bureaucratic civil service pattern and the more particularistic traditional authority structures has produced different kinds of conflict at different levels within the political system. The conflict is sharpest for the civil-servant chief, for it is to him that the two sets of norms simultaneously apply with greatest immediacy. This is so because he is a specialist in the exercise of authority; authority is his profession. The traditional Soga state and the modern African Local Government organisation are, in terms of the definition suggested in Chapter I, specialised political rôles. Thus the norms governing the exercise of authority loom particularly large in the chief's social relations with others. Where such norms are conflicting, his rôle tends to be the focus of the conflict. Thus the chief is faced almost daily with conflicting expectations on the part of persons with whom he interacts. Furthermore, the sanctions which operate in support of the two sets of norms are such as to leave him a very small margin of error in his attempts to balance the two sets of expectations. The civil service norm is enforced by the Administration. If the chief fails to follow it closely, he may well lose his position. The particularistic demands of kinship and clientship are also, however, enforced by senior chiefs and others, who can use their influence with the Administration to punish recalcitrant juniors. The civil-servant chief must therefore steer a course which can successfully be navigated only by the most skilful.[1]

The conflict which centres upon the village or sub-village headman is different. He is also, though in lesser degree, a specialist in authority, but he is not a formal part of the African Local Government bureaucracy and the demands of the civil service norm consequently do not impinge upon him so directly. The difficulties of

[1] See pp. 196–203.

his rôle rather derive from the circumstance that, while he continues to hold his position by inheritance and to "rule" his community in large part according to traditional patterns (or, at any rate, according to what he and others believe to be traditional patterns), the upper levels of the political system have changed in such a way as to deprive him of what he sees to be the just and traditional rewards of his position. Although not directly subject to bureaucratic discipline, he has been deprived of the economic and status-enhancing rewards of personal tribute and is aware that the Administration does not approve of his rights in connection with land. Thus, though not so immediately and constantly subject to the universalistic-particularistic conflict which afflicts the civil-servant chief, he is, in a sense, punished for his refusal to adjust his position to the new civil service pattern. Thus, while continuing, as the head of his community, to participate in the wider political system as the informal local representative of the African Local Government, he does so ambivalently and may react to what he sees as his deprived position by agitating against the African Local Government and the Administration, or by withdrawing into passive inactivity.[1]

Finally, the administrative officer is faced with still a third type of difficulty as a consequence of the structural incongruities which pervade the political system. It is his responsibility to maintain and to extend the civil service pattern of government; he is the active agent in the Westernisation of the system. At the same time, he is responsible for order—for introducing change at such a rate and in such a way that stable government is maintained. To this end he must recognise and, temporarily at any rate, accept features of the system which run counter to the civil service norms to which he is committed, since to attempt to enforce the new norms absolutely would result in disorder. To this degree he, like the Soga members of the system, must try to balance conflicting norms. He must simultaneously endeavour to further Westernisation, yield authority, and remain responsible for the exercise, according to the new norms which he is introducing, of the authority which he is yielding. He must, furthermore, carry out this complex responsibility in a situation where his knowledge of and communication with members of the system which he is endeavouring to change is severely limited, both by cultural and linguistic barriers and by the exigencies of the bureaucratic structure of which he is a part.[2]

In Chapter I, I suggested the hypothesis that bureaucratic structures were incompatible with the traditional Soga political structures—the corporate lineage and the patron-clientship pattern.

[1] See pp. 175–179.
[2] See pp. 209–220.

In general, this is perhaps self-evident and hardly requires formal comparative testing. There are, however, subsidiary questions arising out of the Soga material which do seem to me worthy of comparative testing. I cannot attempt a systematic comparative analysis here, since the relevant data are widely scattered and not familiar to me. In large part they are to be found in the writings of political scientists and historians rather than in those of sociologists and social anthropologists. The reasons for this are obvious. Sociologists and social anthropologists have tended to study either modern Western societies, where bureaucratic structures are relatively well integrated with other institutions, or else non-Western societies where bureaucracy does not exist or has only recently been introduced. Data of comparative interest should soon be forthcoming as social anthropologists concern themselves more and more with contemporary political development in non-Western areas, though as yet little such data has been published.[1] Therefore, though I cannot undertake to test them systematically, I should like to note here a few points which would seem susceptible to comparative investigation.

One such concerns the apparent ease with which the traditional Soga state was transformed in a bureaucratic direction. Although there has been conflict and opposition, on the whole the process has been strikingly rapid and smooth. I have noted some of the particular historical factors which seem to have been involved here: the generally rewarding nature of the situation from the point of view of the rulers and chiefs and the early development of mission education. It is also interesting to consider, however, the degree to which the traditional state was what might be called "structurally receptive" to bureaucratisation. My earlier lumping together of the two traditional authority structures—state and lineage—as being particularistically oriented has perhaps served to obscure this point. While both structures shared this feature in opposition to bureaucratic universalism, they are in other respects not equally incompatible with bureaucratic organisation. For while the patron-client relationship was particularistic, it was also hierarchical and involved recognition of achieved status—both features which are present in bureaucratic structures. The patron-client relationship, once established, was a relationship between two persons as individuals and was often cemented by affinal ties, but in selecting clients, patrons were explicitly concerned with administrative and military ability. The relationship was also a hierarchical one, as compared with the relative egalitarianism of the lineage. One

---

[1] Again comparative data will soon be available from recent studies of other Inter-Lacustrine Bantu societies.

might say, therefore, that the traditional state was an "incipient bureaucracy." The general hypothesis suggests itself that societies with hierarchical, centralised political systems incorporate the Western type of civil service structure with less strain and instability than do societies having other types of political systems, e.g. segmentary ones. Such a hypothesis might well be tested in Uganda, where a similar African Local Government system has been introduced into both the Bantu states and the segmentary societies of the Nilotic north.

I would also suggest that the particular tension which existed in traditional Busoga between lineage and state was a contributory factor. Chapter VI showed that the threat of princely revolt seems to have made Soga rulers anxious to secure more powerful allies. Both Ganda and Europeans were ready to accept such a rôle and were thus enabled to gain control over Soga states. Where the Ganda were concerned, this essentially involved merely the absorption of the Soga states into a larger unit of the same kind, but with regard to the Europeans, it meant something more; although this was undoubtedly not foreseen, it meant ultimately a commitment to a continuing process of change in kind in the political system. Rulers and chiefs, having accepted European authority in exchange for support, were committed to European policies. Generalising beyond the particular events, one might say that the conflict between lineage and state produced a kind of political opportunism in the traditional Soga authorities, and in consequence brought about a fluidity in the system, which made it vulnerable to outside penetration and to change.

I have the impression that the speed and smoothness with which Westernisation has proceeded in Busoga (and in Uganda as a whole) is rather unusual, at any rate in Africa. For example, in the Gold Coast, on the verge of self-government, Ashanti chiefs still debated whether or not to observe the traditional pagan day of rest and were in general much more traditionally-oriented than Soga chiefs, in spite of the fact that the Ashanti have had a much longer period of contact with the West than have the peoples of Uganda.[1] In Ashanti, Westernisation would appear to have proceeded to a greater extent outside of and in opposition to the traditional political hierarchy, whereas in Uganda, at any rate among the Bantu states, the traditional authorities have on the whole been its pioneers. A similar contrast would appear to hold for the Southern Bantu states referred to earlier in this chapter. The difference, perhaps, is at least partly explainable in terms of the particular tension which

[1] Busia, K. A., *The Position of the Chief in the Modern Political System of Ashanti*, 1951, p. 135.

existed among Inter-Lacustrine Bantu between lineage and state and the consequent vulnerability of the state hierarchy to European penetration.

A second point of comparative interest arises in connection with the attempt by the Administration in Busoga to carry the bureaucratic type of authority structure down to the local community level. I have described how the village headmen resisted the attempt to transform them into salaried civil servants.[1] I have also noted the frequent ineffectualness of the Parish chief, who is a salaried and transferable civil servant but who is often overshadowed by the locally-rooted headmen.[2] Aside from the particular circumstances of Busoga, I would suggest that there are inherent difficulties in applying the civil service conception of authority at the level of the local community. The stable local community is everywhere essentially a primary group; its members know each other as total persons as a result of long and intimate face-to-face contact. As a colleague of mine once put it: "In the village everyone is famous."[3] In the lower courts in Busoga, for example (headmen's and Parish chiefs' courts of arbitration and sometimes even Sub-County courts), procedure often assumes that the community knows, or can discover, the circumstances of the case. There is not the same obligation to tell the truth which one finds at higher levels, where anonymity is possible. Litigants and witnesses are more free to lie, since it is assumed that members of the court, knowing the persons involved, can nevertheless discover the truth. The problem is rather to find the most satisfactory means of closing a breach in the social relations of the community. The court applies substantive justice rather than a strictly-defined rule of law. The bureaucratic conception is, of course, quite different. It deals, not with relations between whole persons, but with rules governing types of situation. Acts or attributes of persons falling outside the defined situation are irrelevant. Applied to relations within the local community, however, such impersonality tends to be disruptive of the network of particularistic ties and to result in miscarriages of what the community sees as substantive justice, hence the local community's preference for a leader who knows them and is known by them.[4]

[1] See pp. 173–174.
[2] See p. 196.
[3] Dr. Erving Goffman.
[4] A recent investigator into local government in Uganda recommended, on these grounds, that in the future Parish chiefs should be local men not subject to transfer. (See Wallis, C. A. G., *Report of an Inquiry into African Local Government in the Protectorate of Uganda*, Government Printer, Entebbe, 1953, p. 53.)

Although there would appear to be a general tendency for authority within local communities to be particularistic, the degree to which this is so is undoubtedly relative to variations in social structure. To the particularism of the primary group community, Soga society adds the particularisms of extended kinship and the patron-client relationship between the headman and his people. The resistance to bureaucracy is therefore particularly great. Comparative investigation of community authority within different types of wider social system would undoubtedly reveal other variations of this order.

In thinking comparatively about the integration of bureaucracy with other institutions, it is perhaps well to keep in mind Parsons' view that the universalistic type of orientation which bureaucracy implies is inherently unstable and difficult to institutionalise, due to the circumstance that everywhere persons tend to be socialised in particularistic situations.[1] The early learning of social behaviour takes place in family groups and involves the building up of stable sets of mutual expectations with a relatively small group of individuals. As Freud noted, the extension of this early social learning to social relations in the larger society requires that the individual abstract general social norms from these early particularistic relationships.[2] The latter, however, tend to leave a residual tendency toward emotional attachment to individual persons which makes the learning and maintenance of universalistic orientations difficult.[3] Whatever its psychogenetic roots, such a residual tendency toward particularism has often been noted by students of modern Western societies. Such formally highly bureaucratised structures as the modern state and the business or industrial organisation are notoriously subject to nepotism and to the formation of solidary cliques.[4] The relevance of such considerations here is simply that the conflict between the civil service norm and the particularistic ties of kinship and clientship which has been observed in contemporary Soga society should perhaps not be viewed as a conflict between two equally-weighted social patterns. The special particularisms of Soga society, it would appear, have a natural ally in a universal human tendency which makes the institutionalisation of the civil service norm peculiarly difficult of achievement.

Over the long term, the bureaucratic type of authority structure will undoubtedly become more firmly institutionalised in Busoga,

[1] Parsons, Talcott, *The Social System*, 1951, p. 268.
[2] Freud, Sigmund, *Group Psychology and the Analysis of the Ego*, 1922.
[3] Parsons, Talcott, *The Social System*, 1951, p. 268.
[4] See, for example, Roethlisberger, F. J., and Dickinson, W. J., *Management and the Worker*, 1939; Steffens, Lincoln, *Autobiography*, 1931.

since both the authority of the British Administration and contemporary economic trends work in its favour, but there are various
factors which, in the short term, may condition this process. As
we have seen, one of the major obstacles to the establishment of
bureaucratic structures is the kinship system involving corporate
patrilineages. So long as the lineage system remains intact, it will
constitute a major source of deviation from bureaucratic norms.
The system of corporate lineages, however, has firm roots in the
system of land holding. Though hereditary rulership has disappeared, lineage control of inheritance and succession in the local
community remains undisputed and is backed by the authority of
the African Local Government courts. Although lineages have
broken down in some areas, there would seem to be no reason to
doubt that, in the absence of further catastrophes of the order of
the sleeping sickness epidemics at the turn of the century, lineage
structure will remain intact throughout most parts of Busoga. A
change in the direction of more individual forms of land holding
would, however, undoubtedly weaken the lineage system and
strengthen more universalistic orientations favourable to bureaucratic structure. A body of opinion favourable to such a change
has recently appeared among persons wishing to engage in more
modern forms of agriculture. One might hazard the prediction
that such views will gain wider support in the future with the spread,
through education, of an appreciation of the economic potentialities
of modern farming methods and that the result will be a situation
less inimical to the development of civil service norms.

A second source of future strength for bureaucratic patterns
would appear to be the growing tendency for civil-servant chiefs
to form an élite sub-culture, to some degree dissociated from peasant
life and institutions. I have noted the tendency for chiefs to see
themselves as a solidary group and to form cliques for purposes of
sociability.[1] To the degree that this tendency is increased, it would
seem to form the basis for the development of a civil service *esprit
de corps*, from which the tenuously institutionalised civil service
pattern might draw strength, and a defence against the particularistic demands which spring from traditional kinship and clientship
institutions. This tendency is strengthened by the pattern of
recruitment on the basis of ability and education. To the degree
that chiefs come to feel themselves identified with the civil service
as a body and to see their futures in terms of professional careers
in the service, they will find it easier to commit themselves to the
norms of the system.

---

[1] See pp. 189–190, 201.

So far I have looked at conflict within the traditional and modern Soga political systems in terms of its consequences for the particular institutions involved and for individuals playing rôles in terms of those institutions. In the case of both traditional and modern Busoga, I have centred my attention primarily upon rôle conflict—conflict of the sort which results when incompatible institutions apply to the same persons. In traditional Busoga, persons playing rôles in the state hierarchy also played rôles in the lineage organisation. In modern Busoga, members of the African Local Government hierarchy also have lineage rôles and patron-client rôles. In such situations, the conflict between institutions is, so to speak, absorbed into individual persons. Since both sets of institutional norms are accepted by the same persons, individuals are exposed to conflicting, but equally legitimate, expectations from others and have conflicting motivations within themselves. This is not to say that such conflict is never interpersonal. Interpersonal conflict often results because in a given situation one person may claim over-riding legitimacy for one of the patterns, while persons with whom he interacts may take the opposite point of view. Where conflict is of this kind, however, the positions may well be reversed in another situation. Thus the Soga chief who resists the claims of his kinsmen on one occasion may well assert the same type of claim on another occasion when it seems to him advantageous to do so. The peculiarity of this type of conflict, however, is that it does not divide persons into intransigently opposed groups. Soga society does not consist of one group wholly committed to civil service universalism and an opposed group wholly committed to kinship and clientship particularism; it consists rather of individuals attempting to follow both patterns.

This, it should be pointed out, is not the only pattern which institutional conflict may follow. Conflict between discrete groups committed to opposing norms would appear to be equally common, particularly in colonial situations. Often enough non-Western societies under Western influence become divided into such opposed groups on the basis of adherence to traditional or introduced institutions. I should not imply that inter-group conflict of this type is totally absent in Busoga. As I have noted, persons at different points in the modern political hierarchy are differently affected by institutional conflict. For the African Local Government civil servant chief, the duality of institutional allegiance is most marked. The administrative officer, on the other hand, is more completely committed to the civil service pattern, while the village headman remains more oriented to traditional particularism. In comparative perspective, however, Busoga (and Uganda) would seem to be unusual among colonial societies in the degree to which the conflicts which inevitably arise in such societies have been confined to rôle conflict as against inter-group conflicts.

INSTITUTIONS AND TOTAL SOCIETIES.

Having examined the consequences of conflict for the particular institutions and persons involved, we may turn to its consequences for stability and change in society as a whole. First of all, what is conflict from the point of view of particular institutions and the persons who play rôles in terms of them may, in the total system, operate to maintain stability. In traditional Soga society the conflict between lineage and state would appear to have operated in this way. The sharing by the ruler's brothers of his ascribed fitness to rule, while it represented a threat to the ruler, also provided a ready source of leadership for revolt against what customary norms defined as misrule. Excessive cruelty, burdensome demands for tribute and the like are often spoken of by the Soga as factors contributory to revolt and usurpation. Under such circumstances, chiefs and people might shift their allegiance to a rival prince and thus restore conformity with traditional standards.[1] The conflict between institutions thus provided a check upon the exercise of authority. One of the early consequences of British administration was to remove this check by guaranteeing the chiefs' and rulers' positions. The task of controlling the exercise of authority thus fell upon administrative officers.

While the conflict between lineage and state acted to maintain traditional norms, it did not always act to maintain the stability of states as concrete, territorially-defined units. Princely revolt, though it might serve to put an end to misrule, often resulted in the creation of new autonomous political units. Frequently too, such revolts involved assistance from neighbouring states. Examples of this were cited in Chapter VI. Thus, while traditional political patterns were maintained, concrete political units often were not. Here we encounter the problem of defining the boundaries of the "society." If, following Levy, we define a society to include provision for controls adequate to the maintenance of accepted norms,[2] then perhaps from this point of view traditional Busoga contained no more than a single society. Though at any one point in time the country might consist of a series of autonomous political units, the mechanisms for maintaining conformity with normative

---

[1] This point is made by Fortes and Evans-Pritchard. (See Fortes, Meyer, and Evans-Pritchard, E. E. (eds.), *African Political Systems*, 1940, Introduction.)

[2] Levy, M. J., Jr., *The Structure of Society*, 1952, p. 151.

patterns often involved more than one such unit and often resulted in the creation of new units.

From this point of view, not only Busoga, but perhaps the whole of the Inter-Lacustrine Bantu state area should be viewed, for comparative purposes, as a single society, for the operation of the control mechanisms discussed above sometimes involved areas outside Busoga as well.   Perhaps I should say that within this whole area, common political institutions were operative, but that over time various concrete political units structured in terms of these institutions crystallised out at different periods.   Unfortunately there is too little historical data to test this notion, but I would suggest, as an historical hypothesis derived from structural analysis, that if further historical data were available one would find different concrete states rising and falling, possibly with some rapidity, at different periods.[1]

If this view of the traditional system is correct, then it seems quite possible that, paradoxically, the modern development of African Local Governments based upon Districts as ethnic units may have increased rather than decreased ethnic particularism. The relative cosmopolitanism and the constant shift of political boundaries which seem to have characterised the Lake Victoria region in pre-Administration times have been replaced by stable units around which such particularistic sentiments as linguistic (in many cases dialectal) pride might arise.   Other modern trends have, of course, worked in the opposite direction.

The conflicts which we have seen in contemporary Soga political institutions also appear in a somewhat different light when viewed in terms of their consequences for the total society.   For example, the general pattern by which institutional conflict in the Soga political system has been confined in large measure to rôle conflict— conflict of expectations and motivations within the same persons— has, while imposing a burden of internal malaise and small-scale interpersonal strife upon individuals, acted to prevent the development of intransigently opposed groups which might have seriously limited the possibility of developing a new pattern of institutional integration.

Again, the inefficiency of communication and the lack of mutual knowledge between Soga and administrative officers gives rise to frequent frustration on both sides, but in some cases greater knowledge would only serve to sharpen conflict.   In order to maintain his delicately-balanced position, the civil-servant chief must

---

[1] Leach describes what would appear to be a similar situation in highland Burma.   (See Leach, E. R., *Political Systems of Highland Burma*, 1954.)

sometimes give way to particularistic demands. If such incidents were always detected and punished by the Administration, the turn-over of chiefs would be even higher than it is at present and the functioning of the African Local Government, which in spite of the conflicts within it does manage to govern Busoga with some efficiency, would be seriously disrupted. Administrative officers appreciate this, and though they are aware that many deviations from the civil service norm go undetected, their inability to gain complete knowledge of the events enables them to ignore the less serious cases.

Again, the high turn-over in African Local Government personnel, which results from individuals' falling foul of conflicting institutions and sanctions, is perhaps an inevitable concomitant and pre-requisite of the striking rapidity with which change has progressed in Busoga. Although it involves the loss of persons who in a more fully integrated system might perform quite adequately, it also allows change to occur more rapidly than would be possible if, for example, the same persons were called upon to adjust to all the changes which have occurred in the Soga political system during the past four decades. Although we do not know with any precision the limits within which adults may learn new behaviour patterns, it appears to be accepted that such limits exist. Where there is high turn-over in personnel, the demands for new learning which are placed upon each individual are less severe.

Finally, as in the case of traditional Busoga, we may raise the question of the boundaries of present-day Soga society—the unit to which these functional considerations apply. It is clear that to-day, at any rate, Busoga is irrevocably unified. Though local loyalties continue to exist, persons living within the District think of themselves first as Soga. Furthermore, the African Local Government in the political sphere, as well as economic and religious institutions of many kinds, to-day operate, and in their present form could only operate, across the boundaries of the traditional states. But a further question arises as to whether Busoga is to-day and will be in the future a society unto itself or whether it will finally merge into a unit of wider scope. Protectorate Government policy is clearly aimed at unification and at the development of institutions adequate for an independent Uganda state. The Soga themselves are as yet of two minds on the subject. Tribal particularism at present remains strong, but the vision of self-government is presented to them with ever-increasing urgency. Although the prerequisites for survival as an independent state in the modern world are as yet not clearly understood—perhaps because they are currently the subject of such heated political debate—it would appear that

Busoga alone, with her half-million people, could hardy meet these prerequisites.

Size and population are not the only considerations, of course. There are also institutional prerequisites, though here particularly we are treading upon ground made dangerous by heated controversy. "Institutions adequate to self-government" can only be determined relative to a clearly-defined notion of "self-government." From the European point of view, self-government means essentially government on the Western liberal democratic model. This means representative legislative bodies, efficient civil service systems as well as a moderately-developed economy. The Western view is of course inevitably culture-bound. For the Soga, the self-government which becomes more and more their goal is as yet vaguely defined.

If, however, something resembling the Western liberal democratic state for Uganda as a whole is the aim, then we may say that the prerequisite institutions do not yet exist or are as yet only partially institutionalised. To the degree that they do exist, it would appear that they are at present dependent upon such external institutions as the colonial civil service for their maintenance. We thus arrive at the conclusion that, while in terms of personal loyalty and identification Busoga is a society unto itself, in terms of the maintenance of many of its institutions, such as the African Local Government civil service, it is part of a very much wider society. A beginning in the direction of institutional self-sufficiency has, to be sure, been made. The African Local Government civil service and councils and their counterparts elsewhere in Uganda may become more firmly established and may provide the foundations for similar institutions for the whole territory. On the basis of our present understanding of such matters, however, prediction concerning the speed at which change may proceed is utterly fruitless, since we are aware of the rapid transformations which charismatic nationalism can produce.

APPENDICES

QUESTIONNAIRE USED IN HOMESTEAD SURVEY

Sub-village: Village: Sub-County:
Kisoko: *Mutala*:   *Ggombolola*:

Homestead No.:   Homestead head: Number of huts in homestead:
Namba y'amaka: *Nnyini maka*:   *Ennyumba mmeka mu maka gano*:

		People *Abantu*		who *abasula*		live	
No.	Name *Erinnya*	Lives in which hut? *Asula mu nnyumba ki?*	Relationship to head of homestead? *Luganda ki wakati we ne nnyini maka?*	What clan? *Kika ki?*	What lineage? *Nda ki?*	Born in what county? *Yazalibbwa mu ssaza ki?*	Born in what village? *Yazalibbwa mu mutala ki?*
1							
2							
3							
/							
14							

		Divorced *Abakyala*	or *abaanoba*	deceased *oba*	wives *abaffa*
No.	Name *Erinnya*	Whose wife? *Mukyala w'ani?*	Why absent? *Lwaki taliiwo?*	If divorced, was marriage payment repaid? *Obanga yanoba ebintu bya-sasulwa?*	
15					
16					
17					
/					
22					

		in *mu*	this *maka*	homestead *gano*		
Born in what sub-village? *Yazalibbwa mu kisoko ki?*	Age: *Myaka:* (1) 0–5; (2) 6–15; (3) 16–45; (4) 45 +	Amount of marriage payment? (women only) *Yawasibbwa n'ebintu bimeka? (bakyala bokka)*	Religion *Ddini ki?*	Reached what standard in school? *Yakoma mu ddaala ki mu ssomero?*	Able to read Luganda? *Asobola okusoma Oluganda?*	What occupation? *Akola mulimu ki?*

		Absent *Abaana*		minor *abato*	children *abataliiwo*
No.	Name *Erinnya*	Whose child? *Mwana w'ani?*	In whose hands is he? *Ali mu mikono gy'ani?*	Where is he? *Ali wa?*	Why is he absent? *Lwaki taliiwo?*
23					
24					
25					
/					
29					

Land holdings of people who live in this homestead
Ebibanja by'abantu abasula mu maka gano

No.	Owner of holding *Nnyini kibanja*	Where is it located? *Kiri ludda wa?*	How was it acquired? *Yakifuna atya?*	What allottment fee was paid? *Yawa ensibuzi ki?*
1				
2				
3				
/				
6				

How many cattle are owned by people of this homestead?
Abantu abasula mu maka gano balina ente mmeka?

How many sheep are owned by people of this homestead?
Abantu abasula mu maka gano balina endiga mmeka?

How many goats are owned by people of this homestead?
Abantu abasula mu maka gano balina embuzi mmeka?

How many bicycles are owned by people of this homestead?
Abantu abasula mu maka gano balina eggaali mmeka?

How much money did people of this homestead get from cotton in 1951?
Abantu abasula mu maka gano baafuna ensimbi mmeka mu ppamba mu 1951?

THE AFRICAN LOCAL GOVERNMENTS ORDINANCE, 1949

(No. 2 of 1949)

REGULATIONS

(Under section 6 (2) of the Ordinance)

THE BUSOGA DISTRICT COUNCIL REGULATIONS, 1949.

1. These regulations may be cited as the Busoga District Council Regulations, 1949.

2. For the purpose of these Regulations—

"Council" means the Busoga District Council established by the Busoga District Council Proclamation, 1949;

"Local Government" means the Busoga African Local Government;

"Secretary-General" means the Secretary-General of the Local Government;

"Treasurer" means the Treasurer of the Local Government.

3. (1) So soon as convenient after the coming into force of these Regulations the Council as constituted under the provisions of the Ordinance and these Regulations shall be convened by the District Commissioner.

(2) Three years from the date of the convening of the Council the Council shall be dissolved by the District Commissioner and a new Council shall be convened by him for a further period of three years and thereafter every three years the Council shall be so dissolved and reconvened.

Provided that the Governor may at any time dissolve the Council and order that the Council be reconvened.

4. The Council shall consist of up to 22 *ex officio* councillors, up to 22 nominated councillors and one elected councillor for every 1,500 taxpayers within the District.

5. The Chairman of the Council shall be the Kyabazinga or in his absence the Secretary-General or in the absence of both the Kyabazinga and the Secretary-General the Treasurer.

6. The following persons shall be *ex officio* councillors:—

    The Kyabazinga.

    The Secretary-General.

    The Treasurer.

    The County Chiefs of the Local Government.

    Such heads of the clans set out in the Schedule to these Regulations as have not otherwise become councillors.

7. (1) The District Commissioner shall, so soon as he has convened the Council, nominate up to ten councillors.

(2) The *ex officio* members of the Council together with the elected members of the Council shall meet together prior to the first meeting of the Council or so soon as is convenient after the death, retirement or termination of the appointment of a councillor nominated under this paragraph and shall in the case of a new Council elect ten councillors, or in the case of the death, retirement or termination of appointment of a councillor nominated under this paragraph elect a councillor in his place.

8. (1) So soon as the Council has been convened each County Council established by the Provincial Commissioner under the provisions of section 7 of the Ordinance shall elect from amongst the elected members of the County Council one councillor to the Council in respect of every 1,500 taxpayers within the County.

(2) On the death, retirement, or the termination of the appointment of any elected councillor the County Council which elected such councillor shall within two months elect from amongst the elected members of the County Council a new councillor in his place:

Provided that the District Commissioner may dispense with such an election if such death, retirement or termination of appointment takes place within six months of the dissolution of the Council.

9. Every appointed and elected councillor shall serve on the Council until it is dissolved but may be re-appointed or re-elected to the Council.

10. No person shall become a councillor—

(*a*) unless he is a native of the District and is living in the District or is an African not being a native of the District and has lived in the District for the three years immediately preceding his nomination or election;

(*b*) save with the written approval of the District Commissioner if he has been convicted of a crime and sentenced to imprisonment without the option of a fine and at the time of his proposed nomination or the election less than five years has elapsed since his release from prison;

(*c*) if he has been certified as being of unsound mind.

11. (1) No person shall continue to serve as a councillor who—

(*a*) ceases to live in the District;

(*b*) is sentenced to imprisonment;

(*c*) is certified insane;

(*d*) ceases to hold any qualification in respect of which he was nominated to the Council.

12. (1) The Council shall hold not less than two meetings in every year.

(2) The District Commissioner may require the Chairman to call a meeting of the Council at any time.

13. (1) All acts of the Council, and all questions properly coming or arising before the Council, may be done and decided by the majority of such members of the Council as are present and vote at the meeting the whole number present at the meeting, whether voting or not, not being less than one half of the number of the whole Council.

(2) In the case of equality of votes, the Chairman of the meeting shall have a second or casting vote.

14. Minutes of every meeting shall be kept in a book provided for that purpose; a copy of all minutes shall be forwarded without delay to the District Commissioner.

15. Subject to these Regulations the Council shall with the advice and approval of the District Commissioner from time to time make "standing orders" for the regulation of their proceedings and business, and may with the approval of the District Commissioner vary and revoke the same.

16. (1) The District Commissioner shall establish under the provisions of section 5 of the Ordinance a Committee to be known as the "Standing Committee" which shall consider any proposed business of the Council prior to its presentation to the Council and shall be responsible for the preparation of the agenda of the Council's meetings.

(2) No bye-law or resolution shall be voted upon by the Council unless and until the Standing Committee has had an opportunity of advising the Council on the bye-law or resolution, as the case may be:

Provided that the Standing Committee shall have no authority to prevent the Council considering any matter.

17. (1) The Council may from time to time make bye-laws for the good rule and government of the District. Such bye-laws shall only be made in respect of the matters set out in paragraphs A and B of section 7 of the Native Authority Ordinance and the Native Authority Rules unless the Governor requests the Council to consider making a bye-law in relation to any other matter.

(2) The penalty for the breach of any provisions of any bye-laws shall not exceed imprisonment for a period of six months or a fine or five hundred shillings or both such imprisonment and fine.

(3) Immediately a bye-law has been passed by the Council it shall be forwarded to the District Commissioner who shall inform the Council as soon as possible whether or not the bye-law has been approved by the Governor or the Provincial Commissioner, as the case may be, under the provisions of subsection (4) of section 6 of the Ordinance.

18. (1) At any meeting the Council may consider resolutions in connection with the affairs of the District.

(2) The Council shall consider any resolution or other business that the District Commissioner may request it to consider.

19. (1) The Council shall in October every year consider a budget which shall be prepared by a finance committee established by the District Commissioner under the provisions of section 5 of the Ordinance.

(2) The Council shall complete its consideration of the budget of the finances of the Local Government for the ensuing year by the 31st day of October and shall forthwith forward its resolution on it to the District Commissioner.

(3) The District Commissioner on receipt of the budget resolution from the Council shall forthwith forward it to the Protectorate Government with his recommendations.

(4) In due course the budget resolution shall be returned to the District Commissioner with the instructions of the Protectorate Government thereon.

SCHEDULE

The Gabula	The Kisiki
The Ngobi	The Luba
The Zibondo	The Nanyumba
The Tabingwa	The Ntembe
The Menya	The Nkono
The Wakoli	

Made at Entebbe, this 17th day of January, 1949.

J. Hathorn Hall,
Governor.

(S.M.P.C.3111/1/1.)

DIARY OF A SUB-COUNTY CHIEF

6/2/51   Office . . . . . . tax collection and correspondence.

At County H.Q. *re* checking of all cash (taxes, fines, fees, etc.) sent in yesterday by all Sub-County chiefs.

Back in my office checked cash which had been collected by the clerks in my absence.

Attended to a complaint by . . . . . . *re* hired porters.

. . . . . . complained of his case in Ssabagabo's court.   Advised him to appeal to County court.

7/2/51   Escorted cash to Jinja.

8/2/51   Tax collection and correspondence.

Court: Tried five cases (4 criminal and 1 civil).

9/2/51   Attended County Team meeting.

Checked cash which was collected by the clerks in my absence when I was at County H.Q.

10/2/51   Office—Tax collection and correspondence, plus attending to various complaints.   Paid road gangs and staff.

11/2/51   Attended church service at Jinja on the Celebration Day of the Kyabazinga of Busoga.

12/2/51   At Bugembe Council *re* Celebration Day of the Kyabazinga.

13/2/51   Office—Tax collection and correspondence.

. . . . . . complained against. . . . . ., acting headman of . . . . . . Village for refusing to give him a plot after paying the necessary allotment fee, value Shs. 130/-.   Parish chief . . . . . . Ssabaddu has been requested to send . . . . . . to the office to give an explanation.

14/2/51   Correspondence and tax collection.

Saw . . . . . . *re* complaint lodged against him by . . . . Both parties agreed to go back and settle it out of court.

. . . . . . complained against . . . . . . for cutting a *muvule* tree in his garden without informing him.   Both parties agreed to go back and settle the matter out of court.

15/2/51   Office—Tax collection and correspondence.

16/2/51   Office—Correspondence and tax collection.

Court—Tried one criminal case.

17/2/51   Office—Tax collection and checking of all week's cash.

Sent one . . . . . . to Civil Hospital Jinja by ambulance for operation who was suffering from hernia.

19/2/51   Sent to County H.Q. all cash collected in last week.

Correspondence and tax collection.

Dealt with complaint lodged by ...... from ...... against
...... for harbouring his wife, ..., for 7 months. ......
warned and given 7 days to see that the woman goes back to
her husband, otherwise he will be prosecuted.
Complaint by ...... of ...... against ...... of ...... for
speaking to him in bad language, etc.   Parish Chief Ssabawaali
requested to send in ...... to explain.

20/2/51   ...... of ...... complained against Parish Chief Ssabawaali
for releasing the thief ...... free who stole his bananas
without trial.   Parish chief requested to explain.
In Sub-County council to discuss new bus routes in Busoga.
Saw all Parish chiefs about court debts (unpaid fees and fines—
L.A.F.) in their parishes.
Tax collection and correspondence.
Dealt with complaint lodged by ...... against ...... on
19/2/51.   ...... was reprimanded.

21/2/51   ...... of ...... complained against one ...... of ...... for
entering his compound under the influence of liquor and making himself a nuisance.   Parish Chief Ssabawaali requested to
arrest ...... to be prosecuted for drunkenness, etc.
Dealt with complaint lodged by ...... of 20/2/51 against the
Parish chief ...... regarding the thief who stole ......'s
bananas.   Parish chief asked for permission to look for escaped
thief.
Tax collection and correspondence.

22/2/51   Correspondence and tax collection.
Court—Tried 4 civil and 1 criminal case.
Discussed with ......, Assistant Agriculture Instructor the
problem of uprooting and burning of cotton before the 3rd
March, 1951.

23/2/51   Correspondence, court books and tax collection.
Court—Tried 1 civil and 1 criminal case.
Acting on both District Commissioner's and County chief's
orders, sent Katikkiro to attach ......'s property at ......
for failing to pay Shs. 566/80 in Busoga District Court Case
No. ...... of 1941.   One cycle and 3 office chairs were
attached, plus Shs. 50/– paid in cash.   Gave ...... 7 days to
pay the balance otherwise his cycle and chairs will be sold at
auction on 2/3/51.

24/2/51   Checking of çash collected during week.   Correspondence.

26/2/51   Sent to County H.Q. all cash collected last week.
...... of ...... came and begged me not to sell his cycle and
chairs on 3/2/51, promised to pay a hundred bob before that
date.   I agreed.
......, Financial Assistant, came from Jinja to inspect the
books.

27/2/51 Tax collection and correspondence.
Court—Tried 2 civil and 2 criminal cases.

28/2/51 Dealt with monthly returns. Correspondence and tax collection.
Parish chief ...... sent in ...... of ...... under arrest for being found in possession of ......'s baskets which were alleged to contain cotton. Both accused and owner ordered to go back and bring their witnesses on Friday 2/3/51.

1/3/51 Parish chief Ssabagabo sent in one ...... of ...... badly wounded on the head by one ......, son of ...... for finding him making adultery with his father's wife, ... by name. ...... sent to hospital on remand, and ...... sent on remand to County H.Q.
...... of ...... fulfilled his promise of 23/2/51 and paid Shs. 178/46, therefore I allowed him to have his cycle and chairs and ordered him to pay regularly every month otherwise I will attach his property again.
...... arrived on transfer from ...... to take over from Parish chief .... will go to ....
......, the Kyabazinga's representative in Busoga District Court Case No. ...... of 1950 arrived to hand over to ...... of ...... his 2 gardens which he won from ...... in the above case.

2/3/51 Correspondence and tax collection.
Court—Tried 1 criminal and 4 civil cases.

3/3/51 At ...... with the Kyabazinga's representative in Civil Case No. ...... of 1950.

5/3/51 Inspected road gang Section No. 9.
Office—Correspondence and tax collection.
......, son of ......, of ...... arrested for theft of a woollen blanket and 5 yards of calico belonging to one ...... of .... Remanded for trial on 6/3/51.
Sent Katikkiro to ...... to help police from ...... to arrest one escaped prisoner ......, son of ...... by name.

6/3/51 Tried 1 criminal and 1 civil case.
Sub-County council met to select new sites for bore holes (wells to be drilled by African Local Government) but adjourned until Friday the 9th inst. because no member from ...... came.
Correspondence and tax collection.

7/3/51 At County H.Q. in County Team meeting.
Checked cash collected by clerks when away at County meeting.

8/3/51 ...... of ...... complained against his wife for burning his daughter when away at .... Advised him to pass the matter through proper channels, i.e. through sub-village and village headmen.
Office—Correspondence and tax collection.

9/3/51   Tried 2 criminal and 2 civil cases.
Sub-County council met and passed resolutions.
Correspondence and tax collection.

10/3/51 Sent all cash collected during week to County H.Q.

12/3/51 Mr. ......, Assistant District Commissioner, arrived and checked all books and interviewed staff.

13/3/51 Mr. ......, Assistant District Commissioner, visited ...... and ...... villages *re* complaints made by the people in those villages against .... for taking their land without their consent.
Mr. ...... held a meeting in the afternoon and answered various questions made by the people.

14/3/51 Office—Correspondence and tax collection.

15/3/51 Court—Tried 1 civil case.
At County council to meet District Council representatives on land policy.

16/3/51 Court—Tried 2 civil and 1 criminal cases.
Correspondence and tax collection.

17/3/51 Office—Correspondence and tax collection.

19/3/51 Court—Tried 1 criminal and 1 civil case.

20/3/51 Office—Correspondence and tax collection.

21/3/51 Office—Correspondence and tax collection.
...... complained against ...... for cutting down *muvule* tree near his house.

22/3/51 Court—Tried 3 civil and 1 criminal case.

24/3/51 Office—Tax collection and correspondence.
Checked out cash collected during week.
......, Kyabazinga's representative, arrived and reported to hand over to ...... of ...... his garden which he won from ...... in a civil case. I appointed ......, village headman, to be my representative.

26/3/51 Sent to County all cash collected during last week.

27/3/51 Saw Parish chief, and village and sub-village headmen of ...... village about starting cassava and sweet potato plots, etc.

28/3/51 Went to meet District Commissioner in County Council.

29/3/51 Held a special meeting for the people of ...... village and discussed the problem of early planting of famine foods especially cassava and sweet potatoes in addition to finger millet which has already been sown.   All present were shown how to make bunds of paspalum grass in their gardens to prevent soil erosion.   Home cleanliness was also discussed.
Correspondence and tax collection.

30/3/51 Court—Tried 3 civil and 3 criminal cases.
Office—Correspondence and tax collection.

31/3/51   At County council to hear Kyabazinga's advice *re* forest
reserves and the ownership of plots.

2/4/51   Court—Tried 1 civil and 2 criminal cases.
Office—Tax collection and correspondence.
Dealt with complaint lodged by ...... of ...... against
...... of ...... for harbouring his wife, ..., for 4 months.
Advised both parties to take the matter to the kinship
successor, ..., as it is more or less a clan case.
...... of ...... lodged a complaint against ...... of ......
for harbouring his wife, ..., for 6 months and also for
insulting him when he went to demand his wife. Ordered
him to return to-morrow and say all that in the presence of
....

3/4/51   General office work.
...... of ...... lodged a complaint against his wife ......
who ran away with his property worth Shs. 86/-. Advised
him to prosecute her as she is in her father's house.
...... of .... lodged a complaint against ...... for
abusing her with shameful words. Parish chief ordered to
send in ...... to explain what happened.

4/4/51   ...... and ......, Health Inspectors, came in and discussed
health problems and plans to be taken to improve health
standards in this Sub-County.

5/4/51   Held a special meeting of all Parish chiefs and village and
sub-village headmen for checking of tax registers to find out
why some people have not paid their taxes yet.   Read to them
County chief's letter requesting them to plant many plots of
famine food (cassava).
Tax collection and correspondence.   Paid staff.

A TRIAL IN A SUB-COUNTY COURT

This is a translation of the record of a case between a tenant and a sub-village headman concerning a plot of land. Except for the alteration of personal names and the deletion of place names, the record has been translated just as it stood in the Sub-County headquarters files.

The Court of ...... Sub-County.

6/9/50.

Case No. ....

Accuser: George, of ....

Accused: Henry, Sub-Village Headman, of ....

For having chased me from my land, which I bought from him for thirty-five shillings, without refunding the money which I paid him for it.

Questions put to the Accused by the Court:

Q.: Do you agree to contest this case, and do you say that you will win or lose? You are not forced to speak unless you wish, but remember that what you say will be recorded as your evidence to help the Court.

A.: I agree to contest this case and I say that I will win because when George was coming to me to beg for land I warned him at the beginning not to despise me as the other man whom I had chased away from my sub-village used to do. One day I gave him (George) two shillings to dig a piece of land for me, but he refused. When I asked him the reason, he took out his stick to beat me. I said nothing to him after that. I just went away.

Again, the following day, he came to my place and talked much about the same thing, asking why I had asked him to dig for me. As it was night, I told him to go away until next morning. When morning came, I asked him to call Jacob and Adam, but only Jacob turned up. We went into the matter and this man George agreed in the presence of Jacob that he wanted to beat me. As I was going to refund him the money, I saw Jack and Fred coming. When they reached the place where we were, I handed the thirty-five shillings to Jack and Jack handed it to Jacob and Jacob handed it to George. Then, having refunded the thirty-five shillings which he had paid for the land, I asked him to pay back the two shillings which I had given him to dig for me. After a short time, I heard that he had accused me, saying that I hadn't refunded the thirty-five shillings which he had paid for the plot.

(Thumb mark of Henry.)

Q.: Has the statement which you have signed been recorded correctly?
A.: Yes.

Questions put to the Accuser by the Court:

Q.: You have heard the accused say that he refunded to you the thirty-five shillings which you paid for the land. Is that true?

A.: No, he is telling lies. He didn't refund the money, but one day I had gone from my home. When I returned, my wife told me that Henry had chased us from his land and had forbidden us to cultivate it any more. As I had had trouble with him before, I carried on with my digging the following morning. When he saw me going on with my digging, he stopped me at once. When I asked him why, he said that since he had power over me, I should obey his orders preventing me from digging any more on that land.

Then I took the matter to the village headman, Samuel, but unfortunately he was going on a journey, so he handed me over to Nathan (his assistant) and Nathan called Henry and our affairs were dealt with by him (Nathan). When Henry was asked whether it was true, he agreed and said: "I have chased him from my land and I have already refunded the money which he paid for it." He said this in the presence of Nathan. So I opposed him strongly and said: "No, he's telling lies. He has never refunded my money and here is the agreement which he gave me when I was paying for the land."

So Nathan sent us to the Parish chief's place and that is where we met Adam. At that time, Adam was acting Parish chief and he told us to go back and to return on Thursday. On Thursday we returned to the Parish chief's place. Our affair was looked into and I produced the agreement before the Parish court. The court decided the case in my favour and allowed me to accuse Henry here (at the Sub-County court).

Then, on the following morning, Henry and his wife went into his garden and I went into mine. As I was digging, he raised an alarm and many people gathered. When he was asked why he had raised an alarm, he said, "I am preventing this man from cultivating but he is refusing to stop." Then they asked me why I refused to stop cultivating the land, and I replied: "Because he has not refunded the money which I paid for the land." Again I produced the agreement and gave it to James to read. But as he was reading it, Henry snatched it from him and put it into his mouth and chewed it up and swallowed it. Then I got hold of the two people—James, with his bicycle, and Henry—and took them straight to the Parish chief's place. At the Parish chief's place, James said right out that Henry had swallowed our agreement.

(Thumb mark of George.)

Q.: Has the statement which you have signed been recorded correctly?

A.: Yes.

Q.: Do you have witnesses to prove that Henry didn't refund your money?

A.: Yes, my witness Adam can prove that Henry didn't refund the money because he was the one to whom I handed the money to be handed in turn to Henry, so he is the one to whom it should have been refunded.

Questions put to the Accused by the Court:

Q.: Were the witnesses whom you have mentioned present on the day when you were allotting the land?

A.: Only Jacob was present.

Q.: When you were refunding the money to George, did you gather the people who were present when you were allotting the land to him?

A.: Of the people who were present on the day when I allotted him the land, only Jacob was present when I was refunding him the money.

Q.: If you had already refunded him the money, why did you then take his agreement and swallow it?

A.: We didn't make any agreement, but if the one to whom he gave the money for the land to be brought to me proves that we did, then I will admit that I am wrong.

Q.: You have stated that you refunded the money to Jacob in the absence of Adam, but after that did you try to find Adam to tell him that you had refunded the money to George's representative, Jacob?

A.: I saw him on 6th May, 1950, and informed him that I had refunded the money to George's representative, Jacob.

Q.: Can the people of your sub-village say that no alarm was raised during the month of May, 1950?

A.: Yes, they can say so.

(Thumb mark of Henry.)

Questions put by the Court to Jack, witness for Henry, the Accused:

Q.: What evidence can you give in the case of George and Henry, and whose witness are you?

A.: I am Henry's witness and I am the one to whom he handed the thirty-five shillings to be handed over to Jacob, who refunded it to George.

(Thumb mark of Jack.)

Q.: Has the statement which you have signed been recorded correctly?

A.: Yes.

Questions put by the Court to Jacob, witness for Henry, the Accused:

Q.: What evidence can you give in the case of George and Henry and whose witness are you?

A.: I am Henry's witness and I saw him give thirty-five shillings to Jack, and then Jack gave it to me and I gave it to George. After George had received the thirty-five shillings, he refunded to Henry's wife the two shillings which Henry had given him to dig for him.

(Thumb mark of Jacob.)

Q.: Has your statement been recorded correctly?

A.: Yes.

Q.: How many were you when George was being refunded his thirty-five shillings?

A.: We were four and we have all come to give evidence.

Q.: Who called you to be a witness when George was being refunded his money?

A.: George brought me from my home.

Q.: As you were George's representative, did Henry inform you regarding the refund of George's money?

A.: He told me that George had told him he would beat him.

Q.: What did you say when you were taken to the Parish chief's place?

A.: I didn't go there at all.

Q.: The Accuser stated that you accompanied them to the Parish chief's place and that he had not yet been refunded his money. Now you say that he was refunded his money. Which is correct?

A.: What I have said just now is correct.

(Thumb mark of Jacob.)

Questions put by the Court to Peter, one who attended the Parish court:

Q.: Did you once see Henry being brought before the Parish court in May, 1950.

A.: Yes, he was brought by James and George and was charged for having swallowed George's agreement.

(Thumb mark of Peter.)

Questions put by the Court to Dawson, Clement, Noah and Stanley, all people who first arrived after Henry raised the alarm:

Q.: Do you all agree that in May, 1950, an alarm was raised in that sub-village?

A.: Yes, we all agree that we heard an alarm in May, 1950, in our sub-village and that they were made by Henry. Fighting was taking place between George and Henry because Henry had swallowed George's agreement.

(Signatures of Dawson and Clement.)

(Thumb marks of Noah and Stanley.)

Questions put by the Court to Adam, witness for George, the Accuser:

Q.: What evidence can you give in the case of George and Henry and whose witness are you?

A.: I am George's witness. He came to me in April and asked me to take him to Henry so that he might pay him the money for the land in my presence. After arriving at Henry's place, I handed him the thirty-five shillings in the presence of Ralph and Stephen. Then, four days after the payment, George came to me and said that Henry had allowed him to build a house on the land which he had allotted to him and that he had given him an agreement and that in the agreement were the names of the people whom I have mentioned, as witnesses, and that my name was included. Then, after two weeks, Jacob, the village headman, brought George to the Parish chief's place to accuse Henry of chasing him away from the land without refunding the money which he had paid for it.

As I was acting as Parish chief, because the chief himself was going on a journey, I told them to come back later. But before they returned, I heard that they had fought because Henry had swallowed George's agreement while George was showing it to James.

(Signature of Adam.)

Q.: Has the statement which you have signed been recorded correctly?
A.: Yes.

Q.: As George's representative, apart from having dealt with the case as acting Parish chief, do you believe that Henry had already paid back George's money before the destruction of the agreement?

A.: I don't believe that he had, because at the beginning, when George came to me, he had the agreement with him. But after they came back, I heard that they had fought because Henry had swallowed George's agreement.

Questions set by the Accused, Henry, to George, the Accuser:

Q.: Your witness has stated that when I was allotting you the land, we didn't write the agreement at once, but that we wrote it four days after the date of payment. Can he give the names of the people who were present when the agreement was made and can he give the name of the one who wrote it?

A.: The agreement was written by your son, Theodore, and since I have no power over him I can't say that I will bring him before the court.

Q.: What can your witness, Edward, prove.

A.: He can testify that Jacob said in his presence that you had not yet refunded me the money.

(Thumb mark of George.)

Questions put by the Court to Edward, Parish chief, witness for George, the Accuser:

Q.: What evidence can you give in the case of George and Henry and whose witness are you?

A.: I am George's witness, for George once brought to me the matter of Henry's chasing him from his land which he had allotted to him. Then I went to Henry and asked him whether it was true and Henry agreed that it was true. He said that he had already refunded the money because George had accused him.

Then I asked Jacob whether it was true that Henry had refunded George's money. Jacob answered that he had never paid back the money. Then the agreement was shown to me while we were standing in William's courtyard and I sent them to the Sub-County court.

(Signature of Edward.)

Q.: Has the statement which you have signed been recorded correctly?

A.: Yes.

Q.: As you say the agreement was given you to read, can you tell us who wrote it and whose names were written on it?

A.: It was written by Theodore and Adam's name was on it as a witness, but I can't remember the others.

Q.: On the day when George was showing you the agreement, was Henry present?

A.: Yes, he was present.

Q.: And what did Henry say about it?

A.: Henry agreed that it was made after George paid the money for the land, for George wanted to show it to his parents and relatives to prove that he had some land of his own.

Q.: Did you have a report of an alarm being raised in the sub-village in question during the month of May?

A.: Yes, it was reported to me that it was caused by the fight between Henry and George because Henry had swallowed George's agreement. It was said that the agreement was taken from the hands of James, who was reading it.

Q.: The case was brought to your court when you were about to go on a journey and you left Adam as acting Parish chief. What did you do after you returned from your journey?

A.: I did nothing, because the case had already been sent to the Sub-County court.

(Signature of Edward.)

Questions put by the Court to James, witness for George, the Accuser:

Q.: What evidence can you give in the case of George and Henry and whose witness are you?

A.: I am George's witness. When I heard an alarm being raised, I ran straight to the scene and found Henry still raising the alarm. When I asked the reason, he said: "That man is abusing me." When I asked George whether it was true that he was abusing Henry, he said that he hadn't abused him at all but that Henry was preventing him from carrying on with his digging. Then I asked George to bring the agreement and he brought it, but as I was reading it, Henry snatched it and swallowed it. Then I took both Henry and George to the Parish chief's place. Unfortunately, we couldn't find the Parish chief himself, but we found Peter and told him the story. I told him that the agreement had been swallowed.

(Signature of James.)

Q.: Has the statement which you have signed been recorded correctly?
A.: Yes.

Q.: In whose sub-village were the alarms made?
A.: In Henry's sub-village.

Questions put by the Accused, Henry, to James, the Accuser's witness:

Q.: You say that I took the agreement away from you, but whose names were written on it?

A.: You snatched it away before I had finished reading it.

(Signature of James.)

Questions put to the Accused, Henry, by the Court:

Q.: Have you heard Dawson, a man of your sub-village, and other people, say that an alarm was raised in your sub-village and that it was caused by a fight which occurred between you and George because you swallowed his agreement?

A.: I don't believe what they say. They are just telling lies. They are saying that because they hate me. No alarm was raised in the sub-village in May, 1950.

Q.: Have you no other witnesses who can say that no alarm was raised in your sub-village?

A.: No.

(Thumb mark of Henry.)

Case No. ....
Accuser: George, of ....
Accused: Henry, Sub-Village Headman, of ....
Decided to-day, 16/2/50.

From the evidence given by James, from whom the agreement was snatched and swallowed, it has been proved that Henry swallowed the agreement before refunding George the thirty-five shillings. Therefore the court has decided the case in George's favour. Henry has been ordered to repay the thirty-five shillings and also the two shillings court fee paid by the Accuser. The total amount is thirty-seven shillings.

(Signatures of official members.)   (Signatures of non-official members.)
(Signature of Sub-County chief.)

SUMMARY OF AFRICAN LOCAL GOVERNMENT EXPENDITURE ESTIMATES*

Head	Estimates, 1952		Revised estimates, 1951	
	Other charges	Personal emoluments	Other charges	Personal emoluments
	£	£	£	£
I Administration	12,722	43,263	11,185	38,419
II Agriculture	1,669	681	1,370	620
III Aduit	393	—	393	—
IV Education	32,380	—	25,144	—
V Forestry	1,775	985	1,850	650
VI Medical	9,725	—	9,350	—
VII Miscellaneous	8,935	—	12,705	—
VIII Pensions	5	5,500	300	4,460
IX Police and Prisons	4,295	8,388	3,075	7,524
X Public Works	32,800	5,012	36,938	2,845
XI Tsetse Control	700	—	1,746	—
XII Veterinary	169	222	105	320
Non-recurrent expenditure (mostly new buildings and other capital)	92,680		100,520	
Total	£198,248	£64,051	£204,681	£54,838

* Taken from "Busoga African Local Government Estimates, 1952," Office of the District Commissioner, Jinja.

SUMMARY OF AFRICAN LOCAL GOVERNMENT REVENUE ESTIMATES*

Head	Estimates, 1952	Revised Estimates, 1951
	£	£
I Direct Taxation	145,260	136,562
II African Local Government Courts	8,700	5,250
III Interest on Investments ..	2,180	2,090
IV Grants from the Protectorate Government	36,770	—
V Other Receipts	13,911	11,696
Non-recurrent Revenue ..	91,830	100,423
Total Revenue	£298,651	£256,021

* Taken from "Busoga African Local Government Estimates, 1952," Office of the District Commissioner, Jinja.

AFRICAN LOCAL GOVERNMENT STAFF: 1952*

I. *Administration*

Kyabazinga	1
Secretary General	1
Treasurer	1
County Chiefs	8
Secretary for Agriculture and Forestry	1
Assistant Treasurer..	1
Assistant Secretary General	1
Deputy County Chief	1
Sub-County Chiefs	51
Judicial Officers	3
Senior Accountant	1
Store Keeper	1
Examiners of Accounts	2
Senior Clerk (Headquarters)	1
Parish Chiefs	288
Katikkiros	59
Clerical Staff	179
Office Messengers and runners	64

II. *Agriculture*

Assistant Agriculture Instructors	20

III. *Forestry*

Forest Rangers	7
Forest Overseers and Mechanics	6
Foremen	18

IV. *Police and Prisons*

Chief of African Local Government Police	1
Sergeants and Corporals	86
Constables	187

*Taken from "Busoga African Local Government Estimates, 1952," Office of the District Commissioner, Jinja. These figures are exclusive of casual labour employed in such operations as road building and maintenance.

V. *Public Works*

Supervisor of Works	1
Assistant Supervisor of Works	1
Apprentices ..	3
Market Masters	45
Camp Caretakers	50
Drivers	14
Well Mechanics	4
Artisans	7
Road Inspectors	11

VI. *Veterinary*

Veterinary Scouts ..	7
Total	1,132

CASES HEARD IN THE COURT OF SUB-COUNTY SSABAWAALI, BULAMOGI, DURING 1950

I. *Criminal*

    A. Offences Against Orders and Rules (cotton marketing and cultivation rules, public health rules, livestock husbandry and marketing rules, birth and death registration rules, beer-brewing rules, bicycle safe-driving rules, particular orders of chiefs, etc.) .. 198

    B. Theft 42

    C. Tax Evasion 35

    D. Assault 26

    E. Slander 10

    F. Failure to Do Duty 10

    G. Adultery 9

    H. Arson 7

    I. All other Offences 15

          Total 352

II. *Civil*

    A. General Debt 24

    B. Bridewealth 23

    C. Damage by Straying Livestock 15

    D. Possession of Livestock 14

    E. Land 7

    F. General Property Damage 6

    G. All Other Cases 5

          Total 94

DISCUSSIONS OF THE SUB-COUNTY COUNCIL OF SSABAWAALI, BULAMOGI, DURING 1950 AND 1951

Membership of the Council:

Three elected members from each Parish	21
Seven Parish chiefs	7
Sub-County chief	1
Total membership	29

18/3/50 Discussed election of members for Sub-County and County courts in accordance with District Commissioner's circular.

20/5/50 Discussed County chief's letter concerning election of court members.

25/5/50 Elected seventeen persons to constitute unofficial side of Sub-County, County and District courts.

22/6/50 Discussed following points in the County chief's letter:
1. The problem of raising African Local Government revenue.
    Fifteen in favour of raising the slaughtering fee to two shillings fifty cents per cow and one shilling per goat.
2. African Local Government forest reserves.
    All against increasing reserved forests, as present ones are thought sufficient. But all favour preserving present forest reserves.
3. Registration of village and sub-village headmen.
    All oppose instituting a special register as present practice of recording headmen in poll tax registers is considered sufficient.

27/7/50 Discussed County chief's letter concerning the raising of tobacco in Busoga.
    Seven favour the raising of tobacco. Nine oppose.

10/8/50 Discussed following points in the County chief's letter:
1. Election of a Soga member to the Legislative Council of Uganda.
    All favour the election of a member.

2. The use of poison to get rid of monkeys.
   All oppose.

3. The disposal of land holdings abandoned by occupants.
   All agree that such holdings should revert to village and sub-village headmen.

4. The establishment of trading centres for African shop-keepers.
   All favour the establishment of such centres at Bulumba, Kyani, Gadumire, Namukoge, Buvulunguti, and Nansololo.

14/8/50 Discussed the County chief's letter concerning the holding of a fair and exhibition of agricultural produce.

21/9/50 Discussed the County chief's letter concerning the fixing of the price of meat.
   All reject the suggestion, though the chairman favours raising the price by ten cents per pound for each type.

30/11/50 Discussed the remission of poll tax for aged men.

7/12/50 Discussed following points raised by the County chief's letter:

1. Payment of village and sub-village headmen.
   All opposed.

2. Disposal of land abandoned by occupants.
   All agree that such land should revert to the headmen.

3. The use of prisoners to grow food for government dispensary.
   Seventeen favour allotting four acres to every four prisoners for this purpose. Three oppose this suggestion.

2/1/51 Decided upon remission of poll tax for aged men.

20/1/51 Discussed points raised by the people:

1. The price of chickens brought by people to rest camps for sale to touring officers should be raised to three shillings.

2. There should be a fixed price for all goods sold in shops.

3. There should be a weekly market at Kasokwe.

4. Wells are needed at Butongole, Buyodi, Kasokwe, Nabikoli and Kanankamba.

5. The councils should have the power to elect County chiefs.

6. Arsonists should be made to turn over all their property to their victims.

7. Parish council members should be given an allowance for attendance at meetings.

8. Soga who served in the armed forces should be given a bonus.

9. Eight members favour a return to the system of hereditary chiefs.
Four oppose.

10. There should be a telephone at County headquarters and at the Government dispensary.

11. Each Parish chief should be given a servant to keep his compound tidy.

12. The police constables who guard African Local Government offices should be armed. with guns.

13. There should be cotton-buying stores at Bulumba, Namalemba, and Nansololo.

14. The market at Kaliro should be built of brick and corrugated iron.

15. There should be an eye doctor with proper instruments at the Jinja Government hospital.

16. Fees for brewing beer should be remitted for Christmas.

22/2/51 Discussed the County chief's letter concerning the establishment of new bus routes.
Decided that one bus should run from Kamuli to Namwendwa, Kaliro, Vukula, and Terinyi and return by the same route to Kamuli. Another should run from Jinja to Luzinga, Naigobia, Bukova, Namalemba, Bulumba and Gadumire and return to Jinja by the same route.

14/3/51 Discussed the County chief's letter concerning the price of fish.
Approved the price list suggested by the Parish councils for the sale of fish at the lakes and rivers of origin, but suggested another list for sale in the villages.
Suggested ten new sites for wells.

5/4/51 Discussed the price of fish.

11/9/51 Discussed the remission of poll tax for aged men in the Parishes of Mumyuka, Ssabagabo and Mutuba II.

12/11/51 Discussed the remission of poll tax for aged men in the Parishes of Ssabaddu, Musaale, Ssabawaali and Mutuba I.
Discussed the provision of scholarships for five students at Mwiri College and Budini Girls' School.
Decided that the parents should pay one half and the African Local Government one half.

28/11/51 Approved the provision of a scholarship at Mwiri College for a boy whose father was killed in the war.

INDEX